D0069943

Capturing the

SPARK

Inspired Teaching,
Thriving Schools

DAVID B. COHEN

Foreword by Barnett Berry

Founder and CEO, Center for Teaching Equality

ENACTIVE
PUBLISHING

Palo Alto, CA

Capturing the Spark: Inspired Teaching, Thriving Schools, by David B. Cohen
© 2016 by David B. Cohen.

All rights reserved.
No part of this book may be reproduced in any written, electronic, recording, or photocopying form without written permission of the author.

Books may be purchased in quantity and/or special sales by contacting the publisher, Enactive Publishing, 380 Hamilton Ave., #622, Palo Alto, CA 94301
(650) 468–2322
capturingthespark.com

Publisher: Enactive Publishing, Palo Alto, California

Interior Design: GKS Creative, www.GKSCreative.com

Cover Design: Ruth-Anne Siegel, www.ruth-annesiegel.com

Cover Photography: David B. Cohen; author photo by Jacob Klein-Cohen

Interior Photography: David B. Cohen

Photograph, page 13: Nikki Kanan, used with permission

Developmental Editing: Julie Feinstein Adams, JFA Communications, www.jfacommunications.com

Copy Editing, Project Management: Marla Markman, www.marlamarkman.com

ISBN: 978–0-9976868–0-7 (Print)
ISBN: 978-0-9976868-1-4 (eReaders)

Publisher's Cataloging-in-Publication data

Names: Cohen, David Brett.
Title: Capturing the spark: inspired teaching, thriving schools / by David B. Cohen.
Description: Includes index and bibliographical references.
Palo Alto, CA: Enactive Publishing, 2016.
Identifiers: ISBN 978-0-9976868-0-7 (pbk.) | 978-0-9976868-1-4 (e-book)
LCCN 2016914569
Subjects: LCSH Effective teaching--United States. | Effective teaching--California. | Teacher effectiveness. | Educational leadership. | BISAC EDUCATION / General.
Classification: LCC LB1775.2 .C644 2016 | DDC 371.1—dc23

Printed in the United States of America

20 19 18 17 16 / 10 9 8 7 6 5 4 3 2 1

To all the teachers who welcomed me into your schools and classes and trusted me with your stories, my deepest gratitude.

To my family—Evi, Jacob, and Gil—thank you for your patience, understanding, and loving support, while allowing me the time and freedom to make this book possible.

In memory of Richard Lakin, whose gift was
Teaching as an Act of Love
*and whose legacy inspires
the love of education, peace, and justice.*

Supporters

Substantial financing for this work was provided by:

- Stanford Center for Opportunity Policy in Education (SCOPE; https://edpolicy.stanford.edu/);
  Stanford University Graduate School of Education
- California Teachers Association Institute for Teaching (CTA-IFT; www.teacherdrivenchange.org); Dick Gale, director

Kickstarter Backers

Many thanks to the following organizations and individuals for their financial (and moral) support:

- Ed100.0rg, Jeff Camp
- Educate Our State, Katherine Welch
- Go Public Film Project, Dawn O'Keefe
- Identity Safe Classrooms, Becki Cohn-Vargas

I am also grateful to the following people for their generous support on my Kickstarter campaign:

Randy Banchik	Thor-Ivar Eriksen	Barb Mitchell
Ross Bergman	Andrew Fleisher	Tony Reed
Jeff Charbonneau	Liam Goldrick	Bernie Rhinerson
Dean Clark	Marciano Gutierrez	Susie Richardson
Rob Coelho	Rachael Shepherd Kaci	Michael Roth
Becki Cohn-Vargas	Sheryl Klein	Tien Robinson
Jennifer Cohen	Mark LaMar	Candy Smiley
Judi and Ed Cohen	Melissa Lawson	Sabrina Joy Stevens
Gabrielle Conway	Vicki Mailes Leoni	Barbara Tallent
Bertis Downs	Jenny Maehara	Robyn Tepper
D. Gregg Doyle	Rachel	Silver White
Carrie DuBois	Milliken-Weitzman	

TABLE OF CONTENTS

FOREWORD

Harsh criticism of America's schools is nothing new. The concerns are understandable. Too many students are still ill-prepared for college or careers when they graduate from high school—*if* they graduate. And the academic achievement gap persists, deepening economic inequality. Despite the starts and stops of school reforms, past and present, teaching and learning do not seem to change much.

In the past, student poverty and unequal funding of schools were often blamed for America's educational woes. But we've seen a different story line since the early 2000s, when the No Child Left Behind (NCLB) Act was passed.

Increasingly, policy leaders have pointed their proverbial fingers at teachers as the primary source of dysfunctional schools. These leaders—and the school reform elites advising them—have complained that too many teachers do not work hard enough or have the academic smarts to teach effectively. There should be no excuses for a student's poor performance, they insist. These ideas undergird federal and state policies—including NCLB and Race to the Top (RTTT)—that have instituted high-stakes accountability systems to hold teachers responsible for student test scores. Simultaneously, reformers have advanced efforts to "disrupt" education, such as nonunionized charter schools and shortcuts into teaching.

Yet after more than a decade and a half of this blame-the-teachers approach, reform enthusiasts are beginning to question many market-based policy strategies, as well as the high-stakes accountability systems promulgated by NCLB and RTTT. Student scores on the National Assessment of Educational Progress remain dismal. Charters are, by and large, failing to improve outcomes for students. High-stakes tests have narrowed the curriculum, and in protest, growing numbers of parents are permitting their children to opt out of standardized exams. Test-based teaching evaluations, dependent on unreliable statistical models, fluctuate wildly, and now the courts (e.g., in New Mexico) are issuing injunctions to prevent their use to determine teacher effectiveness.

Even the NewSchools Venture Fund, a reform group that has long promoted education entrepreneurs and competition as solutions to public education's problems, is now raising alarms. In a recent report, CEO Stacey Childress, a leader in the movement to disrupt education, admits that even the best of the "no excuses" charter schools are not getting the job done. These schools might help some high-need students do well on state standardized tests, but various measures of their success in college are "disappointing."

Slowly but surely, the narrative is shifting to acknowledge that outside experts, choice, and competition cannot solve schools' challenges. Instead, reform must emanate from students, families, communities, and teachers. As Childress notes, "Teachers often relish the opportunity to innovate and serve their students better, but struggle to reconcile new approaches with existing requirements—not to mention limited time and resources."[1]

It may be that school reformers are beginning to realize what many of us have known for a long time. Teachers are the solution, not the problem.

And this is exactly what David Cohen's book, *Capturing the Spark,* demonstrates. During the 2014–15 school year, David visited seventy school campuses in fifty towns and cities in his home state of California to paint a picture of how teachers are leading efforts to improve schools. He invites us to join his "tour of some [of the most] vibrant public schools and communities, with innovative programs, thoughtful and supportive staff members at every level, and creative, passionate, life-changing teachers in their classrooms."

David offers an invaluable window into these promising schools, helping us see, hear, and almost touch the powerful interactions between teachers and students. He does not shy away from the complexities of effective instruction, reminding us what it takes to go beyond "teaching to the test" to ensure deeper learning for all students. Along the way, David exposes us to the "thousands of instructional and classroom management decisions" that teachers make every day. He shows us, too, the impact of those decisions: how they help students flourish as readers—and as bloggers, coders, athletes, and dancers.

We couldn't ask for a more qualified guide through California's innovative classrooms than David. A National Board Certified Teacher who has taught for over twenty years, he has substantial experience in analyzing his own and others' instructional practices to identify how and why students do (or don't) learn.

In the latter chapters of his book, David identifies what it takes for "teachers and schools to grow and thrive, sometimes against the odds" and explains how teacher leaders he has observed contribute to the professionalism and stability of schools and districts. His narrative transports us to elementary, middle, and high schools, some with merely dozens of students, and some with thousands. He covers the length of the state, visiting rural, urban, and suburban communities, from the richest to the poorest neighborhoods. In every setting, one consistent theme emerges: Students benefit when teachers have the "autonomy and opportunity to lead." When conditions are right, teachers capture the sparks that make a difference for student learning.

David's portraits reinforce researchers' recent conclusions. As a 2016 research report concluded: "Teaching and learning are not primarily individual accomplishments [of teachers] but rather social endeavors that are best achieved and improved through trusting relationships and teamwork, instead of competition and a focus on individual prowess."[2]

David's vision of schools' potential has been influenced by his deep involvement with the CTQ Collaboratory. This virtual community has served as a "new, national peer group of leading educator advocates, welcoming and generous in spirit, critical friends whose wisdom and encouragement pushed [his] thinking and inspired action."

I am hopeful that the rise of teacher networks—like CTQ's virtual community and growing numbers of others—can engage more classroom experts like David to learn from one another and go public with their expertise.

Ensuring that all American students can fulfill their potential—which is critical to our nation's civic and economic health—means tackling a complex set of problems related to unequal funding and bureaucratic inertia, as well as the many social ills that seep into the classroom and limit the capacity of teachers to teach.

Policy makers and school reformers have the right to take bold action, but they need to turn more often to career teachers like David for solutions, because the right action requires deep knowledge of students and schools. It is time for our nation's accomplished teachers to be the drivers of reform, rather than targets of them.

Barnett Berry
Founder, CEO, Center for Teaching Quality

PART ONE

CAPTURING AN OVERVIEW

Schools, like people, are varied and complex—no two are identical. Yet, while we appreciate their uniqueness, schools, like people, have similarities that are important to understand. Part I of *Capturing the Spark* provides the background for this book and describes how years of experience with a variety of teachers and schools motivated me to take a year off from my own teaching to explore public education throughout California. Elementary, middle, and high schools each have a dedicated chapter, highlighting how teachers and schools spark the interests and learning of students at different ages and developmental stages.

CHAPTER 1

Introduction:

Inspired Teachers, Thriving Schools

*Haydee Rodriguez leads a discussion in her history class
at Southwest High School in El Centro, California.*

RAIANNA WAS THE ONLY STUDENT WHO EVER ASKED ME, "Are you coming back tomorrow?" It was not a question I'd anticipated I'd have to answer, but then again, I wasn't thinking like a first grader. Usually I was a silent observer seated on the edges of the classrooms I visited. Today, Raianna's teacher, Jane Fung, had put me to work, if you can call it work; reading stories with Raianna was a treat for both of us. Now I wondered how to break the news to my brand-new friend that our time together was quickly running out.

I smiled and offered sympathetically, "No, I'm sorry. I'm going to visit the boys and girls at another school tomorrow." She looked down as she thought about my answer, making it difficult for me to read her face; was this was a big deal or not? She looked up again as she thought of another question, and the sudden lifting of her head caused a clicking sound as the long, beaded braids of hair knocked against each other.

"Will you come back another day?"

"I don't know. I'd like to, though." That was true, technically. I would have loved to come back again, to read more books with my new first-grade buddies and to spend more time observing the masterful teaching of Jane Fung. However, repetition was not part of my plans as I spent an academic year visiting dozens of California public schools, and I had no reason to think that Alexander Science Center School in Los Angeles would be an exception. Figuring I'd better not set up false expectations, I added, "If I come back, it's not going to be for a long time. You might even be in second grade by then." Now I'd just made the whole situation puzzling—*second* grade? Raianna gave me a sideways glance and went with a shrug to return her book to the proper bin, leaving me where she'd found me, sitting as I often did, in a tiny plastic chair, trying to capture the sparks of curiosity and learning that animate so many California classrooms.

During the 2014–15 school year, I visited fifty cities and towns in California, spent more than sixty days in public schools, and observed about one hundred classrooms, where I took notes, transcribed bits of conversations, scrutinized interactions, and took thousands of pictures. The goal was to record and share the inspired teaching that I knew was happening all over the state in thriving public schools that defy stereotypes. I wanted to make sure more people know what's happening in the rooms and buildings that most of us walk, ride, or drive past without much genuine insight, despite the depth and sincerity of our hopes regarding public education.

It was a rare and deeply appreciated privilege for me to be able to spend so much time in other people's classrooms and schools. I know very few teachers who have visited more than a few campuses to observe students and teachers. I have taught at five schools (not including summer schools), and until this project began, I had spent days observing classes at perhaps another six or seven schools. Many teachers haven't seen even that many schools. Members of the general public often haven't observed the regular, daily activity in a public school classroom since their student days. Yet we have deep feelings about the value of education, and often, strong opinions about what public schools need to do to improve.

Despite the lack of direct insight, most Americans believe that the quality of our public schools is mediocre or poor. Phi Delta Kappa International (PDK) conducts an annual survey of public attitudes regarding public education. In 2014, as I began my project, 80 percent of respondents gave American schools a grade of C (51 percent), D (19 percent), or F (10 percent). At the same time, however, 50 percent of Americans think the public schools in their communities are better than that that, giving them grades of A (12 percent) or B (38 percent), and only 17 percent say their local schools deserve a D (11 percent) or F (6 percent). So what's happening here? It looks to me like proximity helps: We have a more positive opinion of what we can see or hear about more directly through our friends and family; it's easier to write off our national schools because we have no connection to them, but we hear the negativity and see the most shocking incidents in mainstream or social media.

There's a whole industry of educational consultants and think tanks, advocates, and marketers whose job is to make us all feel acutely the urgency of addressing some problem or another with public education. Our school boards and other elected officials, administrators, teachers, and unions do it too. No group is immune: To persuade us to take action, sign petitions, send donations, or vote a certain way, they often use negative situations to make their case.

There are many ways we could improve education. However, the most pressing issues for many American children are broader than education reform. How much of the public anxiety about teaching and schools is actually displaced concern about wider social challenges may be impossible to say. "The Condition of Education," a 2015 study from the National Center for Education Statistics, found that more than half our nation's entire public school student body lived below the poverty line (using 2013 data). And this percentage was not skewed by a few high population states: The student poverty rate was 50 percent or higher in twenty-one states and still above 40 percent in the next worst nineteen states. There's a crisis of compassion, and even patriotism, if we cannot summon the will to honestly assess and reform the various economic, budgetary, and judicial policies causing this kind of harm to the families of most of our public school children.

Given the severe challenges we face, it may seem counterintuitive that I'm inviting you to read a book full of positive stories about public education. The reason is that to engage productively, together, in the strengthening of the public education system, we have to believe in its viability. Not just in its future potential in the make-believe world of Someday, but in the system as it exists today. The negativity can be overwhelming, suppressing the motivation or ability to think or act.

Several years ago, as I became more involved in education advocacy work, I thought that if everyone simply understood the negatives, they would feel compelled to act, to mitigate the problems. It turns out that the negativity instead causes disengagement. *It's too late. There's nothing we can do. Isn't it awful that our public schools are broken?* That perception is often reinforced by references to American performance on international educational tests that place us behind many modern industrialized nations. However, a deeper analysis might forestall the conclusion that schools are the problem, as it turns out that our schools with low or moderate levels of poverty score among the best in the world. Our main struggle is meeting the broader needs of a huge number of students in poverty, especially with so many of them attending schools with high concentrations of poverty.

But for now, let's set aside the negative. It's time for an antidote to the toxicity of pessimism and cynicism. California's public schools have many talented and dedicated teachers, in many thriving campuses. Let's turn off our pessimistic internal voices and indulge the neglected optimist inside. Welcome to this tour of some vibrant schools and communities, with innovative programs, thoughtful and supportive staff members at every level, and creative, passionate, life-changing teachers in their classrooms.

Inspiration

As an English teacher and literature lover, I know the power of narrative. One way I've tried to open students' minds to that concept is through a TED Talk by novelist and essayist Chimamanda Adichie (recorded July 2009). The talk draws on personal experiences in Nigeria and in the United States to illuminate "the danger of a single story." Adichie talks about how, as a child, she was surprised at the skill and industriousness of a poor family she met, because her single story of the family had initially been simply about their poverty. Moving to the United States to attend college, she found herself the object of pity from an American roommate who had never realized that an "African" person could come from an English-speaking country, listen to American music, or even operate modern appliances. One of her professors later chided her for writing fictional characters who lacked "African authenticity" because they were well-educated members of the middle class. Adichie recognizes that the dynamics of the single story are about power: Who has the privilege to tell other people's stories and what happens when they settle on a limited perspective? Thus, she cautions:

> *I've always felt that it is impossible to engage properly with a place or a person without engaging with all the stories of that place and that person. The consequence of the single story is this: It robs people of dignity. It makes our recognition of our equal humanity difficult. It emphasizes how we are different rather than how we are similar.*

Reading that final statement again, I'm struck by the idea of difference and similarity. The PDK poll might be reconsidered this way: When Americans think about what is local, what is similar, they are more positive and optimistic. It is the other places, the other schools, that are failing, and that perception of failure feeds the inclination to disengage. How many of us have believed the single story of the failing American schools? It's a diffuse narrative, encompassing many settings and characters, but we think we know the outline well enough to conclude it's a rather bleak tale.

But it's not. Don't reach that conclusion. Read about the teachers and schools I visited in one school year, and in Adichie's words, "engage properly" with our public education system; see if you recognize yourself, your own children, and your own community within these stories from diverse schools and classrooms all over California. If we can see the similarities and recognize our "equal humanity," we might then find a productive way forward, together, to build on our strengths and improve public education.

Background

I spent many hours during the 2003–04 school year pursuing National Board Certification as a high school English teacher. Board certification is a rigorous process, above and beyond mere teacher credentialing, so to help ensure my success, I used the support program at the National Board Resource Center (NBRC) at Stanford University. One Saturday morning per month, I brought student work, teaching videos, my own writing, and lots of questions to meetings with my peers and a mentor guiding us through the process. I achieved certification in 2004, and two years later, I became a candidate-support provider to others teachers going through the process. The two years I spent helping others with certification turned out to be the pivotal point that changed my career trajectory and led to this book.

I was, and still am, an English teacher at Palo Alto High School. However, working with peers from other schools and districts around the San Francisco Bay Area turned out to be eye-opening. Palo Alto is a privileged community and school district, both in terms of financial resources and overall professionalism. Observing the contrasts, I began to understand much better how resources and leadership affected teachers and students. Even more important, I began to recognize the negative effects of poor policies. The time I spent most directly involved with the NBRC were the early years of the federal policy called No Child Left Behind (NCLB). The central idea of NCLB was that schools had not been sufficiently accountable for the failure of their students. Congress decided that every American student had to be proficient in reading and math by 2014 and implemented a regimen of standardized testing and reporting requirements that would induce schools to improve or force them to undergo substantial reforms.

The target of 100 percent proficiency was an ill-advised codification of political rhetoric, rather than a responsible approach to legitimate aspirational goals. There was no definition of proficiency and no reason to believe that a standard worth reaching could be simultaneously reached by tens of millions of American children, regardless of poverty, language acquisition, learning differences, or health problems.

As a result of the pressures of NCLB, many states, districts, schools, and even teachers engaged in some unfortunate practices. To be fair, the worst consequences of NCLB were not mandated by that law, though they were quite predictable: Many administrators and school boards under intense pressure allocated time and resources to activities that were believed to raise test scores, often without evidence that such strategies would work. Test preparation and simulation took time away from real learning activities. Creative exploration and experiential learning faded away, while physical education, arts, science, and social studies were cut to make room for more reading and math.

I was fortunate. Working in a district with good test scores and leadership, and ample resources, I was insulated from the deteriorating teaching conditions in many other areas. My good luck was hardly deserved, and in fact, simply highlighted already existing inequities. In my community, most students benefited from every advantage you can imagine in terms of their home life and extracurricular opportunities. It seemed that the students who needed an enriching school experience the most were increasingly the least likely to receive it.

Rather than simply accept the benefits of inequity, I found myself increasingly motivated to address it. After all, the teachers and students negatively affected by these policies were not mere abstractions in "other places," but rather colleagues I worked with and admired, and students I knew at least tangentially through their writing or video of their classes.

My impulse to action and advocacy took place at a time when there were opportunities for me to join teacher leadership projects. After we met through the NBRC, Barnett Berry, founder of the Center for Teaching Quality (CTQ), invited me to join the CTQ Teacher Leaders Network (TLN). I found myself with a new, national peer group of leading educator advocates, welcoming and generous in spirit, critical friends whose wisdom and encouragement pushed my thinking and inspired action. John Norton served as the TLN moderator and cheerleader-in-chief, always finding ways to deepen the dialogue and amplify the perspectives of teacher leaders.

TLN was one of the models that inspired a California teacher leadership network I helped establish, based at Stanford. Accomplished California Teachers (ACT) became my main project outside of school and, for six years, allowed me to meet and work with some amazing teachers from a diverse group of schools and regions in our state. While ACT eventually folded due to lack of funding, the Center for Teaching Quality continues to promote teacher leadership and advocate for the teaching profession, and its Collaboratory online space has expanded opportunities for dialogue and networking among teacher leaders around the country.

The more people I met and the more schools and programs I learned about, the more evident it was that I could help produce a positive counter-narrative about public education. Once I committed to the idea, including taking a year's leave from teaching, it was surprisingly easy to gather suggestions and make arrangements. Friends, family members, colleagues, online acquaintances, and total strangers had school suggestions for me, far more than I was able to visit and enough that I could repeat the process without visiting any of the same places and likely still produce a similar book with similar conclusions.

Methodology

From September 2014 to May 2015, I spent full or nearly full days observing teachers and classes at sixty-three California public schools. (I also went to eight other campuses, but those visits didn't fit the main focus of the book because they were at private schools or my time was too brief or didn't involve classrooms.) During classes, I took narrative and descriptive notes along with many photographs that serve both as illustrations for my writing and reminders of what I observed. (For students whose images appear in the book, I had signed consent forms ahead of time, granting permission for photography and publication, omitting names). Sometimes, my host and I had the opportunity for some fairly lengthy conversations, but there were no formal interviews. Direct quotations in the book come primarily from notes I took at the time. In a few cases, quotes were taken from email correspondence or online forms my hosts completed before or after my visit.

My approach could be described as strength-based. My observations and note-taking focused on the positives; it was decidedly not my intention to evaluate or to offer criticism. There are a number of reasons behind this approach. First, there's a school of thought that focusing on strengths is the superior approach to organizational management and improved performance in a variety of fields, not just education. Naturally there are limits to that idea: You can't ignore egregious problems. You also can't enact a positive vision by simply avoiding negatives.

It was also important for this project that my host teachers and schools could welcome me without reservation. A school day contains hundreds of interactions between teacher and students, and hundreds more among students. (Stanford professor Larry Cuban has estimated that teachers make thousands of decisions a day, with every minute containing options to start, stop, or resume; say something or wait; answer a question or ask another; help this or that student first, observe or intervene, and so on). Even on my best days as a teacher, I know I make mistakes and that some students are, at points, disengaged, confused, distracted, or misbehaving. Teachers needed to trust the intentions behind my visit. Given the professionalism and desire to improve among the teachers I observed, I was asked on several occasions to provide a teacher with some kind of feedback or constructive criticism, yet I always declined. Instead, I would ask about the moments I found most intriguing. It was important for my work that I not leap to conclusions in moments when I had questions or doubts. Here are two short examples to illustrate why:

- Visiting a third-grade classroom, I observe that one of the twenty students doesn't really engage with classmates, preferring to read illustrated books in isolation, under a desk most of the time. The teacher checks in occasionally, but does nothing to encourage interaction with other students or engagement with the main lessons of the day.

- At a middle school, thirty students are supposed to be studying ancient civilizations, taking notes from a textbook. One of the students has trouble focusing, and in a state of distraction and unease has also begun making off-topic comments to a classmate sitting several feet away, trying to work. The teacher tries several times to redirect the student and says the misbehavior is unacceptable, but the problem persists for several minutes.

Even with hundreds of hours of visits and an intention of focusing on the positive, I have to admit that, for a moment, these situations created some doubt: *The teacher is doing something wrong.* We can't ignore a child who's not engaged or tolerate disruption in the classroom. I imagine many observers might have jumped to negative conclusions. I'm afraid some administrators evaluating these teachers would have left the room prematurely, without fully understanding what they were seeing and how it would play out.

But here's why it's important to refrain from judging without sufficient context. In the first example, the student under the desk was back at school for the first time after an extended absence that lasted weeks. There are underlying issues the teacher is aware of (naturally, I receive no confidential details), and the instructional decisions I observe have been made in consultation with a team of professionals involved in the student's education. Apparently, simply getting through the school day and staying in the classroom, at this point in time, represent significant progress for this student.

The second story has a more clear-cut ending that comes about a minute later. It could end with the disruptive student being justifiably sent out of class, given some kind of disciplinary consequences, maybe even suspended if the disruptions constitute a pattern. But the teacher is patient, given that the other students, while briefly distracted, are not at risk of any harm. The disruptive student, for reasons I don't pretend to know, gives up on the problematic actions and decides to attempt the course work instead. Near the end of the class period, the teacher approaches, thanks the student for self-correcting, and asks what it was that helped bring about the positive change. "What worked for you today? How did you calm down?" No clear, simple answer emerges, but there is a lesson here. The teacher has given the student time, space, and trust, and as a result, "catches" the student doing the right thing, conveys the desire to have the student stay in class and learn, and hopefully increases the odds of better academic behavior in the future. Looked at metaphorically, this moment could have either been a step toward graduation or toward dropping out; what some observers might see as a questionable choice by the teacher turned out to be a sign of wisdom that helped this student stay on the right track.

In the chapters ahead, I hope you'll see many more examples of the excellence found among California teachers and public schools, especially when you go looking for it.

The first few chapters are organized by the schools' grade levels—elementary, middle school, and high school—to highlight some commonalities, trends, and observations about students at those ages. Subsequent chapters focus on some of the characteristics that I think help teachers and schools to grow and thrive, sometimes against the odds. The final chapter offers some suggestions about what we can do to help ensure that public education can build on its strengths and improve in the future.

CHAPTER 2

Elementary Schools:
The Real Wonder Years

Sharon Schneider Barrish accompanied me on a visit to Brentwood Science Magnet Elementary School in Los Angeles, where she was my sixth-grade teacher in 1980–81.

I'VE NEVER BEEN AN ELEMENTARY SCHOOL TEACHER, but I've taught at two schools that included elementary grades. Having observed the younger grades for years and with some experience as a substitute at each grade level, I'm sure I would love teaching elementary school—as long as someone else would write the lesson plans, organize the classroom, provide the storage solutions, and teach me all the tricks for quieting a loud classroom and managing transitions between activities. Elementary-aged children are so enthusiastic, curious, and open to change, and it's a pleasure to help them learn as they encounter so many concepts and activities for the first time. They're still discovering so much about learning and themselves, compared to secondary-grade students who generally arrive more set in their self-image and understandings of school.

I recall vividly two days I spent as a sub in a first-grade classroom in 1993 and the lessons I learned from a little boy named Justin. I was supposed to have the class practice simple subtraction. Justin was not interested in doing subtraction, and rather than struggle with the exercise, he decided to walk around the classroom. Walking after him, I made a rookie mistake by turning his off-task behavior into a source of amusement and a challenge. He sped up, avoided me, and for a moment the scene resembled a game of "duck, duck, goose" with Justin racing back to his empty seat as I pursued him, except that he didn't intend to sit down. It didn't take me long to recognize my mistake, and I shifted tactics, sitting down in Justin's seat. With no more game to play and no reward for walking around, Justin came back to me, and I tried my best to help him grasp subtraction, despite my lack of training in how to teach elementary math. Time ran out, the day ended, and I went on to cover other classes at the same school for the next several weeks. When I eventually returned to that same first-grade classroom, I remembered Justin right away. I checked in with him and said he seemed to be doing a great job with his math, as he told me with a smile, "Oh yeah, I like minus now! It's easy!" That kind of turnaround seems rare in high school, and when it happens, it often comes more gradually and with less overt enthusiasm.

Enthusiasm for learning is one of the hallmarks of early childhood education. Everything seems new, and playing is the preferred mode for learning. However, it's the playfulness of the learning that too often leaves early childhood educators undervalued in our system. They're not just playing games. A skilled teacher working with the elementary students needs to understand quite a bit about how children learn, the sequencing and development of various concepts, and reasoning abilities.

Lois Johnson, Transitional Kindergarten
Margaret G. Scotten Elementary School, Grass Valley

I had the opportunity to see the skill that goes into early childhood teaching when I visited Lois Johnson's transitional kindergarten class at Margaret G. Scotten Elementary School in Grass Valley. Transitional kindergarten, or "TK" classes, represent the earliest possible entry point into public education. These classes serve as a bridge between preschool and kindergarten, enrolling mostly students who are nearly but not quite old enough for kindergarten at the start of a given school year. California policy makers decided a few years ago to roll back the cutoff date for kindergarten from December 1 to September 1, and as part of that change, offered the transitional kindergarten option to meet the needs of those children who otherwise would have been eligible for kindergarten.

With decades of experience in elementary school teaching, Lois has all the energy, patience, and organization that are the distinguishing characteristics of great teachers at those grade levels. She finds transitional kindergarten particularly appealing as a teacher, as the focus remains on curiosity, exploration, play-based learning, and socialization. Lois is not the first teacher to tell me that in recent years, kindergarten classes have become too academic. In TK, Lois can make optimal use of her background in music and can build enriching activities that engage children's imagination. The bonds formed with students add to the enjoyment: "This year's class has been my favorite," Lois informs me, adding, "My husband says I say that every year. But it's true."

I'm in the classroom before the school day officially starts, and I observe the students arriving. Some come in with exuberance, glad to see each other and eager to share updates. Two boys greet each other with a big hug. A girl tells her friend that her family has run out of cat food. With wide eyes and arched eyebrows, she exclaims, "My mom *has* to buy cat food! How many *times* do I have to tell her that!?" Those who notice me are curious about my presence. "Whose dad is he?" one boy asks his classmate. Another little boy keeps peeking over the top of his book to watch me.

When the school day begins, Lois uses the singing time to move around the room and greet each student, leaning over to achieve more of a face-to-face meeting, offering a broad smile and a handshake. When the singing is over, it's time to talk, but Lois doesn't immediately worry about hitting certain topics of the day or any agenda. She mentions an art project coming up later: "We're going to be messy today.

We should call today Messy Thursday!" The students have their own agendas for this sharing time: One boy wants to talk about Thomas the Tank Engine, and the next little girl wants to talk about baby dragonflies.

Another student recalls, for no apparent reason: "One time I got to go to Disneyland with my Grandma and Pop-Pop, and I got to take a picture with Ariel." Followed by: "I went to the dentist, and, and, he had toothpaste that tasted like bubble-gum! And I have a wobbly tooth!"

As random as the dialogue may be, Lois responds with genuine appreciation for everything the children say and do. She thanks them for sharing their stories, and when they sing together, she tells them, "You fill my bucket!" The respect that Lois has for her young students and their learning is further apparent in our conversation after school. "Children this young are often not really heard," Lois tells me "These children are learning so much. To see the growth happening is just wonderful. You have to go with the connections kids are making."

However, going with student-generated connections only takes the class so far, and Lois does not leave connections to chance in planning her class. The current theme for the class is the sun, moon, and stars, and it is apparent in the stories, songs, games, art, and even a TK science experiment. Actually, I missed the science experiment, but Lois tells me that earlier in the week, the children used chalk to trace their shadows on the ground in the morning. When they went outside again at noon, they discovered their shadows didn't fit in the outlines anymore. *How did that happen!?* At one point during my visit, Lois shares a book about the sun, and Peter asks a great question: "Have we learned *everything* about the sun?"

The art project of the day is star-related, as students will be finger painting in a swirly style to imitate Van Gogh's *Starry Night*. One youngster suggests Van Gogh might like to visit their class. Lois replies, "I have some bad news: He's not alive any more. He lived way before your grandparents were born."

"We could go back in time!" one of the boys offers, but Lois says that technology hasn't been invented yet. "Maybe in a year," one of the girls suggests. No one reacts. They do react with glee, however, when Lois announces that today's finger-painted starry nights will involve the use of blue paint. Students look at each other in amazement, as if to say, *Wow! Blue!*

Later, there are play "stations" and less-structured activity. I watch a group of children at a sensory table, simply exploring the properties of sand, clay, or dried beans. Over on the carpet, I see some impressive engineering, impossible block structures that circus animals are driving Hot Wheels through and around.

When we enjoy observing this kind of reaction in young children, I think it's because most of us can't have those reactions ourselves anymore. Being amazed by blue paint is so ephemeral, as it should be. These lessons provide lasting value by cultivating the dispositions to ask questions, try something new, make a mess or a mistake, and be part of a community that does these things together.

Jessica Montmorency Nisenbaum, Third Grade
Malcolm X Elementary School, Berkeley

When students reach third grade, the academic expectations are starting to pick up. The consensus in reading research suggests that third grade is the most pivotal year in literacy development, after which gaps and delays become more persistent. The only third-grade classroom I observed for this project was at Malcolm X Elementary School, in Berkeley. The teacher, Jessica Montmorency Nisenbaum (Miss Mont, to her students), showed me how it's possible to hold on to some of the best qualities of that early childhood experience while preparing students for the upper elementary grades as well.

It's the first day of school following the Thanksgiving break, and to get back in the flow of school, Jessica has her students engaged in a warm-up activity, creating a machine of some sort with their bodies and voices. Everyone has to move together to become the machine and see if their classmates can guess what it is. The imagination and creativity of earlier grades are still present in this third-grade classroom, along with the element of fun. The expectations are appropriately more complex now. Students must work together, maintain focus, and consider relationships: parts to the whole, cause and effect. Their attempts at making remote control cars, a camera, or a robot may be a bit uneven in execution, but as a way to start the school week, the exercise serves its purpose well. Students also have a chance to talk to a classmate or two about their Thanksgiving break, which makes for some highly animated conversations. Two girls who seemed to be good friends sit with their hands up, palm-to-palm with fingers interlocked while recounting their weekends, emphasizing the highlights with smiles and wide-open eyes.

As a transition out of storytelling time, Jessica makes quick, effective use of a technique that might come out of meditation or mindfulness practices, asking students for thirty seconds of quiet time, just focused on their breathing. Students clearly know the routine and use it to make a smooth shift into their reading time. Here's where the teaching differs considerably from early childhood education, as Jessica provides specific targeted instruction and offers students strategies to improve their reading skills. Jessica is among the clearest communicators I've observed, with every word well-chosen and every sentence concise, whether working with the whole class, or one or two students at a time.

For the class overall, one of the key points to communicate is a focus for today's reading. Jessica asks students to look for changes in characters and to explain the change using cause and effect. She provides a model sentence with blanks to fill in with details from the readings: "In the beginning of the story, _____ was feeling _____ because _____. Now my character's feelings have changed because _____."

Most students read silently and independently while Jessica works at a table with two students who are getting closer attention today. They alternate reading aloud while Jessica listens to their reading fluency and pronunciation, taking notes along the way. They also talk about the story, with Jessica pushing for more precise articulation of ideas: "Let's use a better adjective instead of 'good.' "One of the girls offers "great" instead. Jessica shifts tactics, going back to ask about causes of these feelings, instead of labels for them. The students conclude this time by writing down a summary of their work today.

At different points in the morning, Jessica is fortunate enough to have the support of instructional aides and specialists who either help out in the classroom or pull out a few students for more intensive help. One teacher who works with students outside the classroom and also supports other teachers is Silver White, who was a colleague of mine when I worked at Stanford's National Board Resource Center. Silver is the one who first suggested that I should visit Malcolm X and arranged for me to spend a day in Jessica's class. Regarding the school overall, Jessica tells me, "The collegial atmosphere here exudes passion, dedication, and integrity. Once I came to Malcolm X (in 2010), I knew I had found a place where my voice could be heard, but more important, the support I was about to receive would be something I'd never forget. I feel at home, and my close colleagues are like family."

The school still has its challenges. As an arts magnet school, Malcolm X has become a popular option in the district and is now larger than the middle schools.

The increased enrollment has affected the ability to house and deliver the arts portion of the academic program, though Jessica says that the staff has pulled together to advocate for the school within the district. She also suggests that the ability to speak up for the school is enhanced by being part of a strong union.

The arts curriculum includes drama, dance, visual arts, and music. I don't have the opportunity to see all those in action, though at one point in the day, as I'm walking down the second-floor hallway, I hear a flute playing the melody to accompany "Deck the hall with boughs of holly, *fa la la la la, la la la la.*" Jessica brings a little extra music into the school day by playing guitar before dismissal and leading students in singing "Stand by Me." It's clear that these students have a teacher who stands by them, providing a school day that makes space for them to have fun with games and music, to build friendships, and of course, to learn.

Sharon Schneider Barrish, Sixth Grade (1980–81)
Nikki Kanan, Second Grade
Brentwood Science Magnet Elementary School, Los Angeles

When we think about schools, it's natural that our own experiences as students play a significant part in shaping our attitudes and opinions. I attended four different elementary schools, with the first three corresponding with my father's years in the Air Force. I settled into my fourth and final elementary school when my father left the Air Force and my family returned to our hometown of Los Angeles. I remember my two years at Brentwood Science Magnet Elementary School much more vividly than anything that came before. I was older, happier, and had chances to revisit the school in later years. I still have some friends from fifth and sixth grade.

My fifth-grade teacher, Larry Kosberg, had just moved to LA from New York and had an accent that made him seem, if not exotic, at least unique. Based on my limited experience until then, I found his teaching methods and persona unusual. He played with us on the playground; he taught us a New York version of handball and later organized a class Olympiad. Mr. Kosberg typed up the lyrics to Simon and Garfunkel's "Keep the Customer Satisfied" and had us sing along with the recording. It seemed a bit dangerous, singing in the character of someone the deputy sheriff disliked, someone who stayed two steps away from the county line, but it was fun. And it wasn't just students who enjoyed the class; Mr. Kosberg seemed to as well.

My sixth-grade teacher, Sharon Schneider Barrish (back then, just Ms. Schneider), exuded a love of teaching and students, and helped cultivate in me a love of learning. I was already a strong student, particularly in reading and writing, so I was challenged with readings like *The Hobbit,* and I memorized and recited Rudyard Kipling's poem "If." Reconnecting with Sharon several years ago through a Facebook group for the school, I arranged to meet her during a trip to Southern California. It was such a pleasure to meet her again in my adulthood, simultaneously someone familiar and beloved, but also new. I discovered just how well she knew and remembered so many of us, as she pulled out photo albums and recalled all sorts of details. It turns out she's kept in touch with many former students and families, and I wasn't surprised that when I mentioned Sharon to my parents and sister, they all remembered her fondly.

Sharon continued to teach at the same school for many years and still knows many of the teachers. So, as I embarked on this project, I asked if she would help arrange for us to spend a day together at Brentwood Elementary, and I was delighted when she said yes.

I arrive back at my old school quite early and have some time to wander around the blacktop, marveling at all that has changed and all that is still the same—more than thirty-three years since I was a student there. Flashes of past games of handball, kickball, and hopscotch replay in my mind. Friends I've kept in touch with suddenly appear in memory as their 11-year-old selves, and other classmates almost completely forgotten begin to resurface. The sounds of children yelling, laughing, and playing all feel familiar, but the playground structures and play areas are all different. I see my old fifth-grade classroom and the fence where we used to stand at recess, sometimes to play a game of "calling" cars as they went by on San Vicente Boulevard—*I call the BMW! I call the Corvette!*—as if we were claiming them, I guess (I never really understood the game). Alternatively, I spent some of my recess time talking about the Beatles with my friends Robbie and Jonathan. The Fab Four had recently become my favorite band, thanks to Robbie, though the radio was more likely playing Michael Jackson's "Don't Stop 'til You Get Enough" or Queen's "Another One Bites the Dust."

The student demographics at Brentwood have changed in the past few decades. No surprise. I think when I was there, the majority of students (though not overwhelmingly) were white and lived somewhat near the school, though there were many black students and some Latino and Asian students. The concept of a magnet school is that it offers a specialized program and pulls students from across the district, not just from the neighborhood; I was told that the percentage of neighborhood students is now rather low. The school's online profile says its student body is roughly one-half Latino, one-quarter African-American, about 10 percent white and 10 percent Asian, and it doesn't specify subgroups in the remaining 5 percent.

My host for the day is Nikki Kanan, a second-grade teacher whom Sharon mentored. Nikki has taught at Brentwood for her entire twenty-year career. I arrive before Sharon, and Nikki couldn't be more gracious in welcoming me (back) to the school and reacquainting me with the campus and academic program. When I was there, the science magnet program included separate weekly science classes, taught by science teachers, in a marine biology lab and an earth science lab. They now have four science programs, but my favorite, marine biology, is no longer in the mix. One important point I wouldn't have appreciated at the time is that when students are in science classes, the primary teachers have prep time, a significant perk in a system that generally neglects teachers' needs. The amount of prep time Brentwood teachers have weekly should actually be provided daily, and many teachers in elementary schools don't even have that much time.

Nikki greets students at the door of her class, a fairly common best practice that helps establish a warm and welcoming atmosphere in classrooms at any level. It also sometimes helps teachers spot trouble literally walking in the door—a student with no materials, or one who is arguing with a classmate, or another who is giving an indication that something is off. In this case, the door to the classroom is at the top of a short set of stairs, in one of these ubiquitous LA Unified bungalows—not portable classrooms but freestanding block-shaped structures that hold only one or two classrooms, and are built with the floor level about four to five feet above the ground. With the sun behind her and the decorated door open wide, it's like students are entering a bright and special place.

There were many times during this journey that I was introduced at schools I visited, or introduced myself, though those times were never as much fun as when I saw how Nikki's students reacted when they found out I used to be a kid at their school. Inevitably, the next question was "How old are you?" Apparently, forty-five is really, really old, but I was reassured that I look younger.

Sharon arrives around nine, and our greeting and hug causes a brief distraction; however, Nikki's students already know Sharon because she has volunteered in their class before. What a tremendous benefit to those children, and to Nikki, to have a veteran teacher coming in as a volunteer.

I had anticipated that Sharon would sit with me during the class, that we might share some quiet observations, and that I might have the benefit of her insights and perspective as I take notes. I realize quickly that's not going to work. She can't just sit and watch. Within minutes, she's looking for ways to be useful: checking students' work, helping kids organize materials, having them read aloud to her. During a math test, a girl raises her hand and Sharon goes to help, clearly a co-teacher for the day. When Sharon consults with Nikki, it's primarily to share information rather than inquire about what to do. If you've ever watched doubles tennis, you've seen partners lean in like this between points, to say something quick but meaningful before setting up the next point.

After a while, I'm more focused on Nikki and less aware of being in my old school with my former teacher. One of Nikki's gifts as a teacher is her ability to interact directly with every student multiple times during the day. She seems to "read" her kids well, anticipating struggles and providing different kinds of encouragement to each based on what they have done. A great teacher develops an informed awareness of which students, at any given moment, need more of a push or more gentle reassurance and support. Nikki shows this kind of awareness as she invites students to her desk individually to review math quizzes and as she circulates among them during reading time. To give some sense of the breadth of reading skills she's working with in second grade, the books students are reading range from Dr. Seuss titles to *Diary of a Wimpy Kid*.

Interpersonal skills are at the fore when Nikki invites students to the front of the classroom to share their "community hero" project. Some are eager to share, and some need confidence and support as they present to their classmates for the first time. Nikki supports both kinds of students effectively.

Sensitivity and patience prove vital again when Nikki moderates a disagreement among students, as she models empathy for them, has them calmly explain the problem, make eye contact, and discuss how to avoid problems in the future. Nikki also has a variety of class rules and procedures that minimize problems throughout the day; she helps students understand and respect personal space and has established routines for students to organize materials and classroom furniture at the end of the day. When all the students are gone, some older students, who used to be in Nikki's class, come to help her out, just because they enjoy visiting with her. Before I go, I have Nikki take a few pictures of me with Sharon, to help capture some of the new memories I've made at my old school today.

What's unique in elementary school children is the overt enthusiasm, the senses of wonder and discovery, the lack of self-consciousness. These descriptions don't apply equally to all children, of course, but the potential is there. Great teachers capitalize on these dispositions to help students learn skills and content across subject areas. It's beautiful to behold and to be around. It was never a bad day when I was in an early elementary class. I made friends, I amazed children by being old, received hugs for no apparent reason, and I thought, "Wouldn't it be wonderful if we could bottle this, preserve it? What if our older students had the same feelings about school and learning?"

By the time students finish elementary school, that portion of their education has spanned more than half their lives. With California school districts now providing transitional kindergarten classes, some of our students will complete seven years of public education by the time they enter middle school. And what a full seven years it is. They come in not knowing all their letters and numbers and leave as young authors, bloggers, inventors, artists, and coders. Barely able to tie their shoes when they arrive, they're now rulers of the playground, athletes in training, dancers on the stage. The child's sense of wonder and curiosity evolves, and instead of marveling at the blue paint or the shadow's changing shape, fourth and fifth graders channel their energy into science projects to save the environment; they write stories and produce videos that evoke tears or laughter. The transition to middle school means new campuses, more teachers, a wealth of opportunities to learn—and plenty of new challenges to address as adolescents.

CHAPTER 3

Middle Schools:

A Brief, Wild Ride

Lovelyn Marquez-Preuher confers with a student in her eighth-grade English class at Dodson Middle School in Palos Verdes (part of the Los Angeles Unified School District). One class period might involve dozens of short interactions like this, keeping students focused and allowing the teacher to monitor learning closely.

THERE ARE PEOPLE WHO WILL SAY TO A TEACHER, "I don't know how you do it. How do you put up with the kids all day? How do you put up with the parents?" Every job has its drawbacks, of course, and most of the teachers I know would say that we don't "put up with" the kids—we *relish* our time with them and find it to be the best part of the day. The work we do outside the classroom—planning, grading, dealing with materials, paperwork, emails, and meetings—is often the more challenging part.

But if you ever hear one teacher ask *another teacher,* "How do you do it?" I'll bet the question is directed at a middle school teacher. I don't have any hard numbers or solid research on that—just a hunch. Based on my experience, anecdotes, and informal questioning, it also seems common for teachers to pass through middle school jobs on their way to high school teaching, as I did, while fewer go the other direction. (Tom Collett, whom you're about to meet, is one who did.) Part of that dynamic may be about status. High school teaching is sometimes perceived as more professional; even within high school teaching, there's often a bias that confers higher status on those teaching upper grades and more advanced classes. However, the questions about teaching middle school are more about the inherent challenges of that age group than about the status issues.

Middle school is a brief but wild ride for children, a time when bodies and minds change rapidly, and emotions can be intense. Body and mind might be maturing on very different time lines. School itself becomes more complicated with the introduction of multiple classes, more challenging work, more focus on grades. There are also more teams, clubs, dances, and activities, along with more responsibility and independence. There are teenagers on campus, and many students begin mixing socially with high schoolers as well. Preferences in music, videos, movies, and games become more mature—if not more tasteful. Access to all sorts of information expands, and it's all new, all happening for the first time, while the parts of the brain dedicated to impulse control and discretion are still underdeveloped.

The teachers I know who like teaching middle school, *love* teaching middle school. They found their niche and answered the call to harness all that preteen (or "tween") energy. They don't just tolerate it—they welcome it and practically feed off it. They develop a keen understanding of how to appeal to both sides of the middle school brain. Not left/right brain, but adult brain and child brain. You can watch the adult brain leap into action for a deep philosophical, ethical, or political debate, and tap into their idealism with projects addressing real-world issues using academic knowledge and skills. You can push their thinking about algebra with complicated, intriguing problems, or challenge them to write a novel in one month (see Laura Bradley, Chapter 7). Then, mix in a little competition, some candy or pizza to be earned, a game to be played or cartoon to be watched, and you'll see the child brain take over quickly.

There's both an art and a science to understanding, teaching, reaching, and loving the middle school student.

Heather Wolpert-Gawron, English Language Arts, Public Speaking
Jefferson Middle School, San Gabriel

There's no question about where to start the exploration of middle schools in this book. In casual conversation, we might say "Heather became a middle school teacher," but few people take on their job as an identity the way Heather Wolpert-Gawron has. Teachers reading this book might already know Heather as "Tweenteacher"—her moniker in online spaces. She is the author of multiple books about teaching middle school and a contributing writer for websites, such as MiddleWeb and Edutopia. These writing accomplishments, the various awards she's won, and her students' accomplishments in publishing their work and winning speech and debate tournaments would all be fine reasons to visit Heather's classroom. The fact that I've also known Heather for thirty years and went out with her in high school just adds to the fun of seeing her teach now.

Heather brings a unique exuberance to teaching and to every interaction with middle school students. Her love of literature helps her connect with many of them, whether she's turning them on to some of her favorite classics, such as *Peter Pan*, *The Hobbit*, or *The Princess Bride*; tapping into their knowledge of icons like Harry Potter or Katniss Everdeen; or delving into something brand-new like the latest book in the *Skulduggery Pleasant* series. Students relate to her goofy sense of humor, pointing out to me various classroom signs with puns that allude to literary places and characters: the classroom door is "Mordoor" (*Lord of the Rings*), laptop computers are stored in "Kartniss," (*The Hunger Games*), and the interactive whiteboard is "Albus Dumbleboard" (the *Harry Potter* series).

In every one of Heather's interactions with students, individually or collectively, it's clear how much she cares about her students and the quality of their school experience. She knows them well, and throughout the day converses with students individually about books they've read recently, or movies or TV shows they've seen. They know her tastes and interests as well and sometimes initiate similar conversations with her. These dynamics are certainly dependent on context; at another school, differences in the students' cultural or linguistic backgrounds might lead to a different approach to bonding with students. But like many thriving teachers, Heather has found a good fit for herself.

The combination of personal charisma and humor will not suffice for classroom management, but it sure helps. At one point in a lesson, Heather realizes that an issue arising with one student has implications for the whole class, who are busily working on their own writing while she's circulating. She raises her voice and says, "Hey! Don't eavesdrop! Why are you listening in to a private conversation?!" Confused for a moment, the class begins to giggle at her irony, but she has their full and quiet attention in that moment as she goes on to share a tip about writing their articles: "I was just talking to Nathan here and telling him that you can always go back to review the models we looked at last week."

About half of what Heather says in class comes with a character voice; her backup career should be doing voice-over work. Students have been working on newspaper articles about superheroes performing amazing feats. To help them understand the writing elements of focus and tone, Heather becomes an eyewitness to a dramatic event. "Oh my gosh! Look! [Pointing emphatically, she pantomimes taking out a cell phone and dialing] *Boop-boop-beep-bop-beep.* Hello? *New York Times?* The most *amaaaazing* thing just happened!" And then she's back to her normal voice for a while to clarify the point of the scene she just created. A while later, she adopts the voice of a little old lady from Brooklyn, and then she becomes a newsreel announcer as she reads headlines written by students. In another class period, in a sour and raspy voice (like Roz from the Disney movie *Monsters, Inc.*), she cautions students, "If ya don't put yer work in the right place, yer not gonna get a grade!"

These moment-to-moment bits of playfulness and humor are not calculated or scripted; they're not even part of a classroom persona. Outside the classroom, Heather will also throw various voices and accents into regular conversation. But there are two important truths about teaching that we can see in Heather's work:

You have to be your authentic self, and your class has to be interesting enough to compete with everything kids are interested in. The idea of being true to yourself applies beyond teaching, of course. If I were to mimic Heather in my teaching, students would immediately detect something false about it—and me. That's hardly a winning approach to teaching, coaching, managing, or leading in any context. Similarly, it's hard to imagine Heather finding as much success or longevity in her career if she were to suppress her personal strengths and passions in a misguided attempt to be some other kind of teacher.

I don't mean to suggest that Heather's class is all fun and games. First, the humor only works because students are comfortable in the room and productive. Students don't actually want a teacher whose primary goal is to have fun. Like adults, students want a sense of purpose, and they want learn and improve. If there were no point to the humor and no progress in learning, the class would turn against the teacher. Heather's demeanor works for her students because she has put in the long hours to plan and organize lessons and instruction that are meaningful and effective.

And when the situation calls for more seriousness, Heather adapts easily. It's almost scary. The last period of the day requires a serious conversation with her speech and debate class. The report from yesterday's substitute teacher was not good, and now, setting aside all the funny voices or any hint of humor, Heather needs to give a speech of her own. As you read it, sprinkle in a few long pauses and visualize some direct eye contact.

> *You guys are in the dog house. I am not pleased. I love you, but I'm frustrated. We are preparing for a tournament that we are hosting, and we are behind. We are not ready. And I can't do anything about it. You have to do it. You'll be competing whether you're ready or not, and that is not an embarrassment we would wish upon anyone, to be up there and unprepared. And keep in mind, this is an over-subscribed elective. This class had two applicants for every space. To get in, you kept someone out, and that was based on your commitment to work hard and work independently. I don't want you out, though. You are amazing, talented kids, and we are glad to have each of you in the class. But you need to show you want to be here. Don't disappoint your coaches and your team, or yourself. It's time to step up.*

For the rest of the period, Heather's students certainly step up. It's a huge class, and almost everyone needs to use class time to practice some kind of memorized speech or performance. The noise would be impossible within the classroom, so the students are outside, seeking enough space to avoid distraction and enough shade to mitigate the 90-degree heat. Heather, dressed in a dark blue suit, endures the heat and sun to make the rounds, observing her students spread out through this section of the Jefferson Middle School campus. They are preparing for a variety of events, with some options that match what you might imagine as a classical speech, in an expository vein, and other options closer to acting or recitation. Students also listen to classmates practicing, helping each other by giving a cue for a forgotten line, or timing a practice run, or making an iPad video to be reviewed later. Heather doesn't intervene much at this point, as the students seem to have recovered their motivation and some sense of urgency about their preparations.

In later correspondence, Heather suggested that some of the students might have regretted going into speech and debate, but it's important for them to see it through. She wrote, "All middle schoolers are works in progress, but that doesn't mean that responsibilities end when kids make questionable decisions. It's important to push them, then praise them for pushing through the difficulties. We celebrate the students who never trophy but grow and push themselves in their abilities more than those who trophy without the effort. You can't give honest praise without pairing it with honest criticism."

The idea of growing through honest criticism is something Heather applies to herself and her teaching. At the end of my visit, Heather and I have only a few minutes to chat; she has work to take home, of course, and two young sons who need their mom, while I'm about to merge into downtown Los Angeles traffic on my way to my next destination. So as we're talking, I'm focused on the positives. That's the nature of my project: I'm not out to evaluate or coach people on the one and only day I spend in their classrooms. But Heather is entirely focused on what could be improved. Could her lesson plans be adjusted, anticipating the likelihood of bandwidth problems for students watching videos on Wi-Fi? Could she shift the sequence of instruction, or break down certain aspects of the assignment into more steps? Provide more, or better, examples?

Usually, this kind of analysis and reflection takes place in a teacher's mind, or sometimes with a colleague who's willing to lend an ear. I feel like a reporter listening to a winning basketball coach at a press conference: "Sure, we're on a ten-game winning streak, but we've got to clean up those turnovers. We also gave up too many easy baskets in the third quarter. We're in trouble if we don't maintain our focus all four quarters, keep up the intensity, communicate on defense . . .". Heather's at the top of her game—and far from satisfied.

Lovelyn Marquez-Preuher, English Language Arts
Rudecinda Sepulveda Dodson Middle School,
Rancho Palos Verdes

The same kind of drive seems to animate many of the teachers I visited, and ultimately, that's more important, and malleable, than the teacher's personality. I think you can acquire an approach to your work and cultivate habits that help you improve, regardless of your teaching style. I can see the similarities and differences between middle school teachers again many months later, when I return to the Los Angeles area. I'm spending a morning with one of the 2015 California Teachers of the Year, Lovelyn Marquez-Preuher. She teaches English language arts at Rudecinda Sepulveda Dodson Middle School (Dodson, for short) in Rancho Palos Verdes, and while her teaching persona is quite different from Heather's, they share a passion for teaching this age group and share a clear vision that guides their efforts to improve.

This is the southern tip of the Los Angeles Unified School District, within sight of the Port of Los Angeles. Many parts of Los Angeles remind you that the entertainment industry drives much of the city's economic activity, but when you get down to Rancho Palos Verdes and the neighboring community of San Pedro, you realize how much the port means to the economy as well. Trucks make up more than half the road traffic when you drive over the bridges near the docks, and numerous train tracks run alongside the highway right up to the railyard next to the port. The largest container ships are about a quarter of a mile long, and they are docked alongside the giant cranes that lift shipping containers from stacks of five or six—each one destined to become one of the cars in a train or the trailer behind a big rig. The work is complicated, dangerous, and well-compensated. Some of Lovelyn's students have parents without a college degree earning a good middle-class income from the port. In fact, many earn more than teachers—a point that Lovelyn mentions because it complicates discussions with students about the economic value of a college education.

Lovelyn has the kind of job that many teacher leaders would love to have—a hybrid position that combines time in the classroom with time working with colleagues on school and district initiatives and priorities. At Dodson, teachers are working to deepen interdisciplinary approaches to teaching; students are more likely to be engaged and develop and retain knowledge and skills when there is overlap and consistency in different classes. Lovelyn has release time from teaching to coach the trainers, helping the teachers who will lead that effort at the school. Additionally, she occupies a district-created position as a "targeted student populations coordinator"—a role that she says gives her special responsibilities to advocate for students learning English and with special educational needs. This work involves parent outreach, monitoring student course placements, and conferring with school leaders regarding budgeting priorities. The extent of her work outside the classroom continually changes: "I keep adding to my own job description," Lovelyn tells me, "but that gets me in trouble sometimes." The bottom line, though, is that Lovelyn has support and flexibility in her work because the focus is always on helping students.

In the classroom, Lovelyn has a calm but purposeful presence. The class runs smoothly because she has taken great care with the lesson and materials, and students receive the support they need as they work. In the first period of the morning, Lovelyn reminds students about writing they did a while ago, trying to make connections that will help students take the next essential step in their progress as writers. The current focus is on providing support for a common theme found in multiple texts. They might draw on articles, poems, and stories they've read as a class, but the specific selections and the theme to be analyzed must come from the individual students. It's a challenging assignment for eighth graders, but well suited for students who are, instructionally speaking, only six weeks from ninth grade.

Lovelyn's commitment to making learning personal is evident in her willingness to make her own story part of the classroom. As an immigrant to the United States, Lovelyn faced challenges in school that many of her students can relate to. She tells me that she once became a bit teary-eyed while reading to her students a narrative about her personal struggles in elementary school, trying to navigate in a new culture and language. If your image of middle schoolers comes entirely from personal travails, or the fictional *Wimpy Kid* series, it might seem like a teacher who sheds a tear in front of her students would be doomed, but in fact, Lovelyn's authenticity builds credibility and a sense community in the classroom.

With each of the three class periods I observe, Lovelyn's instructional choices vary. The overall objective and the source materials are the same, but the pacing, chunking of information, and use of examples varies. This kind of adjustment is among the hallmarks of an accomplished teacher. I know from my own experience that even a well-designed lesson undergoes some fine-tuning during the day. I observe how a lesson works with the first class, make a minor adjustment at midmorning, and perfect it by lunchtime. However, when I ask Lovelyn about these variations in her lesson, it turns out there's even more thought and planning behind what I observed. She hasn't adjusted the lesson based on observations made today. Instead, Lovelyn had planned the lesson in three different versions, taking into account the skills and learning differences in the room. Listening to her talk about her students, I can tell that Lovelyn has made it a point to know them well and meet their needs.

It's more than a question of meeting student needs, though; it's a matter of teacher survival. "I feel like middle school students can smell an unprepared teacher from a mile away, and they will try to take advantage of that, so they push me to overprepare." Lovelyn also points out that a well-prepared teacher, attuned to the students and the lesson, is better able to manage the classroom—almost like a certain web-slinging superhero might: "I've developed what some students call my 'Spidey Senses.' I'll over-hear one say, 'How did she see that?' Or 'how can she hear that from all the way over there?' By being a keen observer of what sets them off or makes them tick, I develop close relationships with my students, and they respect me because they know I care."

Tom Collett, Science
Newark Junior High School, Newark

In the San Francisco Bay Area, I have the privilege of observing another middle school teacher who's been recognized as a California Teacher of the Year (2012). I was at the Sacramento dinner where Tom received his award, along with four other outstanding honorees. (One of those four, Rebecca Mieliwocki, went on to be the US Teacher of the Year. We'll get to her classroom in Chapter 6.) Much of Tom's teaching that we celebrated that night was work at the high school level. As I mentioned earlier, Tom is one of those rare teachers who moved from high school to middle school.

Currently, there's a growing shortage of highly qualified teachers to fill needs in California and in the United States. Of course, the shortages are not evenly distributed among grade levels and subjects; the shortage is nothing new in science and math. So a teacher with Tom's resume and skills can have his pick of jobs. As a high school teacher, Tom taught classes in earth science, astronomy and aerospace science, and marine science and technology. There was also a rocketry club that participated in national competition; Tom's students reached the national finals of the Team America Rocketry Challenge. Later, he handed off the rocketry coaching to a colleague who took the team to a national championship, while Tom focused on a new project in marine science. In addition to teaching students about marine science, he helped them establish a marine science lab that was open to the public.

That's all in the past, though. Tom now teaches eighth-grade science classes at Newark Junior High School, and though it sounds less exciting to me, Tom exudes enthusiasm and pride regarding his school and colleagues. Over the course of the days I spent visiting schools for this project, one of the interesting differences I observed was how much I was encouraged to meet and talk to other people and how much I was sought out on any given campus. I don't want to assume too much about any school from my untested theory; however, I generally took it as a good sign when my hosts made a point of introducing me to their colleagues and showing me around.

Within moments of my early morning arrival, Tom takes me to meet and talk to his principal, Mark Neal. Tom does a fine job of explaining my purpose in visiting and the broader goals of my project, and we stay for several minutes chatting about the school. Both of them have strong, positive feelings about the climate of the school and the direction it's headed. The details emerge with even more clarity at lunch, when Tom brings me to the staff room to meet and talk to his colleagues. With people coming and going, there are repeated introductions and explanations. Every teacher I meet wants to tell me about someone *else* who's doing a great job. Even the first-year teacher in the room has a long list of positives about the school, across departments: She mentions the special needs students who are learning about and competing in the Special Olympics, and the physical education teachers who give up their lunchtime to organize recreational sports and games for students. And more. The music program is going to regional and state competitions. There are new courses under development in science and robotics.

Another sign of good work here is that they take care of students who can't afford new clothes. Not only does the school collect donated clothing, but they also put time and effort into sorting and arranging items neatly on shelves and racks, allowing students an experience more like shopping for something new instead of being handed something old. (About half of Newark Junior High School's 900-plus students qualify for free or reduced price lunches, an indicator of low family income.) It's moving to see this kind of effort undertaken for students and, yet, unsettling that so many children rely on their school for necessities like food and clothes.

Tom asks me about my work this year, what I've noticed so far in my travels. I respond that I find it interesting that there are so many ways to be a great teacher. He agrees, partially. "Well, the methods and styles vary, but I'd say that kindness is inextricably linked to great teaching." What does that look like in the classroom? "I think about the students as if they were my own children. I try to speak their names with the feeling that comes from saying my son's name."

Interacting with large classes of eighth graders (up to thirty-three students), Tom has an energetic, engaging, and humorous manner. He starts all his classes today with some periodic table jokes:

What's the pirate's favorite element? Arrrrgon!

What did the Fort Knox guard say to the runaway bar of gold? "Ay! You! Get back here!" (Gold is identified as "Au" on the periodic table.)

Not much time for jokes, however. Tom's students are just starting to learn about subatomic particles, the relationships among neutrons, protons, and electrons. They're picking it up fairly quickly, partly through an interactive and low-tech demo and discussion, with Tom holding up a two-dimensional model of an atom and sliding magnetic particles to various positions. Then, students have a chance to model different atoms and ions using software on laptop computers. During one class period, a student's question leads briefly to a discussion about unstable, radioactive particles. Seeing some confused looks among other students, Tom apologizes for going into a topic he didn't mean to start yet. I tell him later, "I think it's nice that you apologized for accidentally exposing students to radioactive isotopes." An English teacher can make chemistry jokes, too.

Even in a class where pacing and strategies are well-suited for middle school students, there are occasionally students who make mistakes, lose focus, or mismanage their time or materials. Tom's approach is firm regarding expectations, but as he suggested, always kind. When he talks with students individually about problems, it's concise, quiet, direct, and specific. He sits with students rather than standing over them. "I want a positive relationship, but we also need some compliance with baseline expectations. It's not punishment, not detention. It's a conversation."

As a postscript to this particular visit, I want to highlight one additional comment from Tom, because it speaks to the entire purpose of this work. At the end of the day, in the context of a broader conversation about school variability, Tom says, "There's so much positive energy at this school. I'd be glad to have my son in any classroom at this school. Any teacher. Roll the dice."

Tom's son is still in elementary school, but I have a son in eighth grade, and I pause for a moment to imagine him attending Newark Junior High School. That kind of endorsement, coming from a teacher of Tom's experience and skill, would be persuasive and completely reassuring to me. From an outsider perspective, though, how do people judge the quality of the school?

Using almost any numerical indicator, data point, accountability mechanism, a community member or policy maker won't have any idea. Test scores seem to matter, but they won't reveal the heart and soul of the school. Demographic data will show the diversity, but not the atmosphere, the poverty, or the depth of the staff's caring and supportive efforts.

If we, as a general public, as a state, can't capture the sparks that make a school like Newark Junior High thrive, we risk extinguishing them. If we privilege the lifeless and misleading data to drive policy decisions and ignore the realities of children and teachers, I fear we'll continue making the mistakes of the past. We'll tell Tom Collett and his colleagues they aren't good enough, and they need to try harder, because standardized test scores didn't rise quickly or consistently enough, across all student populations and subgroups.

Tom's assessment of the school carries more weight with me than anything I can look up online. Imagine if we could go to the state's database of school quality indicators, and in addition to finding scores, we could read this:

There's so much positive energy at this school. I'd be glad to have my son in any classroom at this school. Any teacher. Roll the dice.

As my year of school visits wrapped up, I was asked by several people if I planned to return to teaching the following year. That was my plan all along, and I did return to the same teaching assignment I left for a year. However, the exposure to different types of schools sparked my imagination a bit, stoking some curiosity about what it would be like to teach at different types of schools. Despite three years teaching in grades six through eight, and despite having my own sons in grades six and eight during my year of school visits, I had more to learn about middle schools, their teachers, and students. Teachers like the three in this chapter, and middle school teachers in the chapters ahead, showed me how it's done, capturing the sparks that light up learning for "tweens" in these tumultuous years of change. And though it would mortify my younger son, still in middle school, I can now imagine myself as one of those uncommon teachers who might someday return from high school teaching back to middle school.

CHAPTER 4

High Schools:

Launching the Future

*Denise Shaw looks on with satisfaction
at the discussion in her
English class at Vista High School.*

IT'S NOT JUST ONE SMALL STEP, BUT A HUGE LEAP from middle school to high school. The curriculum becomes increasingly varied, with more levels and subjects, simultaneously exposing students to greater depth and breadth in their studies. Those who succeed in advanced placement or International Baccalaureate courses are essentially completing college-level studies. The student publications achieve a level of polished, professional quality, with musicians, actors, dancers, and athletes all performing at higher levels on larger stages, under the gaze of a more attentive public. I'm intrigued by the increasing number of academies and curricular "pathways" within schools, offering students in-depth and practical opportunities to pursue their interests. Some of the possibilities include biotechnology, teaching, environmental science, visual and performing arts, engineering, business, culinary arts, hospitality, medicine or sports medicine, and other careers in the sports industry.

While middle school represented the transition from child to adolescent, high school brings the even larger transition to adulthood, and all that comes with it. At the schools I visited, I talked with seniors on their way to college, career training, or the military; among the juniors, some have clear goals and plans, while others remain undecided about what to do after high school. Still, there's always a sense in high schools that the future is approaching quickly and the stakes are significant.

There are students who dutifully complete all their work and handle school as responsibly as if it were a job; other students already have jobs. Some students enjoy a sheltered experience in their schools and communities; they exude optimism and confidence, though I know from experience as a high school teacher that beneath the surface, they may be quite anxious, feeling pressure to meet high expectations. Some students may seem less interested in school as they're already taking care of themselves, maybe even helping to provide for their families by working or taking care of younger siblings. Some students have become parents well before the end of high school. For some, talk of college and career seems a distant concern while they try to avoid rehab or complete parole without incident.

Though high school represents roughly a third of a student's years in school, I spent about half my time for this project visiting high schools. Teaching and learning fascinate me, regardless of the students' ages, and I can delight in Lois Johnson's transitional kindergarten class as easily as I marvel at the advanced placement classes you'll read about in this chapter. However, when I look at schools as institutions, high schools are the ones I find most interesting, generally speaking.

The high school teacher must continue to understand and accept the child part of the teenager, while preparing the young adult for independence and advanced scholarship. I wish it were easier to know with certainty how well I've done that job for more than 1,000 students in my career. Thankfully, writing this book gave me an opportunity to catch up with one of those former students.

Stephanie Smith, English
La Quinta High School, La Quinta

It's mid-December, and I'm on the road at sunrise heading to La Quinta, south of Palm Springs, to spend the day with English teacher Stephanie Smith, one of my former students from my years at Mission San Jose High School in Fremont. Stephanie decided in tenth grade that she wanted to be an English teacher. She was writing a career exploration essay in her tenth-grade class and came back to interview me, her ninth-grade teacher. At the time, it was easy to be enthusiastic about the future of teaching: Our state budget was flush with tax revenues from the dot-com boom and No Child Left Behind was still a presidential election away from its inception. I told Stephanie that I would always be glad to help or advise any former student, but I would particularly welcome the opportunity to mentor a future English teacher.

As it turned out, I didn't do much mentoring: A year later I left Mission San Jose to take a job much closer to home, and a year after that, Stephanie moved to Southern California to start college. My visit today at La Quinta High School marks the first time we've seen each other since she graduated high school. Like many young adults dealing with former teachers, Stephanie trips up a bit on the choice between addressing me as David or Mr. Cohen, favoring the latter, even though we're now peers. I find it quite easy to make the mental adjustment to Steph-as-adult, however. She meets me near the school gate upon my arrival, and as soon as we begin walking across campus, I can see clearly that she's at home as a teacher here, with colleagues and students greeting her every few steps. Between her teaching and her supervision or coaching for various activities like cheerleading, Stephanie seems to know more than her share of students.

Just to add to the uniqueness of the day, the school is having a holiday breakfast for teachers, which I enjoy as Stephanie's guest. She has also just announced her pregnancy, so the early morning is a combination of holiday wishes, introductions, and inquiries about the due date and how Stephanie is feeling. Later in the morning, a student asks if she can babysit when the time comes. Actually, her exact words are "Can I be in charge of taking care of your baby?" The student goes on to provide her credentials (CPR training) and experience in hopes of landing the job and receives some smiling appreciation from Stephanie, but no promises.

This student's CPR training fits into her curriculum in the Medical Health Academy (MHA) program at her school. La Quinta High School has some impressive career academies, giving students not only exposure to different careers, but also quality training and preparation that can lead directly to employment. To give me an idea of the broader student experience at the school, Stephanie takes me to see the incredible facilities the school has for two of their career academies. The MHA classrooms are more than double the size of normal classrooms, with typical school furnishings in front and hospital-style patient areas in the back, including hospital beds and various types of medical equipment. The Culinary Arts Institute is quite popular with students and has been tremendously successful in cooking competitions against other high schools and even colleges. Given the vitality of tourism and restaurants in the Palm Springs region, graduates of La Quinta's program have good job prospects after high school. The culinary classroom has a large demonstration and cooking area in the front, with a large mirror giving students an overhead view of whatever the teacher is doing in food preparation. The full industrial kitchen for students has the space and equipment for dozens of people to work at once and can support the preparation of full gourmet restaurant-quality meals at banquet scale, serving up to 600 guests. One episode of the cooking TV show *Top Chef* was staged in the La Quinta facilities.

Stephanie has been the English teacher for a group of students enrolled in the Medical Health program for two years now. It's a unique opportunity for a high school teacher to work with the same groups of students for multiple years, and the benefits are clear in the classroom atmosphere. The interactions are easy and relaxed, and even when Stephanie needs to intervene to keep students on task or to rearrange groups of students, she can do so with a smile and a sense of humor that works when teachers and students know each other well. Her students are working on close analysis of *The Catcher in the Rye,* gathering evidence and quotations for use in a future essay or project. While they're working, students are allowed to switch seats and consult with their peers, but Stephanie nixes one move, telling the student, "You don't *really* want to work with him, you just want to go talk." His grin seems to confirm Stephanie's claim, and he returns to his seat. Otherwise, the atmosphere is serious and focused: largely quiet, with occasional hushed conversations followed by the flipping of pages to locate a scene, followed by note-taking. It reminds me of a collegiate study group, except that Stephanie is moving among her students, answering questions when asked and asking questions when it helps to push a student's thinking. Here, we can see much of what high school is about: a mature level of curricular content; an open-ended, intellectually challenging task; and interactions that convey academic expectations, positive relationships, and mutual understanding.

Watching Stephanie teach feels oddly familiar; I don't know that I've had a significant, direct influence, but maybe hints and shadows of my own teaching are present. It might also be that Stephanie and I share some personality traits, and we teach the same subject and age group. We even share an interest in theater that informs our teaching of Shakespeare's plays. As Stephanie's classes are studying *A Midsummer Night's Dream,* they're also performing it, much as she and her classmates performed scenes from *Romeo and Juliet* in my class fifteen years ago. And if I were teaching this year, my students would be working on *The Merchant of Venice* in the same manner.

My school observations usually don't involve more than a little direct conversation with students (and then, always with the teacher's permission and encouragement), but in this situation, I feel a stronger inclination to interact. Just as my former teacher, Sharon Schneider, couldn't resist jumping in to help Nikki Kanan at Brentwood Elementary, I want to be useful, and this is certainly a situation where I have something to offer, as the teacher's attention is spread thin and I have the background to be helpful. Alas, while a second grader will warm up quite easily to a helpful guest teacher, these high school students are not necessarily interested in my guidance. While the second graders were amazed that I once attended their school, high school students aren't necessarily interested in the fact that I was their teacher's teacher once upon a time.

Stephanie's students are mostly working outdoors near the classroom, and I approach a group of five boys struggling with the final scene of *A Midsummer Night's Dream.* It's a confusing scene, including a play within the play. The text requires careful attention, because the characters known as the "rude mechanicals" may at times may be speaking as themselves, and at other moments those characters are playing *other* characters in a short play about the mythological figures Pyramus and Thisbe. It's a scene that has tremendous comedic potential, but inexperienced students may not recognize the humor simply by reading the text. I visit with the group, trying to encourage some experimentation and risk-taking with the text, figuring out ways to make it funny to an audience. I'm barely into my comments, though, before one of the boys turns away from me to talk to his friend. One of his partners says, "Dude! Be *quiet!* He's trying to *help!*" I appreciate the effort on my behalf and offer a quick word or two of advice before moving on, not wanting to be the source of any further disagreement or distraction.

I soon find myself drawn to another group, which I can tell from a distance is making excellent progress. It's clear that one of the students has a drama background, or at least a clear vision of how the scene should play. She's moving among the group members, giving tips and advice, then backing away to view the scene from the audience's perspective. Her partners recognize the quality of her suggestions, and they're eager to listen, watch, take notes, and follow her directions. Step by step they are crafting a fine scene involving the fairy king, Oberon; his servant, Puck; and the Athenian lovers lost in the forest.

Stephanie moves among the groups and helps them with both the text and performance aspects of the play. There are reminders about staging, the importance of staying visible to the audience, and moving almost constantly. She has assigned long scenes, using more of the text than I typically do. We chat briefly about the challenges of this activity, how much support to give, and how to balance teacher guidance and student autonomy. Another significant challenge is that Stephanie is responsible for teaching more students than I've ever had to manage. With class sizes approaching forty, multiplied by five class periods, Stephanie has nearly two hundred students this year.

When we talk about class size in the general public, people often neglect to do the multiplication for high school teachers. While changing one class size from twenty-three to twenty-eight may not constitute a huge shift for that individual group, when applied across five class periods, it essentially means adding another class to the workload: twenty-five more students. With Stephanie's class sizes, if she gives each student's work an average of only six minutes of attention outside of school hours, that's an extra twenty hours of work. The fact that she works that hard and loves her job is a testimony to her personal commitment. That kind of commitment is common in schools and should be recognized and commended; at the same time, we need to acknowledge that we'd be better served if teaching didn't require such personal sacrifice. Unfortunately, that kind of sacrifice is highest among teachers staffing the most challenging schools with the neediest students. They generally earn lower salaries, have fewer material and tech resources to work with, and must cope with inferior facilities and working conditions. When their schools and students struggle, these dedicated teachers are all too likely to have their skills and commitment unfairly called into question by the state accountability system, the media, and the general public.

Other than the large class sizes, however, La Quinta High School has been able to build strong programs and outstanding facilities. The school's career and technical education program has been recognized for its excellence, and they were visited by State Superintendent for Public Instruction Tom Torlakson in 2014. Then, in 2015, the school earned a Gold Ribbon School Award for academic excellence. So, overall, Stephanie is in a setting where she's able use her interests, talents, and strengths to help students thrive academically and personally.

David Atkinson, Science Teacher, Science Department Chair
Lindhurst High School, Olivehurst

Hundreds of miles north of La Quinta, in the small town of Olivehurst, I visited another campus where dedicated teachers are working to overcome systemic challenges as they prepare teens for life after high school. At Lindhurst High School, my host is science teacher, David Atkinson, a graduate of Palo Alto High School, though I was never his teacher. His mother, Carolyn Benfield, has been the principal's secretary at our school throughout my time there. (And if you want to know a secret, the secretaries and custodians are the people who really keep a school up and running.) When I found out about David's career trajectory, I was eager to include him and his school in my project, because he would be so perfectly suited to talk to me about the contrasts between schools and communities. Lindhurst serves the rural towns of Marysville and Olive-hurst, near Yuba City and Beale Air Force Base. The towns have a combined population around 26,000, with median household incomes under $37,000 and median home prices under $130,000. In conversation and emails prior to my visit, David tried to prepare me multiple times: "This isn't Palo Alto."

The day of my visit begins with a drive north from a hotel in Davis. Most of the journey is a straight shot due north, up Highway 99 and then onto Highway 70, passing thousands of acres of farms and wetlands dotted with white egrets, as flocks of geese and ducks fly over in formation. There are plenty of trucks on the road already and not much to distinguish one highway exit from the next during the hour I'm on the road. There are no traffic lights or commercial areas between the highway and Lindhurst High School; it's mostly small houses, some two-story apartments, and a mobile-home park. Some of the houses have several cars parked on the driveways and lawns; some even appear to have makeshift living spaces added onto the sides or constructed in yards.

My navigation app tells me I've arrived, but I'm on a neighborhood street behind the campus, necessitating some extra driving around the school's periphery as the day begins. Students are shuffling toward Lindhurst, some carrying backpacks, some not. A few clusters of students form on street corners, with puffs of smoke drifting up from their circles. For some people, it might be easy to drive by this scene and make assumptions about the school and the neighborhood, with kids who don't carry books and gather to light up before the day has really begun. I'm resisting those assumptions, but I'm aware of them briefly crossing my mind.

Ten minutes later I've found the parking lot, checked in at the office, and I meet David for the first time. His classroom is on the second floor of a new science building, and from the walkway, I can see the exact part of the neighborhood through which I first approached the school. The streets are clear, the kids have come into school, and there's a lot of good happening here.

David has an advisory period before classes start. This program is relatively new to the school and has been introduced in part due to David's advocacy for it. Today's advisory lesson involves learning about different types of scholarships and financial aid, giving juniors some sense of information they'll need to know in more detail next year. But even if they forget the details, the students benefit from advisory because it provides an extra point of contact with the adults at school, with the aim of building relationships. Before the students leave to their first class of the day, David checks in with several of them and always seems to be picking up a conversation in the middle, because he knows the students and their situations. During the transition to classes, one student opens the door just to say, "Have a good day, Mr. Atkinson!" Though more accurately, it comes out as *Haveagooddaymisteratkinson!*

David has a wide range of classes and students during a single school day. His ninth graders come in first, an earth science class for students still learning English, and mostly boys in this particular period. "Ninth-grade boys" may be explanation enough when one of them pauses during some note-taking about the solar system and turns to share with his friend an anatomical rhyme for the planet Venus. Later, after taking notes on the key characteristics of all the planets in our solar system, another boy asks, "What's your favorite planet, Mr. Atkinson?"

"Earth," he replies, dryly. "I'm a big fan of Earth."

Despite the brief digressions or immaturity of some of his students, David accepts them for who they are, can laugh at their jokes (or at least smirk), and keeps them working and learning. This is a moment in a long journey, and David has a firm belief in the potential of these ninth graders. It's evident in his work with older students later in the day. David has worked hard to pursue grants so Lindhurst students can have better science equipment and has actively recruited and supported students who might be reluctant to take his newly introduced AP physics class.

When that class comes in, my observational notes become a bit sparse: I understand the concepts and recall some basic math relating to momentum, but the class moves too fast for me. When they start some lab work involving model vehicles colliding on a track, David moves around the room troubleshooting, but mostly, it's the technology rather than the students that demands his attention. Even with the grants that have funded some upgrades, "we're using equipment that's ten to fifteen years old, and software that's twenty years old," David informs me.

While the AP physics students are on track to attend college, many students in the school are not college-bound. Our discussion of post-high school preparedness touches on competing visions of the mission of high schools. Is college for everyone? It seems self-evident that we must maintain the highest of expectations for all students, and indeed, I don't know any educator who isn't excited to help a student who might be the first in their family to attend college, or even complete high school. Yet for students who contend with myriad problems that limit or derail their academic potential in the short term, it seems just as important to offer options that will make them employable and self-sufficient (not to mention informed and responsible citizens). At a time when college costs rise much faster than inflation, student loans are limited or expensive, and many college graduates are unemployed or underemployed, it seems tone deaf and insensitive to insist that college should be *the one* goal for *all* high school students upon graduation. Yet as soon as we start holding different academic expectations for some students, we should certainly be concerned about which students are tracked toward vocational education and which are considered college material. There are no easy answers.

I do know that the metal shop at Lindhurst is the highlight of my walk around the campus. Just past the softball field, I see and hear a hive of activity. There are close to twenty students hard at work, using a variety of potentially dangerous tools and materials. I borrow some eye protection so I can watch the work and take some pictures, but I have to endure the noise without ear plugs, which all the students have. There are sparks flying in various work areas, with students using a variety of tools for cutting, grinding, spot-welding, and arc-welding. There are both practical and decorative projects under way, and I'm struck by the contrast between the image of teenagers I had this morning outside the school, compared to those in advisory, science classes, softball teams, and metal shop. They're the same kids, in the same community. Driving past a few of them smoking on the street before school, you might fail to realize and imagine that later in the day they are also AP students, teammates, artists, and workers. In some settings, these same young people are distrusted and have to ask teachers for permission to use a bathroom. In metal shop, they're using dangerous tools independently and effectively, mastering skills that might have them gainfully employed in a matter of months.

David is deeply interested in these questions, as we discuss how challenging and gradual change is for schools and communities. Yes, academic standards and rigor matter, though as David points out, "The life challenges our kids are facing make social-emotional learning hugely important for our students. A lot of them are 'couch-surfing'—technically homeless. Some of them are just trying to stay alive or out of jail. It's challenging to maintain a college orientation and help raise rates of college attendance, but still say attuned and relevant to non-college-bound students."

Lindhurst students face challenges that are both daunting and normal in California public schools today: poverty, learning a new culture and language, frequent moves, or homelessness. Recruiting and retaining teachers in high-needs schools is another challenge, even more so in rural areas; however, some Lindhurst teachers have been on staff since the school opened in 1975. David informs me that few of the teachers live in the community, and he commutes an hour each way, carpooling with three of his colleagues. Despite the commute and the challenges—in part, *because* of the challenges—David and teachers like him continue to teach at Lindhurst. It's a shame that some policy makers and members of the general public, looking to improve schools like Lindhurst, often make the mistake of mandating new programs and remedies while overlooking the strengths these schools already possess.

Denise Shaw, English
Vista High School, Vista

I had one other opportunity to visit a high school and compare notes with some-one quite familiar with my school when I spent a day with my friend and former student teacher, Denise Shaw. For several years after her student teaching, we were fortunate to have Denise teaching English at Palo Alto High School, where she quickly became a student favorite and a model of collegiality and profession-alism. Her move to the San Diego area came a year before I started my project. When we meet again, she's in her second year teaching English at Vista High School, already the department chair and helping lead the school's efforts to transform its teaching and learning.

My drive this morning begins around 6:15 a.m., in the town of Murrieta, which means approaching Vista from the country-side instead of the city-side (the greater San Diego metropolitan area). The commuter traffic heading toward San Diego is already starting to build at this hour, but then I exit the freeway and start through Gopher Canyon. When the road emerges on the other side of the winding canyon, the terrain flattens out, and I'm driving past greenhouses, orchards, and fields where workers have already begun what I assume will be a long day of berry-picking. Vista High School is not far from this, but by the time I pull up to the school, I'm in a more developed area.

Among all the visits I conducted for this book, this is the one where I'm most familiar with the teacher and her teaching, having observed Denise many times when we worked together. I know she'll have everything in her lessons well planned, and she will have high goals and expectations. Yet these are new courses in a new setting, and I learn over the course of the day how Denise has adapted and grown as a teacher here.

In the first class I observe, Denise is working with sophomores studying an essay by Roger Rosenblatt, titled "The Man in the Water" (published in *Time Magazine* in 1982). Rosenblatt reflects on the heroism of a man who survived a plane crash in the frigid waters of the Delaware river but bypassed chances to be rescued, helping other survivors get pulled from the water, one by one ahead of him, until he succumbed to the cold and drowned. It's an essay commonly used in English classes, but there are some unique elements to Denise's approach. I'm interested to learn that her students are studying the essay for a second time, having first seen it several months ago. One student remarks that the essay "seems different this time," to which Denise responds, "I don't know. Maybe you're different now." A deep thought there—that the reader affects the text. But what's also unique is that the students' focus for the moment is not on analysis or interpretation of the essay, but rather, identifying obstacles to understanding. It's a method that Denise has been studying as part of a partnership with instructors and researchers at California State University, Dominguez Hills. In any subject, at any level, metacognition, which is essentially thinking about thinking or thinking about how they learn, can be useful to students. With this approach, students might figure out not only what Rosenblatt thinks about heroism, but also how they can manage challenging texts in the future. The key today is for them to recognize why some elements in the essay are difficult, because recognizing the *type* of problem determines the strategies that will solve it. The issue may be vocabulary (what does "aesthetic" mean?), or practical knowledge (why was it risky for a helicopter to attempt to rescue people?), or cultural literacy (who, or what, is "Everyman"?). Denise has tremendous patience and relentless focus, as an exercise like this can easily take off on tangents, and the point is *not* to discuss helicopters or Everyman, but rather, continue to identify what's challenging and why. This type of lesson is also well suited to Denise's sophomores, as the level of text difficulty should increase dramatically in all their classes in the next few years, and they're old enough to handle the slower, methodical approach.

Denise's next class period is a senior AP English class, which looks a bit easier on the surface, though I know how much effort it takes to make such excellent work routine. Her twenty-seven students reorganize the chairs and desks into a large square with an open center to facilitate a relatively unstructured discussion about a play they're studying. The level of discourse is quite impressive, with students not only displaying some sophisticated understanding of a modern drama, but also articulating the different nuances among themselves as interpreters of the text. Denise is working hard at note-taking, tracking the details of the conversation and who's contributing, but for the most part, she is a silent observer. When students find themselves stuck on a particular point and turn to her, Denise refrains from answering and instead redirects them to the text as the definitive source. This level of academic work in a high school is always gratifying to see; if their writing skills are anywhere near as strong as their reading and discussion skills, these students are ready for collegiate work. Denise also makes an effort to promote equity in the classroom, to make sure all voices are heard. To that end, she encourages some hesitant students not to feel that fully formed ideas and interpretations are the only way to contribute to the discussion: "I want to hear from all of you. Even if you're asking a question or offering half of an idea. Maybe someone else will have the other half, and they're just waiting for you, but they don't realize it."

Near the end of the day, I have a chance to observe Denise at work with her principal and fellow department chairs. I knew she had this skill set, and I'm delighted to see Denise in a position of leadership as her school is planning some significant shifts for next year. The specifics of their movement toward individualized learning aren't as interesting to me as the group dynamics. They're wrestling with complicated changes in academics, counseling, and technology, and have committed to a timeline, beginning implementation in the next school year. More than once in the meeting, the group identifies a detail that hasn't been addressed yet or a question for which they don't have the answer, but they trust each other and the process. They seem comfortable with either of two possibilities: They will figure out the answer with further study and preparation or will proceed anyway and learn by doing. Having been in situations where smaller initiatives were drawn out for years, I appreciate the drive on display here. The fact that they allow a stranger to sit in the meeting, take notes, and write about their work was also a good sign. Earlier in the day, I had heard from Denise that the district's superintendent is quite supportive of their school redesign efforts, which must certainly help. I later learned that Devin Vodicka had been recognized by the Association of California School Administrators as Superintendent of the Year. The next month brought news that Vista High School had (like La Quinta High School) been honored as a Gold Ribbon School by the California Department of Education, with additional recognition for an Exemplary

Career Technical Education program. It's revealing that Vista is simultaneously being recognized for excellence and planning for significant changes. These are the kinds of conditions under which students and teachers thrive.

Teresa Gaims, History/Social Studies
Harbor High School, Santa Cruz

The state's Gold Ribbon recognition was also awarded to Harbor High School in Santa Cruz, which was also distinguished as a Title I Academic Achieving School. (Title I is the federal program providing additional funding to schools with a student poverty level of 40 percent or more.) My interest in Harbor, however, was based on my family relationship with history/social studies teacher Teresa Gaims, my second cousin. Teresa and I have talked about public education together many times, and I wonder if our common roots influence our views.

Our grandmothers were sisters, and among all of my four grandparents' many, many siblings, my great-aunt Phyllis, Teresa's grandmother, was my favorite. She and her husband, Phil, lived for many decades in a modest, white house on a quiet street in the same Los Angeles neighborhood as my grandparents. In my young adult years, once I was able to drive myself around to visit my grandparents, I always included Phyllis and Phil in my outings. Though they have passed away, recalling their warm affection still has a palpable effect on me. The reason I mention them here is that their love of knowledge and learning, and their interests in current affairs, were always evident and certainly influential on their children and grandchildren (and me, their great-nephew). I can't discuss my appreciation for Teresa's intellect and her sense of social justice without thinking of our family connection. Though we don't typically see each other more than once a year, our conversations about public education, politics, and civics have always been valuable to me.

I've arrived at Harbor High School quite early on a gorgeous spring morning in Santa Cruz. Teresa has time to show me around and introduce me to a few of her colleagues before we settle into her classroom. I begin to unpack my bag; I have my school visit routine down pat at this point in the year. Laptop, iPad, personal Wi-Fi, camera, all in their places, all batteries fully charged. I'm not even fully settled in before our conversation veers, as usual, to the broader issues in public education nationally, in California, and locally. Much of the conversation concerns ways in which shifts in populations affect school openings and closures, which in turn can distort what's happening in any given school. For example, when one school closes in a community, its former students are not randomly distributed to other schools; students with different levels of family wealth and linguistic backgrounds are often in separate neighborhoods. The schools that receive an influx of wealthier students with stronger English language skills will see a bump in test scores and will appear at a glance to be improving. Conversely, schools receiving an influx of lower-income students and English language-learners will see their test scores dip, suggesting a decrease in school performance. Another example: Teresa tells me about a Santa Cruz charter high school where families are asked (not required) to contribute $3,000 per year, and only advanced placement courses are offered in the upper grades. The charter school peels away a certain type of student from the neighboring district schools, taking both funding and higher-scoring students in the process, leaving the comprehensive high schools with greater challenges and the appearance of decline. These and similar dynamics are masked in school accountability and testing programs. Test scores rise and fall and are used to judge the school, though the individual students and the broader characteristics of the student body may change significantly. School-to-school comparisons are laden with implied or overt judgments, though the measuring stick is a poor one and the schools aren't necessarily comparable in key respects.

Once the school day starts, however, I see teachers and a principal who are responding positively to the challenges they face. The two classes I observe in Teresa's room, AP US history first, and then economics, are fully engaging and challenging. The chronology of the history class has reached the 1960s, and students are comparing Martin Luther King Jr. and Malcolm X, using for the moment the text of a Malcolm X speech and a video clip. The economics class is taking a tangential approach to the curriculum today, using current events chosen by students. Teresa surveys their choices, and in some cases, asks questions to push students toward identifying underlying issues rather than just noting events. Students in this class were also in Teresa's honors government class the prior semester, so they've also completed some more rigorous research this year, focusing on a Supreme Court case of their choosing. "That's the project they remember," Teresa tells me. "When they come back to visit from college, that's the assignment that they say was the best preparation."

Later in the morning, Teresa encourages me to observe one of her colleagues as well, so I find myself in Judith Mayer's senior AVID class. AVID stands for

Achievement Via Individual Determination, a nationwide program that has great success operating at the school level to promote college matriculation for students of color and those who may be the first in their family to attend college. Since it's the first day back from spring break, students are sharing some updates regarding college acceptances, narrowing down their options, or making final decisions. Judith's tone is positive and celebratory, reflecting that even if students are undecided at this point, they've worked hard to give themselves this uncertainty about good options. After the updates, Judith's students resume work on the AVID equivalent of a dissertation—a synthesis research and writing project about a topic of interest. The final product will be around twenty pages long, including an abstract and works cited. Judith circulates to help students reframe their topics and analyze their thesis and evidence. She also takes time to discuss academic vocabulary, ensuring students are comfortable with the specialized terms necessary to study argumentation and rhetoric.

Teresa also arranges for me to have a campus tour and talk about the bigger picture with Harbor's principal, Dick Davis. He shares what the teachers and administrators have done to try to give students a greater sense of belonging and connectivity around campus. Much of what he describes is really about trusting teachers to be creative and independent around curriculum, finding ways to enrich the school's academic offerings within the constraints of the budget and the courses they can offer. At the same time, they have been working to make class routines and expectations more uniform, especially in ninth and tenth grade, when students need more support.

Teresa reinforces the importance of having students feel like school is an institution that is "on their side"—especially for students who are often marginalized:

> *I have seen my students who are undocumented feel empowered to share their stories. In many ways, they are already young adults, with enormous responsibilities. They have transitioned not so much from students to adults, but rather, from feeling disenfranchised to feeling that they belong, that they can succeed, and deserve access to education and career options in this country.*

Looking back at my school visits overall, it's always the high schools where I feel I missed something important or couldn't fit into this book everything I wanted to include. The complexity of the schools and adolescents, and the imperatives that come with preparing students for college, careers, and citizenship are difficult to capture. Since I know it would be futile to aspire for *completeness* in these vignettes, I've aimed to identify what is essential. If nothing else, I hope these views of high schools reinforce the complexity of the institution itself and the issues embedded therein. It was a privilege for me to witness the dedication of these teachers, who confront imperfect circumstances by pouring their lives into the effort to make high schools work for every student.

I'm confident I could state that California public high schools face significant struggles and not find a contrary voice. Yet stating something I'm equally confident of—California public high schools are educating and supporting students—I imagine that I would hear all sorts of doubts, exceptions, and qualifications.

That's "the danger of the single story," which Chimamanda Adichie describes in her TED Talk (see Chapter 1). I've tried in these opening chapters to offer the long-form version of my school visits, what it was like to spend a day with great teachers in schools at every level, small and large, rural and urban, and in between. Their successes are every bit as much of the educational landscape as the troubles that you can find in your news source of choice. Let their positive stories complicate and disrupt "the single story." The chapters ahead will narrow the focus to more specific experiences, programs, organizations, associations, and affiliations that help teachers and schools thrive, and do their best work for students.

PART TWO

THE SPARKS

Inspired teaching and thriving schools depend on a combination of conditions that support excellent practice. Here are the sparks that ignite a passion for teaching and learning and light the path toward sustained quality. Strong training can lay a foundation for continual growth, fostering a reflective approach to teaching and a commitment to equity. Teacher leaders find ways to share their expertise and take on greater responsibility in schools, districts, and our profession. Through National Board Certification, public honors and recognitions, our unions, publishing, networking, and appointed and elected positions of leadership, we advance a vision of public education that meets the needs of the whole child, now and in the future.

CHAPTER 5

STEP into Teaching:

Balancing Theory, Practice, and Reflection

Karl Lindgren-Streicher confers with his students at Hillsdale High School in San Mateo. His preparation in the Stanford Teacher Education Program (STEP) provided a solid foundation for effective teaching and continual growth in the profession.

DURING A STRETCH OF TIME FROM THE START OF COLLEGE until my late twenties, I changed addresses twelve times and became quite adept at packing my life into boxes and car trunks. I even had favorite, sturdy cardboard boxes that I kept in closets and attics, waiting for the inevitable next move. On June 17, 1994, I had my Honda Civic loaded up for a move from Los Angeles to Palo Alto, as I prepared to enter the Stanford Teacher Education Program (STEP). That year provided the defining transitions in my personal and professional life, and I retain many vivid memories about that entire period.

The intensity of a one-year master's degree and teaching credential helped forge strong relationships among those of us going through the program. It was a challenging but highly productive time, as we spent mornings of every school day in our student teaching placements, then went to Stanford in the afternoons and evenings for our own coursework. We alternated constantly between the roles of teacher and student, designing and grading our students' assignments, then completing our own. I've known and worked with STEP graduates who completed the program in the 1980s and in every decade since. STEP alumni over the years may have had different instructors and different course content, but there's a consistency in our thinking about the nature of our work and the professionalism it demands of us.

We graduated from STEP well prepared to begin and sustain our careers, with a solid balance of teaching practice and education theory. When it comes to theoretical aspects of education, I've heard many teachers express a preference for what they consider a more practical "toolbox" of methods and materials that will make them effective in the classroom. However, one of my professors, Lee Shulman, a giant in the field of teacher training, pointed out to us that there is nothing as practical as a good theory. It's great to have a whole set of instructional approaches at your disposal, but it's essential to have some idea of the rationale behind them to improve or drop them as needed in the future. In our classes and supervised student teaching, we were encouraged from the beginning to apply theory to an analysis of challenges we faced in our student teaching placements, and the emphasis on reflective practice shaped the way I work to this day. The STEP graduates I know, and the ones described in detail here, all share that reflective mindset.

April Oliver, English Language Arts
Los Altos High School, Los Altos

As I planned my school visits for this project, I was eager to observe teachers from STEP, and at the top of my list was a fellow member of my English teaching cohort from the class of '95, April Oliver. Collaborating with April several times during graduate school, I was always impressed by her intellect and professionalism. For twenty-one years, April has been teaching at Los Altos High School (the first year was as a student teacher), but visiting her is a time-warp kind of experience for me, as I haven't seen April in many years, and she seems virtually unchanged.

Though curious about her teaching because of our shared training, I'm even more eager to learn what has kept April in one place all this time. Part of the answer is probably something like destiny or kismet—the good fortune to have found such a good fit at the start of her career. But it's more than that. Teaching a full-time load of high school English classes is an incredibly demanding job, so much so that many teachers, including myself, find ways to modify their teaching assignments. To avoid teaching a full load of five English classes, we look for other assignments, take on various support roles for students or peers, or drop down to part time if we can afford it. In April's case, a strong background in dance has been quite useful, as she teaches dance classes to round out a full-time schedule. Opportunities like these make a significant difference in a teacher's work satisfaction and quality of life, and it's a smart move on the part of the school to keep a teacher of April's skills and experience on staff.

Such longevity and stability in her teaching career is a sign that April has been able to find continual growth and challenges in her work. Fairly recently, she's had an opportunity for ongoing collaboration with the education research and policy organization WestEd; four years of work on a literacy and writing initiative culminated with April copresenting the team's findings at the 2014 annual meeting of the American Educational Research Association. She has also had the experience of being an AP English exam reader for the College Board. Teachers who participate in AP reading describe it as a powerful learning experience, involving considerable discussion about teaching and student work with teachers from around the country, followed by an intensive experience reading hundreds of student essays in a short time.

April brings this learning back to her AP English students. It's a spring morning, and the AP exam is coming up soon. As students review a poem and practice the interpretive work that would lead to an essay, April shares insights from her experience as an AP reader. There's other work going on today as well, as some students are performing scenes from *Hamlet*. It's no surprise that seniors in an AP class are skillful and motivated, and their scenes are quite polished. I'm struck by their focus and attention during classmates' performances as well. The emphasis in their presentation is on the delivery of the lines, as opposed to a more developed staging with costumes, props, and furnishings. April's students have prepared not only by studying the text, but by also watching multiple interpretations on video; their analyses of these other interpretations accompany the write-up that explains their interpretive choices, turned in at the start of the class period. At times during the period, I hear April encouraging reflective learning practices in her students, as she pauses to have them think back over prior work and performances they've observed and helps them anticipate a culminating activity in which they will recognize exemplary work by their peers.

April also teaches an American literature course, and for some students, today brings their turns delivering speeches about "Facets of the American Experience and Identity," as reflected in *The Great Gatsby* and compared to the present day using a variety of examples. Again, the instruction has taken place already, but I can see the care that has gone into writing well-organized speeches, delivered with skill, clear arguments, and (mostly) well-selected evidence to support comparative claims.

The day of my visit is not ideal for talking with April about teaching, as she has no more than a few minutes here and there for conversations. Even her lunch is taken up with dance auditions, and then after lunch, it's time for her dance classes. I've seen few performing arts classes during my year of school visits, so I'm eager for the opportunity to observe. There are distinctive elements in each subject area in education. For example, English classes present the challenge of balancing the goals of reaching common understandings about literature while validating students' uniquely individual responses to what they read. In science classes, the unique elements include the central roles of inquiry, experimentation, and measurement. In the performing arts, student publications, and athletics, teachers are called to work in different ways. What stands out in my observations of these performance- and production-based classes is the intensity of the collaboration, with everyone involved and contributing, ideally, to the broader shared enterprise. The teacher must work in a way that is especially inclusive; if one student struggles with a history or English lesson, there are many ways for us to give that student more individualized attention at another time, in another way. In a dance studio, when everyone needs to make the same move at the same time, the student who struggles must be supported immediately, directly, and in front of the whole class.

The dance studio seems a little bit small for its purpose, accommodating about twenty dancers per class. Before today, I had tried to picture April as a dance instructor. Having never taken a dance class, I drew upon images from movies or TV: Pounding a cane on the floor, the teacher or choreographer sets the tempo and glares at the dancers, calling out each step, noting each flaw, criticizing individuals—a demanding perfectionist feared by all. Instead, April is dressed for dance, at ease working on the floor in front of or alongside her students. She models everything students are doing throughout the warm-ups, then demonstrates some new choreography. Not every class gives our students a chance to watch us do *exactly* what we're trying to teach them; teaching academic subjects that way more often would be helpful.

In the latter portion of the advanced dance class, students are learning some challenging parts of a new performance piece. At one point, April gives some instruction and demonstrates what she wants, but right away, several voices call out, "wait, wait!" I love that it's acceptable to call attention to your difficulties or confusion in a situation like this; it's essential that *everyone* eventually masters the dance, and there's a tacit understanding that not every dancer will pick up the moves quickly and simultaneously. After a period of instruction, April divides the class into groups and sends some out for independent practice nearby while she works more closely with another group in the dance studio. Now her instruction is more detailed and technical, involving windmills, fan kicks, ball changes, *pliés*, touch turns, etc. The direct and specific instruction I see here reflects the early stages of a piece of work and contrasts with the English classes where I saw the end result and little if any of the instruction. In both cases, however, it's clear that April is a gifted instructor who has figured out how to guide her students' learning in whatever form it takes.

Karl Lindgren-Streicher, History/Social Studies
Hillsdale High School, San Mateo

About a decade after April and I finished STEP, Karl Lindgren-Streicher went through the program to train as a history teacher, completing his student teaching at Hillsdale High School in San Mateo. Like April, he has stayed in the same school ever since. His STEP classmate, English teacher Sarah Press, completed her student teaching in the same school and same year, and has stayed as well. They continue to work together as teaching partners in an interdisciplinary small learning community within Hillsdale.

I've known Karl for a few years and visited his classroom multiple times prior to this book project simply because he's the kind of teacher who relishes openness and interaction with professional peers. Outside of Hillsdale High School, Karl is a leader in the education community, locally and nationally, through CUE (Computer Using Educators) and the Edcamp Foundation. (I discuss Edcamp in more detail in Chapter 13). The way Karl focuses on reflection and peer learning for himself and other teachers has a strong corollary in his approach to teaching high school.

My visits to Hillsdale have generally found Karl in the midst of some kind of creative or open-ended project, so while his primary content area is history, my insights have more to do with the ways that Karl empowers students to take ownership of their learning. On the day of my visit, Karl is introducing students to something called "20% Time" or "Genius Hour." The idea comes out of the private industry, where some companies encourage employees to take on more initiative for creative, self-directed projects one day per week. Google was perhaps the best-known practitioner of "20% Time," though they no longer use it as widely. The benefit for the companies is that they own the results when their employees come up with innovations through this self-directed work. In Google's case, products like Gmail and AdSense (which allows Google to place targeted ads on websites) came out of "20%" projects. In education, many teachers have gravitated toward similar projects as a way to boost student motivation and ownership of their learning. For Karl, the decision to incorporate this type of project comes from constant reflection on ways to engage students in their education and make both the content and the skills relevant. He would also be the first to say he's not sure how it will turn out. But as he has told me, and as he has emphasized in many of his blog posts, we have to model the constant inquiry and experimentation that we suggest will help students become what we also aim to be: lifelong learners. We constantly examine our teaching, consider our students as people and as learners, and look for ways to improve.

Perhaps STEP is a teacher training program that attracts individuals with this mind-set. Regardless of our starting points, however, STEP cultivated the kind of thinking and teaching that Karl engages in. "I think STEP did a great job of creating reflection as a norm for me," he explains. "Examining lessons became something that was normal. Making tweaks wasn't weakness; it was trying to reach all students."

Both personal experience and anecdotal evidence suggest that students appreciate and ultimately benefit from long-term, self-directed projects, but I know that the early stages of such work are difficult for them. I see that in Karl's classes as well. When teachers refrain from giving detailed instructions and specific expectations about the focus and dimensions of a project, students experience a period of disorientation. If the teacher doesn't provide all the requirements and answers, then what exactly are the students supposed to do? They need some time to generate multiple ideas and then sort out the ones that are challenging and complex enough to hold their interest but manageable enough to bring to fruition. They want something personal enough to be unique and highly motivating but still academically purposeful. Karl's time today is largely spent inspiring and encouraging students to follow their passions in creative ways, though he does ask them to be mindful of obvious constraints: "Horseback riding projects are kind of hard to pursue or develop during class time," he points out as one example.

Still, as he goes around the classroom, very few ideas are shot down. Student drive and creativity seem to fascinate and energize Karl, and for the moment, he's likely to say, "Let's worry about that later," instead of rejecting any ideas. Students are helping each other with this brainstorming phase, sitting in groups of four. Some of the project ideas relate to psychology, child development, animals, art, sports, computer coding, and mobile app design. Students change their minds quickly, which is expected and appropriate at this initial phase of the project. Karl moves from group to group, embedding himself and speaking so quietly most of the time that I have trouble hearing if I'm not right there as well. But when his eyes light up and he smiles broadly, I can hear him saying, "*Very* cool!" or "That would be *incredible!*"

While the primary history curriculum has been set aside for today, Karl is still checking in with some students about their prior or upcoming work. Then, during his prep period, Karl's focus returns entirely to history and student writing as he collaborates with colleagues, including a group of STEP student teachers, around essay-grading calibration. This exercise helps teachers build in greater consistency in their expectations and grades when evaluating student work.

Karl does a fair amount of his own writing as well, much of it on his teaching blog (historywithLS.blogspot.com). On the day of my visit, *California Educator* magazine has a reporter and photographer visiting as well, a sort of meta-observation of me observing Karl, based on the fact that we both blog about teaching. In my case, blogging has been more about sharing information that I hope will influence people's understanding of schools and teaching, but for Karl, not surprisingly, it's more about reflection: "Blogging is talking. It's a way to clarify your thinking to others, and ultimately to yourself. Finding like-minded people, and even some you disagree with, helps you learn, not only about them but also about yourself."

Marciano Gutierrez, History/Social Studies
Alta Vista High School, Mountain View

Originally from Fresno, Marciano Gutierrez came to the Bay Area to attend Stanford, first as an undergraduate, and then entering STEP. Now he has found a teaching home at Alta Vista High School, just ten miles away. STEP's emphasis on social justice in public education had a strong influence on Marciano's path, leading him not only to his position at Alta Vista, but also to a brief hiatus when he worked as a Teaching Ambassador Fellow (TAF) for the US Department of Education. I met Marciano through mutual friends in that program but have known about his school quite a bit longer. (The TAF program is discussed in further detail in Chapter 11, in the section about Linda Yaron.)

Alta Vista began as a continuation school for students whose disciplinary problems, truancy, or lack of academic progress in the first two years of high school led to placement in the program for grades eleven through twelve. It has since expanded to provide alternative educational placement for students in grades nine through ten as well. The school serves not only its home district (the two-school Mountain View-Los Altos High School District), but also my home district, Palo Alto Unified, which also has two high schools. I had heard of Alta Vista over the years, though I knew few details. Some students who failed multiple classes in ninth and tenth grade at my school ended up transferring there, and our school counselors said it was a strong program. Nonetheless, I couldn't help imagining something less than inspiring, a building full of unmotivated or frustrated juniors and seniors trying to scrape by to earn a high school diploma. It turned out to be a much more vibrant and academic place than I imagined.

For students who need educational alternatives with greater individual attention, flexibility, and extra support, Alta Vista has much to offer. It's a small school, about 170 students, which facilitates personal connections and relationships with the staff. There is a clear focus on setting and reaching goals, and a caring, encouraging atmosphere. Marciano's first class of the day is US history, and there are only eleven students in the room when class begins. The energy level is a bit low, about what I'd expect from teens first thing in the morning, but Marciano is all revved up. He engages every student in the room and moves around constantly while reviewing the rise of the American labor movement following the Industrial Revolution. They move on to analysis of political cartoons, aiming to examine differing views on *laissez-faire* economics through the ways various artists use symbols, analogies, and irony. As the lesson moves along, a few more students arrive, and Marciano responds to each differently. To one, he simply says, "I'll catch you up later," while he asks another, "Was the bus late again?" At first glance it might seem that a teacher, especially at an alternative high school, should be more concerned about enforcing rules and doling out consequences for tardiness. What I'm seeing is that Marciano knows and understands his students as individuals. He's reacting based on awareness of their individual challenges: how much school they may have missed or attended recently, which bus they rely on and how unreliable it is, what obstacles they face during their transition into or out of various impermanent living arrangements. "Knowing the kids is the key to working with them. When it's a struggle for them to be at school at all, you don't lay into them for being late. When they don't get along with a parent, you might call that parent with good news, but you don't use 'I'm going to call your parent' as a threat."

With all the students now present and working, Marciano circulates through the classroom helping students with their historical analysis, but he's always collecting more information about them as well, checking in with a simple "how are you doing?" or asking more specific questions when he knows there's something important to follow up about. By building these relationships, Marciano makes school into a safe and supportive place for his students. Knowing their challenges in life and not just in school, Marciano recognizes that their success is that much more urgent, and therefore, really a triumph when it comes. So, sympathy is not a goal unto itself: Marciano's investment in students as people first creates a level of trust and credibility that helps him push every student to meet high academic expectations. With every student he works with, Marciano makes them clarify positions, generate precise interpretations, support claims with visual evidence, and articulate how the evidence supports their views.

The following class period, Marciano has ninth graders studying world history. They begin work right away using laptop computers, writing about the Cuban Revolution. With this class, the real academic push that I observe most often is Marciano demanding more precise writing. One student has the phrase "spend more" in a sentence, and Marciano wants to know the best way to specify "more": Is it the actual difference in amounts or as a percentage of overall spending? And "What do you mean by 'health care'"? The student ends up clarifying a point about access to preventative care and vaccinations. As students review statistics to include in their writing, Marciano points out that with economic indicators, bigger numbers are not always better: A higher GDP is good, but higher inflation or unemployment are not. Marciano has a great rhythm and pace as he works with students individually. He starts with one observation about something a student has added or improved, checks for understanding regarding one fact or argument, and offers one writing tip to help students with specificity or grammar. In this manner, he's efficient with time and effective with instruction.

On the day of my visit, there's an end-of-the-quarter assembly to celebrate the success students have had in various classes. Their success might be in overall achievement, making academic progress, completing a requirement, or overcoming an individual challenge. The teachers and students are enthusiastic and sincere in celebrating each of the recognized students in this event. Marciano also credits his principal, Bill Pierce, for setting the tone at the school and providing a positive vision for Alta Vista. When it's Marciano's turn to celebrate students during the assembly, he stands in front of the school with a large envelope labeled, comically, "Top Secret." As all the teachers have, he proceeds to offer some brief remarks detailing a student's success before giving out the creatively named, "Pedal to the Metal" award to a student whose success has been accelerating, or "Movin' On Up" for a student who completed some independent study. There's a touch of humor and plenty of warmth in the way he calls students up to receive a certificate and enjoy the applause. I'm left wondering why our system often needs to label children as failures and remove them from "regular" schools before we start focusing on the supports and conditions that enable them to succeed.

Like April Oliver, Marciano seems to have landed at the perfect spot. The quality of preparation teachers experience helps produce a clear idea of what we're looking for in our work, and what kind of places and practices are most compatible with that vision. Marciano sees a direct line between his training and his professional life years later: "STEP views teaching as a profession that has the potential to make life-changing impacts on the lives of students and prepares its candidates accordingly." The same impulse that led Marciano to the US Department of Education temporarily has also kept him at Alta Vista. And while sometimes a clear vision of professional purpose is what keeps us in a place, it can also trigger a move when the time comes.

Haydee Rodriguez, History/Social Studies
Southwest High School, El Centro

Haydee Rodriguez entered STEP looking for a career change and came out not only as a teacher, but also as a powerful advocate for our profession and for students. Her STEP experience came at a pivotal time that included Stanford's leadership in the opening of a new high school in East Palo Alto. Having such an early and powerful grounding of her teaching with the broader issues of school design and education reform, Haydee has continued teaching while taking on leadership positions in a number of organizations. She serves as on the board of directors for the National Board for Professional Teaching Standards and is also a commissioner on the California Commission on Teacher Credentialing. While these leadership opportunities give her insights and influence regarding teaching statewide and nationwide, Haydee's first commitment is to address the needs of her students in the small border town of El Centro, just minutes away from Mexicali, Mexico.

My drive from San Diego to El Centro one April afternoon brings me so close to the border that my mobile phone switches to a Mexican cellular provider, which sends a text message welcoming me to Mexico and displaying international roaming charges. So I have the phone off for the next forty-five minutes or so, until I arrive in El Centro and call Haydee to meet for dinner. It's early enough that Haydee wants to show me around town a bit before dinner, so she begins a driving tour around El Centro. We pass through a number of distinct neighborhoods, but they're probably less than a square mile each and all right next to each other. We pass through a section of "downtown" near the county courthouse and the central post office, and then a moment later, we're in a residential area with small, older houses, and some run-down, two-story apartment buildings. Within a few blocks, we turn right and the street widens quite a bit, while the houses and front yards seem to double in size. We drive past Haydee's school, Southwest High School, and see some relatively new houses as well. The edge of town is precisely that—it just ends. We're driving up a road where, if I look between the houses to my left, I can see fields and mountains to the west, and the last bit of daylight. Haydee says, "I wanted to drive you around El Centro for a while and show you everything, then I realized there's not much to show you—it's El Centro." Sure enough, another right turn, and we're just about back where we started on Imperial Avenue.

A popular high school teacher having dinner at a popular restaurant in the small town where she grew up, Haydee unsurprisingly runs into friends, former students, colleagues, district administrators, and a school board trustee. In between the various greetings and benign interruptions, Haydee is laying out a powerful story about the importance of education for her students and community. It may be a small town, but they know the world is larger than El Centro; many people here cross the border to Mexicali often just for visits, shopping, or affordable medical care. At the same time, Haydee sees many students searching for a vision of where else they might go and what they might do. The local economy is driven by agriculture, correctional facilities, and federal activity relating to immigration, customs, and border patrol. Students with other interests may feel some pull to leave El Centro, and teachers might encourage that; yet there's a civic cost to consider if many of the most ambitious young people in the community aim to leave. The nearest state universities are in San Diego, over one hundred miles away. If the town is to thrive in the future, it may depend on students who are academically prepared enough to leave and personally connected enough to come back.

For Haydee, that's an autobiographical summary. She is keenly aware of what she represents for her students: an independent, professional Mexican American woman who left for college and graduate school; has lived in San Diego, Santa Barbara, and the Bay Area; and has now chosen to return to El Centro. Another part of her personal story, well-known in her community, is that she nearly died in a terrible car accident several years ago. While she was in a coma in a Palm Springs hospital, word of her condition spread, causing her former students and broader community to flood the hospital phone lines with concerned calls and inquiries. One of Haydee's doctors said he hadn't seen anything like it, even with celebrity patients.

During my day at Southwest, Haydee is eager for me to get a feel for the whole school and what it represents for the community. I start my day with a student-led tour and realize how few of my schools visits have involved such extended student interactions. Alyssa is a senior at Southwest and a former student of Haydee's who also happens to have an open period in her schedule. She often spends part of her morning in Haydee's classroom, simply for the company and something to do, and for somewhere to sit and prepare for the rest of the day. Today, Haydee has recruited her to act as tour guide. With her high school graduation weeks away, Alyssa is looking forward to moving about 300 miles away to attend college, but in the near term, her excitement centers around the school's upcoming production of "Alice in Wonderland." Having a background in theater myself (high school, college, and my first teaching job), I'm immediately full of questions about the play, the drama program, and the recently built, 2,000-seat theater that Haydee has already mentioned to me. Alyssa loves the theater, though she speaks in similarly positive terms about almost everyone and everything at Southwest.

Like La Quinta High School (see Chapter 4), Southwest has a number of academies or pathways from which students can choose, giving their studies a certain degree of focus and providing some career skills in the process. Over the course of my day at Southwest, I see three of them. The Southwest Academy for Visual and Performing Arts seems to be the largest, pulling together a variety of artistic disciplines. The room right next door to Haydee's is a dance studio, where I see student auditions for an upcoming show. The instructor, Jessica Brooks, has professional dancing experience and runs the audition in a professional manner, with students having to state their names at the start of their audition, even though they're in her class. Later in the day, I watch other students in the arts academy rehearsing "Alice in Wonderland," directed by teacher Christopher Spanos, in that huge, gorgeous theater, which is a gem of a resource not only for the school, but also for the town. In classes for other career academies, I talked with the culinary arts teacher Amanda Hill, who brings not only professional experience to the job, but also a focus on healthy eating, and I had my wrist taped by a football player named Robert, a student in the health science and medical technology program. This class, introduction to sports medicine, is taught by Andrea Corella, who has taken students from El Centro to college and professional sports events and facilities around Southern California so they can see the application of what they learn in school.

My time in Haydee's classroom is similarly enlightening and revealing. I could describe student presentations about governmental issues relating to health care and the economy, but what stands out the most is how safe her classroom is for students who have frank disagreements. It would be wonderful if adults could listen to each other without interrupting, offer opposing political views without making the debate personal, and feel comfortable taking the minority view among the majority. In one conversation, the topic of teachers' unions comes up, and students feel comfortable expressing views that they anticipate Haydee may disagree with. She does and explains why, and they continue talking about it in a respectful way. Haydee brings me into the conversation on that issue, but as a guest I'm more comfortable avoiding either side of the argument. Instead, I offer the idea that education systems and organizations vary widely in size, resources, personnel, local histories, and workplace cultures; there are no simple answers, and almost any generalization about education policy or politics can be countered with many exceptions.

In a way, these interactions in Haydee's class reflect a mindset I can trace back to STEP. Our teacher training provided both practical experience, theoretical foundations, and an inclination toward inquiry and reflection. Each of the STEP alumni profiled in this chapter is an excellent teacher, leader, and advocate, precisely because of the cycle of inquiry and reflection. Stanford business professor and author Robert Sutton talks about the importance of leaders having "strong opinions, weakly held." In other words, we are clear about our principles and have formed strong opinions based on knowledge and experience, yet we remain open to the possibility that new learning and experiences will continue to inform, or even change our opinions.

My focus on STEP in this chapter is intended to highlight the ways in which a strong teacher education program can provide some of the sparks that lead to excellent teaching and rewarding work in the profession. New teachers, like other professionals, should be thoroughly trained and ably supported by experienced mentors. A solid foundation leads us to pursue continual learning, reflect on our profession and career pathways, and bring about improvement in our classrooms, schools, and educational system.

CHAPTER 6

Teachers of the Year:

Vision, Voice, and Opportunity

Jose Rivas directs a student engineering challenge as part of his work as a science and engineering teacher at Lennox Mathematics, Science & Technology Academy in Inglewood. In 2011, he was named an Outstanding Teacher of America by the Carlston Family Foundation.

As my year of school visits progressed and I made my way up and down the state multiple times, it became increasingly common for people to ask me, "What's the best school you've seen? Who's the best teacher you've seen?" I generally avoided answering the question, finding it difficult to compare such a diverse group of teachers and campuses. My approach to this project was to look for the best in each person, in each classroom and school, and I was never disappointed at the end of a visit.

At various levels in our educational systems, however, there are processes for identifying and honoring Teachers of the Year in our schools, districts, and counties, along with each state and the nation. I've had the privilege of meeting many of California's honorees from the past decade and have worked closely with a few of them. I've met some of our recent national Teachers of the Year as well. Are they the answer to the question, "Who's the best?"

I'm still not going to answer that directly, though I can say with confidence that I find Teachers of the Year to be consistently skilled as advocates for students, schools, and the teaching profession. It makes sense, as the selection process for the Teacher of the Year includes not only recommendations and classroom observations, but also applications and interviews, requiring nominees to articulate clear ideas and insights about education. In this chapter, we'll see inside the classrooms of four state and national Teachers of the Year, and we'll glimpse the work of four other teachers recognized through an outstanding statewide program run by the Carlston Family Foundation.

TEACHER OF THE YEAR AWARD

Rebecca Mieliwocki, English Language Arts
Luther Burbank Middle School, Burbank

When you reach the point in teaching where you're so good that you know what's happening in your classroom without directly observing, it's like having eyes in the back of your head; Rebecca Mieliwocki teaches like she has a 360-degree array of closed-circuit cameras and recording devices. I'm observing her seventh-grade English language arts classes at Luther Burbank Middle School, in Burbank, and witnessing a flawless display of classroom management from the 2012 California and National Teacher of the Year.

There are thirty seventh graders working in groups to present research they've done to prepare for their study of *The Pearl,* by John Steinbeck. The research phase is over, and students have the first half of the class period to finish presentation posters and put the final touches on their oral remarks. Each group has a separate topic that provides context or useful background knowledge for reading the book: Steinbeck, pearl diving, scorpions, colonialism, the concept of fate, and the region and people of La Paz, Mexico. The structure of the activity and its place in the larger unit of study are both pretty typical, but Rebecca runs it masterfully. It's only early October, but the class hums with productive energy reflecting how well they've absorbed the organization, routines, and expectations in their class. Within the groups, there are specialized instructions that only apply to students in designated roles, and Rebecca sometimes calls out those students by name, without referring to any notes or records of student roles in each group. At the end of one class period, she spots a scrap of red construction paper beneath a desk, across the room—something that should have been cleaned up at the midperiod transition but escaped detection until now. Rebecca pauses for about a second. Then, as if she has consulted her mind's closed-circuit video recording, she identifies the student who would have been responsible for that single scrap of paper half an hour ago and asks her to take care of it. I can't tell if the students are impressed by their teacher's abilities, but sitting in the back corner of the classroom, I'm adding multiple exclamation points to my notes. When students leave, they're careful to put the room back in order, but Rebecca still moves among the rows of desks and adjusts for perfect alignment after the students have departed. It's like the final move in a choreographed dance that begins and ends with quiet order, and in between features constant sound and movement.

For the casual observer, I think accomplished teaching is most associated with classroom management—what the teacher says and does to make class time efficient and conducive to student learning. The reality is that teaching is more multidimensional, involving continual learning, planning, design, assessment, collaboration, and leadership. In my visits with teachers honored as Teacher of Year by their district, county, state, or a private organization, what stands out is usually something beyond their classroom practice. Make no mistake: Teachers like Rebecca or Lovelyn Marquez-Preuher (see Chapter 3) demonstrate excellence in the classroom, but most schools have some teachers with similar skills. In my experiences observing Teachers of the Year and working with some of them on various projects, I find they generally share two distinguishing characteristics: First, they have a detailed and clear vision regarding quality education, and second, they are driven to use every dimension of accomplished teaching to address both the learning needs of their own students *and* the broader needs of students and teachers.

Lovelyn has channeled that commitment into her hybrid teaching position, which has her teaching students and teachers, and advocating for all the students in her school. She writes, presents at conferences, and participates in regional teacher leadership efforts. Rebecca has been a powerful advocate for the teaching profession in every conference room, stage, or venue she's able to reach. In her remarks to the National Educators Association (NEA) in 2012, commenting on the lack of teacher voice in education policy making, she said, "It's so striking to me that, in our ferocious and noble zeal to leave not even one child behind, we may have accidentally left the teachers behind instead." The same theme finds its way into our lunchtime conversation on the day I visit. I've had many conversations like this over the years, though Rebecca offers a practical suggestion that's new to me and reflects her understanding of where teachers need to be in order to have the impact we want: Rebecca suggests that future Teachers of the Year in California should have advisory seats on the State Board of Education. As one of the few teachers who reads agendas and minutes and tunes in to webcasts of those board meetings, I heartily endorse the idea.

Jessica Pack, English/Social Studies, Sixth Grade
James Workman Middle School, Cathedral City

The California Teacher of the Year honor goes to five teachers each year. Over the course of this project, I was fortunate enough to spend the day with six who have received that distinction, though—to my knowledge—only Jessica Pack, a 2014 honoree, has had a street renamed in her honor. Driving up to James Workman Middle School, I notice that the short street running alongside the school bears Jessica's name, a tribute from Cathedral City (near Palm Springs), which also declared "Jessica Pack Day" when they unveiled the sign. It's a touching gesture, indicating the esteem in which she is held by her community, and hopefully a sign (pun intended) that the community values teachers in general.

Among the Teachers of the Year I've known, Jessica is the first I had heard of before she was recognized by the state. With a drive toward constant learning, innovation, and technology integration, Jessica had already established a reputation through her work with the organization CUE (Computer Using Educators) and DigiCom Learning Institute, which trains teachers to use digital media and technology with their students. She also blogs about education and is an active Twitter user. (In Chapter 13, we'll meet other teachers who use their online presence and social media savvy to build mutually beneficial personal learning networks.)

While I think education technology is where Jessica's unique strengths and leadership shine brightest, it is more precise to say that her interest lies in using technology to give students greater autonomy and voice in their education. Although Jessica has been ahead of the curve for several years in piloting various tech tools in the classroom, she focuses on their purpose more than their functionality. Students are able to do more research; have more control over what they read, write, or create; and collaborate on projects that have a broad reach. "It's about what they're doing, not what I'm doing," she tells me later.

But it's not all about the technology. Students only go online when it is makes sense. Other times, a simple dry erase pen and a whiteboard are perfect for the task at hand, such as a quick brainstorming session for a small group. When the audience is the class, paper and bulletin boards suffice, but to reach an audience beyond the classroom or campus, publishing work online makes sense.

On the day of my visit, students are learning to address important topics in the format of a public service announcement (PSA) video. In preparation for that activity, students view and discuss some actual PSAs. With the goal of helping students analyze what they're seeing, Jessica starts with an easy one, showing how fathers can be more involved with their children by simply playing with them more; the target audience and the message are clear. The next PSA dramatizes the potentially deadly consequences of texting while driving. This time the intended audience is less clear to the students; the PSA showed a teen driver, so are they the only intended audience? Isn't texting while driving also dangerous for adults? Could the PSA be aimed at all drivers? Can passengers help prevent texting while driving? Maybe they're part of the audience too. The goal is not for the students to come up with a definitive answer, but rather to practice the deconstruction of a message: the images, words, and context. With that skill, they're better prepared to discuss all sorts of media, audiences, and messages; and in the short term, they'll have the language and common points of reference to plan their own PSAs.

It takes a certain boldness to seek and accept the title Teacher of the Year, bringing attention to yourself and your practices, and Jessica and I talk about that for a while after school. She's cognizant of how much more public her work is now, how her opinions and writings are more visible, a reflection on her professional peers and the Teacher of the Year program. But that's the point, too, to have new, broader audiences and expanded influence over the conversations and policies that drive schools and bring about change. While there's a legitimate debate about the overall impact of technology in education, it is evident in Jessica's class and through her students' use of technology that they're developing academic and technical skills, along with creative and collaborative dispositions that will serve them well.

Kathy Marvin, Science
Jeffrey Trail Middle School, Irvine

The more we hand over control to our students, the more trust we need; most of the time, our trust is rewarded, as students who internalize high expectations for themselves will often exceed our expectations. California Teacher of the Year (2010) Kathy Marvin is a science teacher at Jeffrey Trail Middle School in Irvine, and she provides an excellent example of how that's done.

Jeffrey Trail opened in 2013, with Kathy coming over from another school in Irvine to provide some of the leadership in designing the science program. The campus, classroom facilities, and new equipment all make the school quite appealing, though I wonder how Kathy handles a total student load of two hundred and supervises extracurricular groups.

Kathy's classroom is the eighth-grade science lab, and today it's full of noise, collisions, and broken eggs. Students are participating in a physics challenge: create a cardboard car that can protect its driver (a raw egg) from injury (breakage) when the vehicle slams into a wall at low, medium, and high speeds. There are rules about the construction and size of the car, but otherwise, students have plenty of flexibility and many creative approaches to design and decoration. To start the experiment, each car is strapped onto a wooden block, which is pulled away from a wall, stretching a piece of attached rubber tubing; when the block is released, it will slide toward the wall rapidly, with the speed increasing the further the tubing is stretched. Most cars succeed on the first trial, where the distance traveled is about two feet. Many fail on the second trial, covering perhaps three feet. Most of the vehicles that succeed on the second attempt end up failing on the third. Each trial, at any distance, produces a loud bang as the wood block slams into a simulated wall.

Kathy is seated nearest to the point of impact, and her face shows combinations of delight, amazement, and sometimes dismay as each launch begins and ends. Though there are dozens of trials during each class period, Kathy's students follow almost every one with cheers, laughter, or an appropriate exclamation: *Whoa! Wow! Ew!* Sometimes the crushed egg makes enough noise that the trial's results are immediately apparent, but sometimes Kathy must check with her fingertips to determine if the egg is intact, cracked, or even crushed. The eggs are in plastic bags, but a couple of times the impact is sufficient to produce a splatter of raw egg that hits Kathy or a student. All in the name of science!

The scientific principles involved in this experiment are mass, velocity, acceleration, and force, but the instruction around those concepts happened prior to my visit, and the students' scientific analysis of the experiment will follow after I'm gone. Kathy offers some insight about the design elements that seem to help some eggs live while others die. Although the language is vehicular (crumple zones absorbing the force, for example), the materials are more simplistic (cotton balls, popcorn, gummy bears, etc.).

If I had seen only Kathy's regular science classes, I would have had a great experience at her school, learning about how a Teacher of the Year contributes to the success of her students and her new school, but the day's real revelation is the Science Olympiad class. This advanced science elective is quite popular, and since there's only one session, it's a huge class. The class has already rung up some impressive results in Science Olympiad competitions for the year, winning the middle school division for Orange County and taking third place in the state. Now the class has quite a project ahead of them, organizing and hosting a Science Olympiad competition for elementary schools. The class, the competitions, and this event are all student-directed. Kathy moves around the room, serving as a resource and answering questions but giving no instructions, at least that I hear. At one point, students come to her with a piece of broken plastic, a fixture or joint of some sort that held together the parts for some piece of equipment used in one of the events. Kathy's reaction to the broken equipment is perfect; there's no need to question or criticize anyone, as it's clear that these students go about their work with serious intent and care. Accidents happen. They advise her of the problem, and she merely asks them to investigate options to fix or replace the part. A little later they come back having done some research into adhesives and present their best option, noting that this type of glue will hold the pieces but might also expand when dry. I'm impressed by the collegial kind of trust between the students and teacher, collaborating like scientists and engineers. Such trust evolves by design in an academic culture thoughtfully cultivated by a master teacher.

Several weeks after my visit, I emailed Kathy to find out how the event turned out. She replied:

> *They ran the whole event, and all the adult event supervisors became redundant observers. The kids ran all the events, scored tests, and inspired young scientists. The huge take-away is that we need to give them MORE opportunities to lead and create, and trust them to do it. Our job needs to be more of a true facilitator, and we need to have the ability to step back and let kids lead. Naturally, this doesn't happen overnight or without training and great kids. It's tough some-times because this is a class of 45 "chiefs." But each student has had multiple opportunities to lead small groups or pairs in the past. On the day of the [Elementary Science Olympiad], they took it to a new level . . . My motto is train them well and then get out of their way and let them amaze themselves and everyone!*

Valerie Ziegler, History/Social Studies
Abraham Lincoln High School, San Francisco

At the high school level, a Teacher-of-the-Year mentality and drive can lead schools and students in even more interesting directions. Valerie Ziegler was a California Teacher of the Year in 2010 (the same year as Kathy Marvin) and notable among her accomplishments is that she helped establish both the Teaching Academy and the Green Academy at Abraham Lincoln High School in San Francisco. In both, students are grouped together for some of their regular class-es, then have specialized sequences of classes and internships or other practical experiences outside the school. The approach is similar to what was described at La Quinta High School and Southwest High School (in El Centro).

The Teaching Academy students are interested in teaching careers and spend some time working in classrooms at nearby elementary schools. With their parents' permission, of course, juniors and seniors are dispatched to nearby schools once a week during their midmorning break. At the partner school, Lincoln students work in classrooms for sixty to ninety minutes, then return to school in time for their first class after lunch. Valerie and her Teaching Academy colleague, Dina Wright, make the same trip, going to the various partnering school sites to supervise their students and check in with the teachers there.

Naturally, I schedule my visit with Valerie on a day when her students are doing their own teaching, so I end up with a bonus visit to another school, Dianne Feinstein Elementary. The school secretary greets Valerie and Dina warmly and tells me that she hopes to have her own son in the Teaching Academy someday. Around the school, we find the Lincoln students all in their assigned classrooms, some working more directly with students than others. The variables affecting their work include the student's own inclinations and work habits, the needs and personalities of the elementary school teachers, and the demands of any given day. No matter how much actual "face time" is involved, students are developing good experience relating to children and education. Many Teaching Academy alumni can be found working in the district's after-school programs, and some have gone on to become teachers, including one alumna who has returned to Lincoln as a full-time Japanese teacher.

The Green Academy offers a focus on environmental issues and sustainability. The practical work is more grounded at the school, with students studying health and pollution issues relating to water consumption. Students are advocating for more water-bottle filling stations on campus and have studied the costs and benefits of different water delivery methods. My parting gift for the day is a refillable aluminum water bottle to discourage my use of plastic bottles with the chemical additive BPA. In an end-of-year update, Valerie informed me that that Green Academy engineering students later conducted a windmill design challenge, and, in a competition sponsored by the organization Generation Citizen, the Green Academy seniors received a Change Maker award in recognition of their activism to end water waste.

I have a chance to talk with Principal Barnaby Payne, and while he is quite proud of the school and the academy programs, he is quick to point out that their success hinges on the teacher leadership present at the school. The innovations, instruction, problem solving, and much of the paperwork and fundraising all depend on the teachers; his job is to say yes and support the teachers as much as possible. I can almost imagine that Valerie alone would take up half his time with all her ideas about establishing and improving academies. It's labor intensive on both ends.

While I've focused on Valerie's unique leadership in the academies, I should also note that she excels in her core discipline, history, and has contributed to the broader field of history and social studies education by helping to develop a literacy and history curriculum with the Stanford History Education Group.

I've suggested that Teachers of the Year have a shared ability to articulate and enact a vision for quality education, and I should add that they seem consistently driven and energetic. I don't think Valerie sits down at all during the school day, except perhaps during the short drive to supervise the Teaching Academy students. Even during lunch, she's on her feet, helping students with makeup work, checking in about projects, and observing other collaboration happening among students spending their lunchtime in her room. I wonder for a moment where Valerie finds the energy to be so constantly engaged, then realize it may be the constant student engagement that provides the energy. She, in turn, is providing the sparks that have so many students energized about what they're doing and learning.

OUTSTANDING TEACHER OF AMERICA AWARD

In addition to the state Teacher of the Year program, there are also local level recognitions and private organizations that honor teachers annually. Among these, the Carlston Family Foundation has the award that I find most interesting and compelling, although it is given only to high school teachers. Recipients of this award (called the Outstanding Teacher of America award, though given only to Californians) must be nominated by former students who went on to college; typically, the nominee is a teacher who made the most significant impact on that student during high school. After the foundation receives the nomination, foundation director Tim Allen conducts more research by traveling to interview and observe the teacher, and in a step that makes the Carlston process unique, he also interviews the teacher's current and former students, colleagues, and administrators. Tim has been traveling statewide to learn about great teachers for over a decade. I've attended some of the foundation's annual events and have collaborated with Tim to plan a teacher symposium one year, so I was eager to take advantage of his insights and network as part of my own work. Like state teachers of the year, Carlston honorees are consistently skilled and visionary, dedicated to their students and doing whatever it takes to help students succeed beyond high school.

Jose Rivas, Science/Engineering
Lennox Mathematics, Science & Technology Academy, Inglewood

Jose Rivas understands what it takes for his students to overcome challenges in the economically disadvantaged community of Lennox, an unincorporated square mile of Los Angeles County just east of Los Angeles International Airport. (His school's address is in the city of Inglewood, right next to Lennox and Los Angeles). Born in El Salvador, Jose came to the United States as a child and grew up in the neighborhood where he now teaches. After graduating from Loyola Marymount University, Jose began an engineering career with Boeing. He felt a calling to give back to his community by focusing on quality education, so he ran for a position on the local school board, and won. His time on the school board convinced him that he needed to be in the classroom to have the impact he hoped for, so became a teacher instead.

I can't imagine a California high school that wouldn't love to hire a teacher like Jose, who has roots in the community, is able to teach multiple subjects, is bilingual in Spanish and English, and has work experience in a technical industry. (He's also a black-belt in the martial art of *aikido* but hopefully that's not often necessary at school.) In addition to the Carlston recognition in 2011, Jose was the Lennox School District Teacher of the Year in 2012, and he assisted with the charter school conversion process that led to the current academic program at his school. With this background in mind, and having already met Jose through the Carlston Foundation, I'm particularly excited for this visit, even though it begins particularly early on a Monday morning.

Lennox Mathematics, Science & Technology Academy is a small high school, under five hundred students, with most classrooms in a single concrete building, along with some portable classrooms along one side of the campus. The neighborhood is a mixture of residential and commercial: On one side of campus is Acacia Avenue, full of modest houses and apartment complexes, while on the opposite side is Hawthorne Boulevard, with a check cashing store, multiple auto shops, and an "adult super store." Inside, the school is bright and full of positive energy. Jose and I meet up before school starts, and I have the chance to watch him greeting students at the start of the school day. Standing in the enclosed hallway outside his classroom, Jose offers salutations for students on their way to his class right now and engages others he'll see later in the day. But these are not standard greetings; each interaction seems like the resumption of a conversation about electronics or robotics or some other project or assignment. One girl turns the corner and Jose shoots her a huge smile and just points at her with a knowing look. The gesture reminds me of a greeting someone gets after stepping off the medal podium or returning to the dugout after a home run. She returns his smile and offers a pumped-up, "raise the roof" gesture. They exchange a few words, then she continues on her way while Jose connects with many other students passing by.

The blessing and the curse of being a talented teacher at a small school is that Jose teaches five different courses (a typical high school teacher has five class periods teaching two or three courses). One of these centers around an engineering competition to build a solar-powered boat, housed in a workshop created in a portable classroom. While robotics or rocketry competitions engage similar skills, there's an extra edge to a competition that puts a student into the final product—and then into the water. It raises the stakes for success or failure considerably. Students working on the boat during my visit are all seniors who have been in Jose's classes prior to this year, and they're working in small groups focused on different elements of the boat. Some are working on the engine and the throttle cable, some on the structure of the craft itself. Jose moves around the room asking and answering questions; all the while I'm thinking that a former Boeing engineer is a great person to be teaching a group like this. It's a professional atmosphere, with students using a variety of technical (and not-so-technical) tools and equipment around the room. When they need to test various methods of cutting and attaching different materials, a few students head outside and spread out on the grass field nearby.

No matter which subject or grade level he's working with throughout the day, Jose thrives on the students' energy, telling me later that the more they're doing, moving, and talking, the more he likes it. He lightens the atmosphere and builds students' confidence through his warm interactions with them. When someone has the right answer, he says, "Listen to this guy! He's ready now. I'm gonna have you teach my class!"

Another student is not so sure about his answer and says to Jose, "If it's wrong, don't put me on the spot."

Jose replies with a mischievous grin, "Would I do that to you?"

Several students overhearing this interaction answer for their classmate, "Yessss!" as Jose feigns a sense of betrayal that they would say that about him.

Sometimes in science classes, the precursor to finding answers is knowing precisely what your question is. To help students begin to formulate questions, Jose uses engaging demonstrations. In one class, he picks up a barbell with maybe thirty to forty pounds of weights attached and starts doing some bicep curls, with the theme from "Rocky" playing in the background for good measure. Once the novelty of the moment passes, there's a serious point: Jose challenges his students to identify how energy and work (in the technical, scientific meaning of the word) are observable in weightlifting. For another classroom demonstration, Jose removes a five-pound weight from the barbell and suspends that metallic plate from a cord attached to the ceiling. He stands a few feet to the side of where the weight rests when not in motion, then he pulls the weight up to his face, with the cord taut at perhaps a sixty-degree angle away from vertical. When he releases the weight, it will fall away from him and begin a pendular motion; the question is, should Jose be worried about the weight striking his face when it swings back toward him and completes one cycle? After some discussion and predictions, Jose lets the weight go, and even though I know it won't hit his face, I can't help but wince as it comes right back within an inch of his nose. He doesn't flinch. Students react with laughter and comment to each other briefly. The next question from Jose: "What if I give it a little push this time?" He does, and when the pendulum swings back toward his forehead, he dodges and lets it go by. Maybe that's where the *aikido* training comes in handy.

Jose doesn't always come off as such a thrill-seeker. His AP physics students will be taking a field trip to Knott's Berry Farm amusement park soon, a common springtime activity for students taking this course around the country, at least when there are thrill rides close enough to school. They will enter the park before it opens to the general public, gather measurements, and analyze data relating to the rides, then they can enjoy whatever extra time they have after doing their work. Jose jokes with them: "I'm going to be sitting under a tree reading at Camp Snoopy. But if you're scared to go on a ride, I'll hold your hand and take you on the ride." The offer is made with tongue firmly in cheek, but in a way, Jose holds plenty of hands at Lennox Academy, nurturing his students in the best sense of the word; most are aiming to be part of the first generation in their family to attend college, and Jose ensures that they have the personal and academic support not only to reach college, but to persist in higher education and thrive on their own.

Shannon Morago, Science
Six Rivers Charter High School, Arcata

The northernmost point in my school visits was the town of Arcata, just north of Eureka and home to Humboldt State University. It was also a trip that took me to an area I'd never visited before. The northern coastal region of California, with its combination of mountains, redwood forests, rivers, and beaches, was even more beautiful than I anticipated, and I could see the appeal of living and working in such an idyllic setting.

My destination was Six Rivers Charter High School, to spend the morning with science teacher Shannon Morago. Unique in comparison to most charter schools, Six Rivers is a district-created and directed school, operating independently on a portion of the Arcata High School campus. The goal of creating the school was to provide a small school experience for students who would benefit from the extra attention and focus that comes in such an environment. Six Rivers has fewer than one hundred students, so students in each grade level are together constantly. The teachers and principal know everyone in the school, and in fact, the principal makes daily visits to classrooms to check in individually with students and teachers.

Students and families who choose Six Rivers are interested in and benefit from individualized help and attention; they may have had less interest and success in the large, traditional, comprehensive schools they attended before. Shannon recognizes and embraces the challenge of having a high proportion of students in whom solid academic habits and college aspirations are not a given. Noting the tendency for larger schools to track certain students into lower level classes, Shannon appreciates having everyone in the same class, with the same expectations—and those expectations are high. Shannon informs me that her sophomores in biology and juniors in chemistry all find these classes challenging. It's not only the concepts, but also Shannon's insistence on high-level scientific writing.

During my visit, I observe students in biology and chemistry classes who are doing some peer review of writing, a strategy common to English classes, but one I haven't seen in non-English classes. It gives me a chance to circulate and understand the students' work a little better than if I had been simply looking at scientific content. One student enlists me to answer a writing question about his paper, so I have a chance to see the impressive level of detail in his scientific observations.

Shannon is pushing for similar attention to detail in their writing, and from what I can see, her students have grasped her expectations.

Class grades are based on more than writing up observations, though. My visit takes place in October, at a time when students are still adjusting to their classes, and Shannon is completely open about figuring out what works with these particular students. Shannon is an experienced teacher with plenty of ideas and resources, and she studies her students' progress in search of ways to serve them better. She and her principal speak together briefly about students with Ds and Fs, tackling the challenge together by considering instructional strategies and student support, rather than simply lowering expectations or writing it off as a student problem. There's a high degree of confidence evident in Shannon's willingness to adjust her teaching to her students when something doesn't seem to work. That we need to adjust to our students first—not vice versa—is an ironic truth that great teachers working with challenging students must understand and accept.

"I find I use the word *teach* less and less," Shannon explains. "I want school and education to be about learning, not teaching. I don't think as much about *teaching* as I do providing a lot of opportunities to learn. I challenge, encourage, cajole, support, push, and question. The more I understand about human learning, the more I focus on how to bring joy and rigor in thought into the classroom. And, in turn, the more I laugh with and wonder with my students, the more I am astonished by what they can do."

Over the course of a year, a teacher like Shannon helps students understand the content and produce work at a level they didn't know they could reach. That's the common thread among Carlston award-winning teachers. As one of Shannon's former students told Tim Allen, "She had so much energy and absolutely loved what she was teaching us. She was an inspiration because I never liked math or science until she was my teacher. She made me love chemistry and is the reason I chose chemistry as my major."

After lunch, Shannon and I have ample opportunity to discuss teaching philosophies, professional trends and developments, and the value of reflection in our practice. After teaching in the mornings, Shannon heads to her other job: program leader in the teacher education program at Humboldt State. It's only a ten-minute walk from high school to university, and the daily switch between the two settings serves Shannon and her students well. Her constant immersion in teacher training and theory keeps her teaching sharp, and her daily work with students keeps her university work grounded in effective, real-world practice.

Martin Brandt, English
Independence High School, San Jose

Effectiveness is certainly the goal in teaching, but I wouldn't want to confuse the word with "efficiency." Efficiency suggests accomplishing an objective with no wasted time or effort. In situations where we enjoy our work and we're building relationships, there's something to be said for the quality of the experience. Without becoming inefficient, we want to enjoy the process, slow down sometimes, recognize, and relish the moments that matter.

Martin Brandt, who teaches English at Independence High School in San Jose, is the embodiment of this feeling in teaching. I met "Marty" through the Carlston Family Foundation, as he has continued to work with them since winning their award in 2003. Many teachers in the region know Marty through his work in the Bay Area Writing Project, and as a cooperating teacher in the San Jose State University teacher credential program. One of my former student teachers, Sima Thomas, started out in Marty's classroom.

An atmosphere that is comfortable for students is typically also comfortable for the teacher, and Marty's classroom is a perfect model of that; it's not always efficient, though. When Marty presents a set of writing instructions and tips using PowerPoint slides, he sets the presentation to music (today's accompaniment comes from Carlos Santana) and will stop the slides to synchronize the music so the crescendo matches the key slide. He could have moved the PowerPoint along more quickly; instead, he takes an extra moment to enjoy the experience himself, and make it more interesting for his students, who laugh with him as he "geeks out" over the music-and-slide synchronization. Maybe the lesson is both effective and efficient; maybe the content and skills stick with students more the first time around because Marty keeps them engaged. And it's not as if he's relying on PowerPoint to do the work. Marty spends much of the class moving through the room to consult with students individually about their writing and to answer their questions. Dedicating some extra time here and there to make a class more interesting and personal is worthwhile.

Observing his AP language class, I could see Marty's passion for great writing, the world of ideas, and the learning process. His delight in language is infectious:

After Marty shares a particularly excellent example of a creative sentence structure for an opening line, one student exclaims, "That's *tasty!*" Marty's classroom is also a place where students are comfortable expressing themselves, even if the idea they share may be unpopular. One student demonstrates that idea in a discussion involving me. Keeping in mind what he heard about my work when Marty introduced me to the class, a student approaches me after class to challenge the premise of my book: "Are you only visiting good teachers in poor schools?" he asks. I find out that he has attended at least three high schools in as many states and has concluded "There's not much good out there, especially in English classes." He says most classes are routine in their procedures and pedagogy, and English classes in particular lack objectivity and clarity in meaning and purpose. He's very confident in his conclusions. Trying to steer him toward something positive, I ask what subjects he does like; he responds, "It depends more on the teacher. A good teacher can make you enjoy a dull subject, and a bad teacher can make a good subject awful." With all the confidence that a worldly 16-year-old can bring to a debate, he calmly refutes all my points, and though we may not have changed each other's thinking, it's clear that Marty's classroom is a place where students can take chances and be assertive.

One of Marty's colleagues in the English department at Independence High School, Harriet Garcia, also plays a role in this book. Though I visited the two of them on the same day, I had different purposes in each visit. We'll meet Harriet in Chapter 12.

Vicki Leoni, English
Tulare Western High School, Tulare

Vicki Leoni recognizes the importance of a positive atmosphere to help students learn and, like Marty Brandt, achieves much of that positivity by being authentic, self-caring, humorous, and unflappable. She was a 2014 finalist for the Carlston Foundation teaching award and is an English teacher at Tulare Western High School. Tulare is a town of 60,000 people, and the second largest in Tulare County, southeast of Fresno. It's an agricultural area, and some of the students commute quite a long way to attend the school. In addition to teaching English classes, Vicki has also taught AVID classes and served as the program coordinator for her district.

As briefly explained in Chapter 4, AVID helps students reach college, especially first-generation college students who might need additional academic support and guidance. In Tulare, only about 15 percent of adults have a college degree, and there are no four-year colleges within an hour of the town. As a result, Vicki finds that many students think of college as a remote possibility, an abstraction of uncertain purpose or value. AVID provides students with more information about college eligibility and financial aid, extra tutoring during school, and academic coaching to support student skills, such as note-taking, organization, time-management, and self-advocacy.

Tulare Western has a block schedule—with ninety-minute class periods a few times per week instead of shorter class periods daily—and my visit comes on a day when Vicki has all English classes. However, I can tell at a glance that AVID classes also meet in this classroom, as there's an abundance of college information on the walls, along with encouraging posters and class pictures from recent years. At the same time, I can tell it's an English classroom by looking at the student work on the walls and the student groups named after authors.

Today, Vicki's English classes are dealing with challenging, dense texts, including Machiavelli, and engaging in discussion and collaboration around difficult topics, like the ethics of leadership. The level of expectations for academic discourse is quite high: Vicki discourages summarizing and taking shortcuts, and requires students to refer back to the text consistently as they generate questions and responses—all very appropriate for students nearing the end of high school.

As much as Vicki is prepared to help all her students reach for college, there's a certain reality in the community as well: There are students who won't go to college (at least in the short term) and have made an informed decision about that post-secondary path by the time they're seniors. Vicki understands her students and community, and her college advocacy does not inhibit positive relationships with every student in her classes. Some students are working while in high school, helping to support their families, and have plans to continue working full time after high school. (Tulare County is relatively poor, yet also among the most productive agricultural centers in the nation.) That's the case with one student in Vicki's first-period class this morning. She notices and comments on his absence at the start of the period, and his classmates begin to speculate about his eventual arrival: "What time do you think he'll be here today?" "What kind of drink will he have?" Sure enough, a tall young man comes in ten to fifteen minutes later, carrying a cup of coffee. He settles into class and gets to work without much discussion or interruption, but I ask Vicki about him later in the day. She tells me he works an early-morning shift as a truck driver, and because of variabilities in the work, including the frequently dense Central Valley fog, he doesn't always arrive by the start of class. (The fog is so serious that the school starts later for part of the year based on its probability.) In a situation like this, Vicki recognizes that her student is also a fellow adult with a job, and ensures that he feels welcome in her class, rather than punished for missing the bell sometimes as he juggles serious responsibilities in his life. She's doing all she can to make sure he'll get as much as possible out of these last few months before graduation.

Her sense of caring is evident in every student interaction, and every time she talks to me about an individual student. Vicki's greatest concern at the moment is a student whose father passed away just last week, though there are obvious limits to what she can do for him other than offer sympathy and flexibility as he copes with this family tragedy and tries to carry on in school. As she circulates around the classroom checking in with students, I can see they welcome her helpful and cheerful presence, rather than seeing it as supervision. At the end of each period, she has the same advice for each of her classes as they head off for the weekend: "Make good choices. Be good people."

Vicki has ambitions to help her school and district as well. She collects data from her classes and shares her findings with colleagues as she aims to identify more effective instructional strategies and grading practices; the next step is to pull teachers from other schools into the effort, gathering more information and trying to reach consensus about what works. She tells me, "I'm hoping this becomes a common way of communicating and working together in the future. It's exciting to be in a district that shares this vision." Beyond the district level, Vicki is encouraged by an uptick in state spending for education and the decreased, misguided focus on standardized test scores in state accountability. Looking at the big picture, Vicki is quite optimistic: "Despite all the negativity out there, it's a great time to be a teacher in this state."

These highly honored teachers come from cities and schools that vary in almost every way, and their skill sets and personalities are similarly variable. Observing them in their classrooms didn't convince me that Teachers of the Year are significantly better instructors than the other teachers I spent time with this year. Their most unique quality as a group is the clarity of vision that drives their teaching. Some find their spark in the love of learning and dedication to helping students master an academic discipline. Others focus on transforming the ways that we do schooling and manage learning. Some have an abiding commitment to their community or the neediest students therein, and they display a relentless focus on setting and achieving worthy goals in that context. Others have a gift for caring about and supporting "the whole child"—the person that child is now and the adult to come, rather than merely the student. The recognition of individual Teachers of the Year brings well-deserved attention to some outstanding people. It should also be seen as a celebration of the profession, highlighting the myriad ways that teachers collectively dedicate their energies to education, bringing their varying passions and talents to the work of improving schools and students' lives.

CHAPTER 7

National Board Certified Teachers:

Building Professional Status

Stories come to life when National Board Certified Teacher Leslee Milch reads to her kindergartners at Gilbert Elementary School in Buena Park.

THOUGH MY MOTHER AND AUNT BOTH HAVE SOME TEACHING EXPERIENCE, physicians dominate our family tree. My father and sister are both MDs, as are at least seven cousins and in-laws. So when I think about a profession and what it means to be a professional, I often think of doctors first. I know, at least second hand, the time and training that goes into entering the medical profession and the additional challenges of board exams, ongoing education, and renewing board certification. For teachers, there is a corollary organization and experience, but so far it represents the exception rather than the norm in our profession.

During my graduate school studies, one of my professors was Lee Shulman, an internationally recognized leader in research and policy around teacher training and professional learning. Much of his research, like my own "imprint" of professionalism, was based on examining the history of the medical profession and the steps involved in achieving professional status. A century ago, doctors had much lower status, few barriers to becoming a doctor, no agreed upon body of knowledge or best practices, and little regulation. In the same way that doctors took control of their profession, Shulman hoped teachers might establish and adhere to higher standards, assert greater autonomy over certification and practice, and thereby create a level of trust and status on par with other professionals. The National Board for Professional Teaching Standards (NBPTS) was created in 1987, with Shulman among its architects. I entered the Stanford Teacher Education Program and met Shulman in 1994. The idea of eventually becoming a National Board Certified Teacher (NBCT) was encoded into my professional DNA; regardless of the challenges and expenses, I took it for granted that certification would be the logical next step for me after a few years of teaching.

National Board Certification has evolved in its nearly thirty-year history, but in each iteration, certain requirements have been central to the process. First, teachers must study and understand a set of highly detailed standards of practice unique to the age group(s) and discipline(s) they teach. These standards documents are dozens of pages long, with rich descriptions of highly accomplished teaching practice. Teachers must submit a variety of entries to create a portfolio of their own teaching, with ample print and video evidence of the teacher's expertise having a clear impact on student learning, along with additional evidence of how teachers engage with parents, colleagues, and the profession as a whole. Finally, teachers take exams based on the skills in their discipline. For example, my certification involved a six-part exam that required me to evaluate student work samples and then design lessons to address the identified weaknesses in their work. I also had to demonstrate my own analytical skills applied to a poem and propose a set of lessons centered around a universal theme, incorporating both literature and works from other art forms such as music and film.

Teachers who achieve board certification almost always describe its value in advancing their teaching and helping them as education leaders and advocates. Just as important, teachers who attempt certification but don't achieve it still generally attest to its value and validity. In different states and districts, there are varying incentives to pursue certification, but unfortunately, there is not yet any state or district where NBCTs make up even close to half the teaching force.

I hope we do reach that point—and beyond. Teachers who pursue certification develop, or refine, their ability to think analytically and reflectively about their teaching. Because it's essential to certification, teachers learn to look for evidence of student learning and seek effective partnerships within schools and communities. The shared standards and understandings give us a common language and framework for talking about teaching and making our teaching better every year. Naturally, when I began this project, I made sure that NBCTs would make up a critical mass among the teachers I observed.

The National Board Standards are age- and subject-specific, but they are all based on the same set of five core propositions:

1. Teachers are committed to students and their learning.
2. Teachers know the subjects they teach and how to teach those subjects to students.
3. Teachers are responsible for managing and monitoring student learning.
4. Teachers think systematically about their practice and learn from experience.
5. Teachers are members of learning communities.

Whether certified or not, great teachers excel in these domains, though stronger in some than in others. When I'm visiting NBCTs, I know that they have proved themselves in each of these areas, and I know that we're able to discuss teaching in these terms. To illustrate what the core propositions look like in practice, I've organized this chapter according to the five propositions and selected NBCTs whose teaching clearly demonstrates each one.

CORE PROPOSITION 1: TEACHERS ARE COMMITTED TO STUDENTS AND THEIR LEARNING.

David Berk, Third Grade
Cleveland Elementary School, Pasadena

With National Board Certified Teachers figuring so prominently in my thinking about accomplished teaching, it's fitting that my very first school visit outside of my own geographic area is in the third-grade classroom of David Berk, at Cleveland Elementary School in Pasadena. Having practiced a few observations in my own district and then one in a nearby district, I'm energized to be on the road after months of planning. Dave and I have known each other for a few years through our shared interests in education, advocacy, activism, and National Board Certification, and it's wonderful to see him today for the first time in a few years.

It's a warm, surprisingly clear morning in early October. I arrive at Cleveland Elementary quite early, well ahead of the school starting time at 8:45 a.m., and I use the time to settle in and prepare for the activities to come. When the students arrive, they swing into action almost immediately. The day begins with a lesson in how we talk about stories, the specific vocabulary of fiction. Students read a story in pairs, and Dave circulates to listen to them discussing "character, plot, conflict, and theme." They've clearly started this work already, as there are pictures on the wall illustrating the themes from past stories. My favorites are "Never be mean to your teacher" and "Never give six dinners to a cat."

The lesson itself doesn't stand out for me as much as what happens in the transitions to subsequent lessons during the day. Whenever it's time to move on to something new, Dave has an assortment of songs and videos ready to play, and the students dance their way through the transitions. As I watch Dave jump and dance and make silly hand movements with his students—choreography they seem to know pretty well already in early October—I wonder if I could ever do this. I'm probably too self-conscious, but Dave is right there with his kids at every move in "The California Milk Song" and "The Sid Shuffle" (Sid is the sloth character in the *Ice Age* movies). I ask Dave about these transitions later, anticipating an answer that speaks about the value of giving children a chance to move their bodies and reset their brains a bit in between academic tasks. It turns out there's even more to it, and

Dave proceeds to give me a quick lesson in bilateral coordination—movements that cross the midline of the body—and how this all links back to student learning and skill development. I thought they were just working out the wiggles, but Dave is watching for much more than that. What looks at first glance like a commitment to having fun with students is also a commitment to student growth.

Knowing students well, as people and as learners, is essential to our instructional effectiveness. When I think about building these relationships over time, October seems like it's still quite near the beginning of the process. Maybe that's because my experience is in high schools, where students are getting to know six or seven teachers, and a typical high school teacher is working on relationships with 150 or more students who are rotating through for smaller portions of the day. So I can see a great advantage in this regard when the teacher has a single class. To capitalize on the value of knowing students well, Dave and his third-grade teaching partner at Cleveland Elementary have moved together from second to third grade, along with this cohort of students. They were also given the flexibility to determine class assignments and move some of the kids around to create balanced classes. As a result, Dave has known some of these students for over a year. It shows in the way he talks to parents at the beginning and end of the day, in the way he talks to colleagues and instructional aides about which students are excelling or lagging in a certain lesson, and especially in his interactions with the children in the room. As Dave begins a new math lesson, he has students seated on the floor facing him and a screen behind him, where a document camera and projector are showing the math problems and his methods of solving them. I'm sitting to the side, not ten feet away from Dave and from his students, and he's managing the kids and math at the same time. At least three or four times, Dave intervenes to prevent distractions or misbehaviors, and I can't even see what the trigger was. When it's time to move on to individual practice back at their tables, the students are all on track and ready to work again. Dave asks, "Boys and girls, which problems are you going to do?" They answer in chorus, drawing out the response: *"Twooo-and-threeee."*

As students stand up and move about, I ask a quick question regarding the prescience in his classroom management, and Dave laughs. "Oh, yeah! You have to see the trouble before it starts. There are some I just know, when they scoot closer to someone else, they're going to be whispering or playing or doing something with their hands." No time for elaboration, though—Dave is off to help students.

Their efforts are so earnest, working on the concept of place value, using grouping and manipulatives to help represent how the digit "8" means something different in the numbers "28" and "85." I'm circulating around the room, too, occasionally looking at student work and enjoying students' pride in their work as they show me a variety of mathematical representations for different numbers. They differ in the ways they work, with some talking to themselves to solve a problem, others working out addition on their fingers. One girl's jaw drops when she finishes a problem, like she can't believe what the answer turned out to be or maybe can't believe she hasn't solved it yet.

Dave now returns to a student he was helping earlier. "You figured it out! You figured that out! You kept working it! Are you proud of yourself?" he asks his beaming student. Next, Dave approaches a girl who needs some help: "I see you, Natalie. I see your effort. That looks like a hard problem for you to work out." She nods. "Can I give you a suggestion?" She nods again, this time with a smile. "Try drawing a picture to help you." Natalie says nothing and immediately starts working on an illustration.

It doesn't take a National Board Certified Teacher to make these efforts to know students well and demonstrate this level of commitment, but that certification means that the teacher understands the *how* and *why* of that commitment and is thoughtful and intentional around these efforts.

Leslee Milch, Kindergarten
Carl E. Gilbert Elementary School, Buena Park

When I first began planning this book, one of the first teachers I contacted was Leslee Milch, a kindergarten teacher in Buena Park. Leslee wrote the book on National Board Certification. I mean that literally: Leslee cowrote the book *Understanding National Board Certification: A Guide for Teachers and Those Who Support Them* (along with Tara Barnhart and Mark Ellis). Leslee was also my coleader in organizing the California contingent of NBCTs visiting congressional offices ahead of the 2011 National Board conference in Washington, DC. Clearly, she's dedicated to advancing the profession and advocating for teaching and teachers, though I think her actions in the classroom and community are even more persuasive than the words in her book or in her conversations with policy makers.

Walking into Leslee's classroom at the start of the day is slightly difficult, because not only are there over thirty students (in a kindergarten class), there are also at least ten parents or grandparents in the room reading with the students. There are also about six younger siblings in the room, some in strollers. It's a regular feature, part of Leslee's *daily* routine to have adults in the classroom to start the day. Some of the parents and grandparents know Leslee well by now, partly because it's near the end of the school year and also because they've had older children come through her class. In fact, Leslee has been teaching at Gilbert long enough to see former students come back as parents. The crowded classroom makes the morning more hectic for Leslee, but there are significant benefits for everyone involved. The students have extra opportunities to read to an adult, share their learning, and connect school and home. The adults have a better understanding of the school and Leslee, and a chance to see their children's progress on a regular basis. They also benefit from seeing the levels and varieties of books that help their children learn to read, and they are able to interact with Leslee regularly, sharing information that helps Leslee know her students and their families. This kind of information can be so vital. When a student is struggling, a teacher who knows the student well can be more effective by understanding and addressing the root cause of a problem rather than simply expecting the child to change a behavior. One boy is having trouble paying attention from the start of the day. Leslee gives him a couple of verbal prompts within about two minutes, trying to help him focus; when those attempts fail, she quickly deduces that he didn't eat breakfast this morning and that his sister rather than his mother took care of him this morning. When morning recess comes, Leslee sends the boy to "second breakfast" instead of the playground.

A morning meeting allows Leslee to review the day's agenda, in the middle of which Leslee tells her kindergartners, "And *if you're good,* I'll let you go to lunch after that." But they're not fooled: "We *always* get lunch!" A little later, with the whole class still seated on the carpet, a couple of students are distracted and bothering each other when they need to listen. It's subtle, but Leslee notices and has them stop. "I saw that," is all she needs to say, and a few students note, "You see *everything!*" Another time when she needs to be a bit stern, she reminds them, "I'm the boss. You can be the boss tomorrow." Some students raise their fists and cheer, while some other students cleverly point out, "Tomorrow's Saturday." It's clear that students have developed an understanding of Leslee's sense of humor and also find their own ways to contribute to the fun atmosphere.

One of the highlights of observing Leslee is seeing her during story time. When Leslee reads stories aloud, she puts great energy into it, making the books come alive with comedic voices and sound effects. She also pauses here and there to show the connection between specific punctuation marks and how she reads the text, the pace or inflection appropriate to a comma, period, question mark, or exclamation point. They talk about images and shapes, using terms like "symbol, horizontal, vertical." And given that it's now April, I'm not surprised to see some of the students handling these concepts well. Some students are especially quick to offer answers and ask questions, so Leslee consistently reinforces the need for some students to keep quiet at times for the benefit of others who need more time to think of what they want to say and how to say it. With this balanced approach, Leslee's kindergarten class is simultaneously fun and academic. She tells me at one point, however, that she's not entirely comfortable with the increased push of academics into kindergarten—a concern reminiscent of Lois Johnson's (see Chapter 2) and a subject of much debate in recent years. Still, Leslee manages to work in some academic topics and vocabulary without draining the joy.

Leslee's commitment to students and their learning extends out into the community. For over fifteen years, Leslee has organized "Read with Me," an outdoor reading activity held in a local park on summer evenings. Like her invitation to parents and other family members to be a regular part of her classroom, this effort makes reading fun and social. It started as a relatively simple way to connect kids, families, and books, during the summer months when many students were at risk of "summer slide"—the loss of learning and educational momentum they had during the academic year. And perhaps to some extent, the weekly event is more symbolism than substance if we think of it strictly in terms of reading. The real value of it is in the sense of community connectivity. Over the years, "Read with Me" has grown quite popular, attracting over one hundred families to the park on those summer evenings. Several community organizations, including the local library and even the FBI's community outreach department, have donated books for Leslee to distribute to families. Additional community partners have stepped in to provide healthy snacks and parenting support and information for adults while Leslee reads with the kids. Another local elementary school has adopted the whole idea, putting more teachers in a position to show their commitment to students and their learning.

CORE PROPOSITION 2: TEACHERS KNOW THE SUBJECTS THEY TEACH AND HOW TO TEACH THOSE SUBJECTS TO STUDENTS.

This proposition makes an important distinction between knowing something and being able to teach it. So often we assume that the people who excel at something are automatically the most qualified to teach it. Were that the case, you might expect the best coaches in sports would be consistently those who were the best players, but we know that's not the case. In the field of mathematics education, Dr. Deborah Ball's study of the mathematical knowledge necessary for teaching provides a fine example of that distinction. Ball's research helped demonstrate that students learned elementary school math best when they had teachers with both a deep understanding of mathematics *and* a solid grasp of how children learn math. When the same measure of teaching knowledge was given to classroom teachers and to mathematicians, 60 percent of the mathematicians did poorly on the test. If you haven't worked with and learned *from* children, it's often unclear how they could misunderstand something that seems so simple and obvious to an expert. In my own experience, I recall the "lightbulb" moment, several years into my career, when I figured out why some students exclusively used character dialogue, to the exclusion of a story's narration, as evidence in their essays about fiction. The reason is that we English teachers hammer into students' minds the importance of using *quotations,* so when students go looking for potential quotations to use in an essay, some of them are looking for quotation *marks* in the text. It seems obvious now, when I have more experience thinking like a student, though for years I scratched my head trying to figure out why students quoted inconsequential bits of dialogue and passed up more revealing narration and descriptions in the same passage.

With this particular core proposition, I want to briefly revisit two NBCTs I wrote about earlier, both of them also California Teachers of the Year. Lovelyn Marquez-Preuher (see Chapter 3) teaches middle school English language arts at Dodson Middle School in Palos Verdes. I described her commitment to her students and peers, and her knowledge of her subject and how to teach it has also been validated through her National Board Certification, and her work as an adjunct instructor of teachers at both Mount Saint Mary's University and California State University at Dominguez Hills. I also described how Valerie Ziegler's vision has spurred the growth of innovative academies within Abraham Lincoln High School in San Francisco (see Chapter 6). Valerie is an NBCT whose combined knowledge of her subject—and how to teach it—made her a valuable partner collaborating with university faculty and doctoral students in the Stanford History Education Group's "Read Like a Historian" curriculum development project.

Since we've already seen a great deal about these two NBCTs and how they demonstrate Core Proposition 2, let's move on to the next one.

CORE PROPOSITION 3: TEACHERS ARE RESPONSIBLE FOR MANAGING AND MONITORING STUDENT LEARNING.

Here's the hardest work in teaching, especially for secondary school teachers. The sheer number of students and assessments can be overwhelming: Imagine having 150 students to manage and monitor, and suppose that on one-third of your school days, each student produces something requiring grading, assessment, data entry, etc. That's a realistic estimate in my experience, and it means a gradebook or other records will contain over 9,000 pieces of information, each one representing student activity or assessed work. If each item requires an average of three minutes (some much more, some less) of teacher work to review the item, provide feedback, and record the information, that's the equivalent of more than eleven forty-hour weeks of work. More time than most summer breaks.

For teachers in primary grades, the main challenge is not the number of students, but rather the variety of information. Speaking strictly in terms of efficiency, I think it's easier to process one hundred of the same assessments given to different students than it is to process twenty-five assessments for the same number of students, covering four distinct skills or content areas. I need to know how my students are progressing in English language arts (ELA). My colleagues in elementary teaching need to know how students are progressing in ELA, math, science, social studies, and a range of other domains that might come up on an elementary grade report.

Tammie Adams, Literacy Coach
Brookfield Elementary School, Oakland

When it comes to managing and monitoring student learning, I think it's not a coincidence that the two NBCTs that come to mind are both teaching in schools that benefitted from California's Quality Education Investment Act (QEIA). I'll discuss the law in more detail in the concluding chapter, but in brief, this act, resulting from a successful lawsuit brought by the California Teachers Association on behalf of needy schools, poured extra money into struggling schools—for a limited time. One of these schools is Brookfield Elementary, a campus in west Oakland, directly abutting the retention wall of Highway 880. In a community with inadequate resources and high poverty, students face daunting challenges that demand more of our schools than we generally enable them to provide. Tammie Adams is an NBCT who has taught at Brookfield for almost two decades. Even with QEIA funding, Brookfield has faced immense challenges in the varied governance and shifting policy landscape of Oakland Unified.

I've known Tammie for nearly a decade, having worked with her as a National Board candidate support provider first, then collaborating with her on crafting policy reports with Accomplished California Teachers. She is an optimistic realist, observant and wise when it comes to understanding the challenges in her school and her students' lives, and never flagging in her efforts to address those challenges head-on. The day that I visit Brookfield, it's easy to observe those challenges and understand them better through Tammie's eyes.

It's early in the school year, and Tammie is adjusting to new position as a literacy coach at Brookfield. Coaches and other teachers with special assignments are increasingly common in schools across the country. They typically focus on a particular school or district priority, such as reading, math, technology integration, or new teacher mentorship, and provide support for teachers in either a single school or in a district. The coaching position may be part time, replacing some of the classes that a secondary school teacher would be teaching, or full time, as in Tammie's case. Often, we think of coaches as working outside the classroom, but Brookfield has had trouble keeping teachers in a particular second-grade classroom. Since Tammie taught many of these students last year and doesn't have a classroom of her own, she's been pressed into a quasi-substitute role, helping this class and their substitutes, while also trying to figure out her new role as a coach.

When she's in the classroom, I can see how well she knows the students, anticipating their needs and questions, helping them find reading material that will interest them and provide the right level of challenge for them. When we're in the hallways or dropping into other classrooms, we run into plenty of her former students, and Tammie remembers their names and their families. And when we return to her office, I can see how Tammie combines personal knowledge and observations with more concrete data, tracking the progress of every student in the school. The view behind the scenes shows the variety of tools and resources that Tammie draws from to help teachers schoolwide with literacy instruction and assessment, and she has her own notes and records regarding individual students. I think there's much to be said for having someone like Tammie in this role, because her longstanding connection to the school and community provides valuable context and prevents her from focusing so much on the data that it obscures the actual people behind the numbers.

She can't do the work alone, of course, nor can a school be solely responsible for the well-being of the children it serves. Brookfield Elementary has been able to partner with outside agencies to provide additional social services, which means bringing that extra care into the school; Tammie points out to me who else is on campus: social workers, counselors, a speech therapist, behavioral specialist, psychologist. I wonder what will happen to this level of support when the QEIA funding runs out.

When student test results don't match the demands of inflexible policies or laws, the pressure on teachers and students grows, staff turnover increases, and a reform fatigue sets in as various initiatives and programs come and go quickly. Site and district administrators tend not to last very long on the job. Over time, outsiders and policy makers begin to view the school and its community primarily in terms of their deficits. There's the troubling issue of institutional racism involved as well, reflected in the ways that schools and school staff composed almost entirely of people of color are denied equitable resources, and then held solely responsible for not overcoming inequity, often with the implication that any shortcomings reflect some inherent inferiority within the community and school staff. The equity gap and the problems of poverty demand attention; the positive stories in the community and school deserve similar attention. Tammie's career-long dedication to Brookfield and its students, and her leadership as a National Board Certified Teacher, are essential parts of a narrative that must be shared.

Ashley Alcalá, First Grade
Riley Elementary School, San Bernardino

Far to the south of Oakland, in a similarly under-resourced community, San Bernardino's Riley Elementary School is another QEIA site, with another National Board Certified Teacher among the school's leaders. Were I to wander the school without guidance, peeking into classrooms up and down the hallways, I'd have no trouble finding my destination: It's the classroom sporting a crazy amount of red and silver Washington State University signs and posters, banners and pennants. I post a picture of her classroom online without mentioning this teacher's name, but all our mutual friends seeing the WSU colors know immediately I'm spending today with Ashley Alcalá. Many of these friends know Ashley through her work with our state union, and some also know her as a National Board Certified Teacher and advocate for certification.

I probably couldn't have picked a worse day to visit, but I have to take what I can get while I'm in the region. In addition to the driving rain that will keep all the kids and teachers indoors all day, it's also a Friday, the day before winter break, and its Career Day, with a variety of guest speakers coming to speak to students in multiclass assemblies and also in classrooms.

All those factors might set the stage for a long and challenging day, but Ashley jumps into her normal routine, hoping for the best. Students seem eager to start as well, showing fine energy and focus in their warm-up activity that combines reading, writing, and coloring. There are only eighteen students in the class, a low number resulting partially from absences, though mainly due to QEIA funding for class-size reduction. The benefit is clear: Fewer students means that each one receives more of Ashley's time and attention. If there's an activity under way and Ashley needs to make it through the room to monitor every student's progress at least once, she can take a moment or two longer with students who need a little more help, or finish the activity in less time and move on before students lose focus.

Even on this unusual day leading into winter break, Ashley is continually among students, watching, giving feedback and instruction, collecting student work, and making notes about their progress that will inform her future teaching. As she puts it, "Continuous monitoring of student learning is imperative to young children learning to read. It provides key information for the teacher to plan interventions when students struggle."

It doesn't hurt that Ashley's students are a fun, social group. Some approach me with questions about their reading and math lessons. As I move around the room, they welcome my questions and like to show me the books they're reading. I always enjoy these brief opportunities to work with really young students, those at an age when it seems everything is new and possible. Ashley's passion for early elementary grades is grounded in that same idea: "I enjoy teaching first grade because of the growth I see the students making socially and academically. At other grade levels, you don't see as much growth in the majority of your students. My students are *fun* to teach, because they have a joy for learning and are eager to learn to read, despite the many challenges they face on a daily basis in their community."

All of Ashley's collected information about student progress will help her individually and will also be put to use in collaboration with her colleagues (see core proposition 5). Ashley tells me,

> We have a very collaborative and reflective principal [Aldo Ramirez] and staff who work together very well. We have collaboration time every Monday, and that is truly what it is. We interact with each other as professionals to analyze data and plan instruction for our students. Our principal is not afraid to be reflective about himself and encourages others to do the same.

CORE PROPOSITION 4: TEACHERS THINK SYSTEMATICALLY ABOUT THEIR PRACTICE AND LEARN FROM EXPERIENCE.

Laura Bradley, English Language Arts
Kenilworth Junior High School, Petaluma

Though the term *metacognition* is not used, it is the idea at the heart of this core proposition, which also addresses teaching and learning together. In a sense, it suggests that accomplished teaching depends on the teacher's ability to *learn—* to think about our thinking, to understand the connection between our teaching and the results, and adjust accordingly. We aim to help our students develop the same habits and skills: Think about what has come before, understand how they've reached a given point, and plan for future success informed by the past.

Students can use metacognition to improve their problem solving or argumentation, and also to improve their study habits. Teachers rely on metacognition at every step but especially after teaching a lesson or unit of study: *What was I thinking would happen when I taught this material in this way for these students? What actually happened? What parts of my instruction were most effective, or least effective, and why? What should I keep and repeat next time, and what do I need to change?*

Imagine you're teaching eighth-grade English language arts, and as you think about past practices, you realize you've observed more effort and vibrancy in student writing when it's not just an exercise for which you are the sole audience. You've seen how students crave opportunities to use their creativity and how they feed off each other's energy. You recognize that students relish challenges and will come together as a community to meet worthy goals. Maybe you've been teaching long enough to realize that worksheets and study guides produce minimal learning and engagement. You know that most major language arts textbooks are bloated collections of bland content—too many excerpts, too little context, too busy visually, and too constrained in scope and organization. If you're *thinking systematically about practice and learning from experience,* like a National Board Certified Teacher, you might recognize an opportunity to fundamentally alter and improve on the traditional practices in language arts classes.

That's what Laura Bradley has done at Kenilworth Junior High in Petaluma. As a veteran teacher married to another veteran teacher, both from teaching families and both with lifelong ties to the community, Laura has had decades of experience to reflect on teaching and students in her community, and she has taken bold steps to reinvent language arts classes for seventh and eighth graders.

We English teachers know there's no substitute for writing practice to improve writing, but reading all that student writing can be a barrier for some teachers worried about assigning more than they can read. A middle school teacher might have students write several significant pieces each semester, ranging from one to three pages typically, perhaps a total of a few thousand words. Laura has her eighth graders write novels—in a month. Working within the framework of the Young Writers Program within the National Novel Writing Month project (NaNoWriMo), Laura has, for several years, successfully challenged her students to write an entire novel in the month of November. With adequate planning and access to technology, plus administrative support for a solid month of classwork devoted to one purpose,

Laura has guided hundreds of students in recent years to the completion of short novels, many of which are available to order online and can be found among the thousands of books filling Laura's classroom library. Her project has been noticed by the *New York Times, Edutopia,* and other publications, and has generated some serious engagement and enthusiasm among her students.

The value of this exercise is immense. It strengthens students' perceptions of themselves as writers and improves their writing speed, fluency, proficiency with writing conventions, editing skills, and understanding of the writing process. They gain a sense of maturity and competency, achieving a bold goal that few adults even attempt. They build a sense of community within their classes and even, virtually, with writers across the country.

I don't mean to suggest that every eighth-grade English language arts teacher should copy Laura's NaNoWriMo idea (though her Kenilworth colleagues did). Her teaching, like all good teaching, is a product of her knowledge and skills, her personality, her strengths, and the context in which she works: the school, community, and students. The personality piece is important, though I can imagine some instructional gurus cringing when they read that. While it's true that there are some fundamentals to good instruction that must be independent of personality, guaranteed in any classroom regardless of the teacher, it is just as true that teaching and learning thrive on strong relationships, and these relationships cannot grow when we stifle rather than embrace individuality. In Laura's case, there's a blend of ambition, optimism, creativity, and humor that runs through her work, which is evident in her classroom and in her work with adults, as I learned from working with her as National Board candidate support provider. She has charisma that makes people want to work with her, and she brings out the best in others. And if the novel-writing assignment had been required of her rather than initiated by her, it's questionable whether or not she would inspire the kind of consistent success that has followed since she took that initial plunge with her students.

Since the leap into novel writing, Laura has also jumped with both feet into a variety of technical and media innovations in her teaching. She's a Google Certified Teacher, skillfully incorporating a variety of digital applications into her language arts teaching and also creating an elective course in digital media. Laura also advises a broadcasting club that's on the verge of becoming a new elective course. I didn't know it at the time of my visit, but Laura was a nominee for the Henry Ford Teacher Innovator Award; the announcement of her first-place selection came two weeks later.

My visit to Kenilworth is near the end of the school year, a perfect spring day in California's wine country. The school is on Riesling Road, and yes, Chardonnay, Cabernet, Merlot, and Zinfandel are all nearby. I arrive early to make sure I'm ready for my one-day job as a guest anchor on the morning newscast at KTV. Since the broadcast is produced by student volunteers in a club rather than a class, there's not much time for them to prepare the broadcast. Laura helps the students compose the script and has also raided my Facebook profile for pictures of me, including one showing my recent stiff but moderately successful attempt to learn how to surf. With the help of the KTV students, I find my first time on the morning news is less awkward than my first time on a surfboard.

Evidence of Laura's constant reflections on improving teaching show up throughout the day. There are new Chromebook computers that she's piloting for the school, and she has offered her class for a trial period to test out new furniture that's more comfortable, lighter, and easier to move around the room. In her English class, Laura's students, already novelists, are now producing magazines; it's a format that still calls for their writing and editing skills but provides new challenges in terms of audience, formatting, and visual content.

The digital media class is even more open-ended, with students trying out a variety of video projects and, for the most part, failing. The current challenge is to create a short video that uses some editing tricks to produce humorous, surreal effects. Two girls are outside trying to set up a row of dominoes, planning to record their fall, and then edit in a surprise ending. However, the dominoes keep falling prematurely at the slightest gust of wind. In the classroom, a few students are trying to set up a Rube Goldberg machine, sort of like an elaborate mousetrap where objects fall, twist, swing, or bounce in sequence to set off other objects and motions. They don't have enough space and aren't able to create the effects they can imagine. But this is what learning looks like. Laura could easily have anticipated these problems and could step in to tell students how to fix them, but then the projects would become a collaboration of teacher and students. When they own the process and the project, they're learning *through experience* about planning, testing their ideas, and improving as they go. They'll rely on metacognition to help them achieve better results next time. Just like their teacher.

CORE PROPOSITION 5: TEACHERS ARE MEMBERS OF LEARNING COMMUNITIES.

Keila Snider, Principal
Jessica Simpson, Instructional Coach,
Student Activities Director
Desert Springs Middle School, Desert Hot Springs

I can't think of an educator whose story illustrates the power of a learning community better than Keila Snider, the first principal who figures prominently in this book. She became a National Board Certified Teacher in 2000 and made certification an instrumental part of her leadership when she became a principal. She began at Julius Corsini Elementary School in Desert Hot Springs. She had been a teacher there and knew well the challenges they were facing: The school was growing rapidly, in a high-poverty and high-crime neighborhood. Students were struggling, parents were not engaged, the campus didn't feel safe, and staff turnover was around 75 percent annually. Many policy makers look at schools like Corsini and want to bring in outside programs, more training, and external solutions that look at the existing staff as part of the problem. Teachers whose students produce the lowest test scores might be targeted for intervention, and then removal. Keila looked at the teachers as the solution, and in the spring of 2007, convinced every one of them to take on National Board Certification as a way to improve their practice. (It is no small decision to attempt certification. The entire process can take hundreds of hours outside of class time, and many teachers already struggle to balance time for work, family, and personal care. The process can also be expensive, though costs have come down more recently. The financial details, various supports and stipends, and out-of-pocket expenses vary considerably across districts, and have changed a few times at the state level as well.)

The result of the certification push at Corsini was a dramatic turnaround in campus climate, parent engagement, and teacher retention, which was 100 percent the following year. For some policy and leadership audiences, it would also be important to note that a significant and sustained improvement in test scores helped make the case that having groups of teachers pursue National Board Certification can be an excellent approach to school improvement. Keila's sister, Danielle Snider, is also a school principal in the same region, and her school staff undertook a similar certification effort, producing similar results. Keila has moved on to a new school, but Corsini has held on to its success for the past four years, thanks to the now-certified staff and the improved school culture.

I've known Keila for several years and arranged through her to visit Desert Springs Middle School (DSMS). However, my host and guide for the day is Jessica Simpson, one of the National Board Certified teachers who helped improve Corsini and who is now an instructional coach at Desert Springs. It's an unusual situation for me to spend so much of a school visit with a teacher I don't know and haven't contacted myself. It helps that we met with Keila for dinner the night before my visit, and when it turns out that we have a mutual friend, my former student Stephanie Smith (see Chapter 4), we reach an even greater level of comfort for the day ahead of us.

Though some of the challenges at DSMS resemble those at Corsini (which is a feeder school for DSMS), the solution is not identical. It wouldn't have made sense for Keila to come in to her first middle school leadership position and expect the teachers to do what had worked for her at a smaller school, serving elementary school students, with a different group of teachers. Too often, well-meaning people assume that if something works in one place, it makes sense for leaders to mandate the replication of the same methods in a new setting. What I can see at Desert Springs, however, is that the method is secondary; what matters most are the driving values and commitments made by the staff. So even if they're not all working as a team toward National Board Certification, there's a sense that the school is working as a team, one that happens to be led by NBCTs putting the core propositions into practice.

The teamwork is evident in the school atmosphere, where, despite the stresses of poverty and homelessness that further complicates the lives of almost a third of DSMS students, they are fully engaged and working hard all over the school, being challenged by skilled and caring teachers and enjoying a relaxed and safe campus. I saw a couple of individual students who exhibited behavioral problems or signs of emotional distress, but I also saw the adults on campus responding quickly and thoughtfully.

As an instructional leader, Jessica models the fifth of the National Board's core propositions all day long. In every classroom we enter, Jessica knows the teacher's schedule, where they are in their curriculum, and what their strengths are. She has a collegial pride in her colleagues, evident in her avid agreement when I note the level of challenge and student engagement in Andrew Lee's math class or when I observe how Antonio Mendoza withholds simple or correct answers from students in his technology elective, directing them instead to find or construct their own answers. I see the patience of the music teacher and the sincere warmth of an English teacher, and every time I'm outside the classrooms or walking the halls, I'm struck by the pleasantness of the atmosphere. Not for the first time, or the last, I have to admit that it's hard to shake preconceptions about what a school will be like in an economically depressed neighborhood.

Finally, at the end of the day, I have a chance to see Jessica as a teacher, her one class being the student leadership course. There are ninety students enrolled, but a mere sixty in the room today (the thirty sixth-graders are working elsewhere). They have a variety of projects to work on, and Jessica's main focus is to check in with student leaders for each facet of each project, to make sure they're watching timelines, monitoring progress, anticipating deadlines, and managing their teams. Once the students start working, they are focused (for middle schoolers!), independent, and inclusive. Clearly, Jessica's understanding of how to work in a learning community among teachers has filtered through to help her students develop a similar sense of community.

Kay Hones, Librarian
San Francisco Unified School District, San Francisco

Months later, I have the chance to spend time with a National Board Certified Teacher who extends the idea of learning community far beyond the walls of a school. Kay Hones is a teacher librarian in San Francisco Unified School District, with a full-time position made up of part-time assignments at multiple alternative high schools. Like me, Tammie Adams, and Laura Bradley, Kay has served as a National Board candidate support provider at Stanford's National Board Resource Center. Helping other teachers go through certification is a powerful way to participate in our professional community and also to continue reflecting on our own practice and improvement. Kay explains that, as a result of working with candidates, "I am constantly learning new ideas for my own practice. When I'm planning my library lessons, scheduling library events, writing grants, I constantly ask myself, 'what is the impact on student learning?'" (Recall that impact on student learning must be evident in the certification portfolio.)

Beyond connecting with teachers through the National Board Resource Center, however, Kay plays an active role in building and strengthening the profession, as both a teacher and as a librarian. Actually, all the librarians I've ever known or worked with have this shared characteristic, which I think serves them well in their particular teaching roles and also probably serves as a survival mechanism. Teaching can be a surprisingly isolated activity, practiced mostly with one adult surrounded by dozens of children. While classroom teachers don't have enough time to observe each other or collaborate adequately, most of us have professional peers next door, around the corner, or down the hall. However, not every school in California has a librarian, and when a school does have one, they rarely have a fellow librarian on campus. It's not surprising then that librarians are adept at seeking and building strong learning communities beyond their individual campuses. Unlike teachers in core subjects, they must advocate for their professional existence, when instead, librarians should be considered the most indispensable teachers in a school, due to the ways they can support every student and teacher in a school.

While Kay may share some characteristics with other librarians, her personal background makes her unique among teachers I've known or worked with. In addition to being a high school librarian, Kay has been an elementary school art teacher, and has experience teaching in Oahu, Detroit, and Hattiesburg, Mississippi. In her time in San Francisco, she has worked in both elementary and high schools and finds herself drawn to the more challenging, alternative educational settings. Her current position includes work at three such schools. Hilltop High School serves pregnant students and young mothers. Civic Center Secondary School serves students in transition out of juvenile detention. Downtown High School, where I'm spending the morning with Kay, is the landing place for students who have been counseled out or expelled from other San Francisco high schools.

To digress briefly from the focus on National Board Certified Teachers, I have to say how impressed I am by Downtown High School. It's unfortunate that it takes some kind of significant problems for students to end up here, a reaction similar to my thoughts on Alta Vista High School (see Chapter 5). Like Alta Vista, Downtown High School is a small school focused on providing extra support for students, with a dedicated and creative staff. Students have a variety of curricular choices delivered in a project-based learning approach. Each semester, students are offered courses in various interdisciplinary focus areas. Their basic subjects like English, math, science, and history/social studies are tethered to concentrations in the environment, community-building, or social justice, with projects that might involve outdoor education, cooking, performing arts, visual arts, and—in one room I visited—the construction of a boat that was due to launch into the San Francisco Bay later in the spring. Downtown students can also link some of their academic activities to job training and placement. There are adults throughout the school creating a calm and safe atmosphere, connecting with students, and providing a variety of support and outreach, including personal, informational, and even nutritional. It's no mystery what most students need to thrive in school, or life. And it's a shame that for so many students, we withhold it until they're in trouble, if they ever get it at all.

The academic program requires some unique support from the librarian. I have a chance to observe Kay's work with a class that needs to research the criminal justice system, as part of a writing project that will eventually lead to a spoken-word performance piece. In this work, and in the basic establishment and maintenance of a library for Downtown High School, Kay fulfills the most basic role of a school librarian. However, what's behind that work is a combination of networking and proselytization. Kay relies on community and administrative support, and has to reach out to teachers constantly to find ways to support their work. For teachers who may not be as used to having libraries and librarians available, Kay focuses on letting them know what's possible, what resources exist both in the library space and in her capacity to assist them. "You have to catch the teachers first," and then the students are more likely to visit the library, which increases the odds that they're reading. Kay knows that libraries need to be warm, clean, comfortable, and inviting spaces, so she attends to the physical aspects of the library, in addition to the hospitality. "Some of it is as simple as connecting with kids by noticing haircuts and new shoes," she tells me. There are also creative ways to try to reach more students, like the "Blind Date with a Book" idea: High-interest fiction and nonfiction books are wrapped in plain paper, with short intriguing descriptions written on the paper to try to entice a potential reader into a "blind date"—without knowing the author or title, or seeing the cover.

Beyond the school, Kay is active in various district committees and community organizations that support school libraries and public libraries. The San Francisco

Public Library has a new program called The Mix, bringing a variety of informational and creative resources together in one place to support and engage the city's teens. At the time of my visit, The Mix was in its final planning stages, and Kay was already spreading the word to students. Her participation in a broader professional community helps that community and makes her a better resource for her students.

Most great teachers are not National Board Certified Teachers, but most National Board Certified Teachers have something great about them. As leaders on their campus, in their districts, and in the broader community, they demonstrate a deep commitment to students and to our profession. Certification, for many of us, is the spark that ignites interest and action in leadership and advocacy. Making certification the norm rather than the exception in our profession would undoubtedly spark further improvement in teaching and schools.

CHAPTER 8

Teacher-Powered Schools:

Putting Educators in Charge

Casey Link is surrounded by his fifth graders as he finishes giving instructions for an activity at Chrysalis Charter School in Palo Cedro.

MY INTRODUCTION TO THE IDEA OF TEACHER-POWERED SCHOOLS occurred when I learned about Math and Science Leadership Academy (MSLA), a teacher-founded and teacher-led school in Denver. The school was created by the Denver school district, not only with the blessing of the union, but at the suggestion of the union president at the time, Kim Ursetta Manning. Her partner in this enterprise was Lori Nazareno; I met Lori and Kim through their connections to the National Board and the Center for Teaching Quality. In both local and national media, MSLA has been deservedly praised for its success in serving high-needs students with an innovative model of school design and governance. It was also among the schools studied in the book *Trusting Teachers with School Success* (by Kim Farris-Berg, Edward J. Dirkswager, Amy Junge), which served as my guide to teacher-led schools in California.

The book details several models of teacher-led schools, with varying degrees of autonomy and authority in areas of curriculum, instruction, budgeting, and personnel decisions. These schools may operate within the fold of a traditional district, may be chartered through districts or counties, or have other governance structures. With some friendly assistance from *Trusting Teachers* co-author Kim Farris-Berg, I was able to arrange visits to three teacher-led schools in California.

Alysia and Paul Krafel, Teachers, Co-Founders
Casey Link, Fifth Grade
Chrysalis Charter School, Palo Cedro

There are people who will refer to the San Francisco Bay area or Sacramento as "Northern California," and relative to Southern California, that holds true, but there are vast expanses of our state still north of "northern," and that's where I headed for my first visit to a teacher-led school. I had just spent a couple of days on the Humboldt County coast—nearly three hundred miles north of San Francisco and still one hundred miles short of the Oregon border—when I headed inland through the mountainous Shasta-Trinity National Forest. On this sunny Tuesday afternoon, I drove alongside a shimmering Whiskeytown Lake and soon came upon the Trinity River Lumber Co. in Weaverville, where I pulled over to watch as specialized machines lifted four or five tree trunks at once, stacking them in mounds fifty feet high, maybe taller. I emerged in Redlands, crossed the Sacramento River, and turned south on Highway 5 toward Cottonwood, my destination for the evening. Alysia and Paul Krafel were among the teachers who established Chrysalis Charter School, and they were also my hosts for the night before I visited Chrysalis. To reach their home in Cottonwood, I drove several minutes up one dirt road and then turned and went down another. Shortly after my arrival, Paul took me on a short walk around the area, past the pens where he and Alysia keep chickens and goats, through scrub brush and along a wash where he pointed out signs of deer and feral pigs.

Visiting with Alysia and Paul at their home proves to be an excellent introduction to the school and the community. The school itself is such an extension of its founders that I benefit from seeing how they live, learning about their family and the founding of the school. It also helps me, as a city-dweller, to understand more about the area and the families there. Chrysalis is chartered by Shasta County and draws students from all over this rural area. The open spaces and quick access to national forests and wilderness areas have shaped the curriculum of the school and its ethos. The school's name evokes a natural process of metamorphosis and emergence, and the school mission is "encouraging the light within each student to shine brighter."

The approach to helping "each student" has much to do with the sense of community at Chrysalis, creating an environment in which individuals can all shine in their unique ways. It's a small school with one classroom per grade level, kindergarten through eighth grade. To foster a sense of community, each day starts with the whole school gathered together outdoors for a "Tree Assembly." There's singing, information about current happenings at school, attention to the seasons, weather, and plants. Paul pulls a few blades of grass and explains that it's a non-native, European species called plantain, brought to California by settlers because of its medicinal qualities. One of the older students jumps in to say you can chew it up and apply it to an insect bite or sting to make it feel better. The morning assembly also includes checking in on a science experiment involving a patch of no-longer-green grass that hasn't seen daylight in a while. I'm included in the gathering as well, as Paul introduces me to the entire school. I'm not sure if the youngest students are really taking note of my presence, but at recess, later in the day, I receive a personal welcome and unexpected hug from one of the fourth-graders, giving me a greater sense of the familial atmosphere at Chrysalis.

However, any thoughts that Chrysalis might be too "touchy-feely" and therefore less academic are put to rest in Casey Link's fifth-grade class. There may not be as much seat time or as many worksheets often associated with traditional academic work in elementary school, but students at Chrysalis are working on challenging content. To help students receive appropriate instructional support and challenges in math and reading, they may spend part of their day with students at a different grade level, and that arrangement is subject to change with the students' needs during the school year. The small campus and interior doors connecting many of the classrooms make it logistically simple, while the emphasis on a caring and friendly atmosphere ensures there's no stigma for students who work with a lower grade level for part of the day.

In Casey's class, the math lesson for the day involves word problems based on the idea of painting a wall in three colors. There are many variables—the cost of a can of paint, the square feet that can be covered per can, the various ways you can employ a three-color pattern on one wall. To experiment with this spatial part of the problem, Casey has all sixteen students sitting on the carpet with him, using rods of different colors and lengths to build a facsimile of their wall. Students seem to be fine with the multiplication involved, but Casey pushes them to recognize the practical limitations implied in the problems: For example, if you need to paint twelve square feet and can only cover eight square feet per can (small cans, I guess), you'll have to buy two. Buying one and a half cans is not a realistic option. As students complete their problems and share their designs, Casey pays them for their design work—in actual Japanese yen (presumably small amounts!). He has spent time in Japan and has a variety of Japanese art and photos around his classroom.

I also observe reading and writing time, which includes some independent reading and some direct instruction. Casey's students review strategies to identify a compound sentence; they are advised to "put your finger on the conjunction," then look for complete sentences on either side of the conjunction. Following that advice works well for a few examples, first involving the conjunction *and,* followed by *or.* The lesson is derailed by some major giggles when the time comes to "put your finger on the 'but.'" If you know any current or former fifth-graders, you'll understand, and if you happen to work with fifth graders, I think Casey would let you borrow that can't-fail joke.

Later in the day I have the pleasure of watching the series of science experiments and demonstrations Casey has set up at stations around the classroom. Students are learning some of the properties of gasses and liquids. The balloon-balancing station shows that air has weight. Using large syringes (no needles), students find it's possible to compress air, but not water. An upside-down empty cup lowered carefully into water won't fill with water because the air won't be displaced. These and other experiments lead to conversations and theorizing about what's observed, then students wrap up their conversations in time to write and illustrate their conclusions for today. This portion of the day may show the students at their most serious and scholarly, and they're clearly enjoying the process and the challenge.

At lunch, I join Paul, and the entire student body, outside. Students sit and eat where they choose, and teachers mix in as well. Paul is technically more administrator than teacher at this point, but the school has one full-time administrator to help him out. Paul and I are eating lunch with a few students who are new to the school. It's late October, and they say they've enjoyed the difference. They find Chrysalis more engaging in the classroom and more friendly campuswide. When everyone has finished with lunch, Paul joins some boys playing Frisbee on a football field, so I join in too—the only time in my year when I played with students at lunch recess, probably because it was the only time that a teacher I was visiting was playing with students too.

While they might be having plenty of fun at Chrysalis, teachers are putting in just as much work as their peers elsewhere, and with a broader array of responsibilities than teachers have in a traditional school. That point is reinforced again and again in my conversations with Casey, Paul, and Alysia. Teachers collectively or in smaller committees deal with the school finances, food services, facilities, transportation, administrative and clerical matters, and of course, the academic program. I don't mean to suggest that the teachers have daily responsibilities in all these areas. Just like any school, Chrysalis has staff to handle nonteaching jobs, including a lead administrator to oversee all the nonteaching work. Paul also handles some administrative duties while continuing to teach part of the day. However, the administrators are not in charge of the staff; the staff hires and evaluates the administrator instead. (The details of administrative roles and governance vary among teacher-powered schools, though I think it's essential to point out that a school can thrive without the traditional model of administrative oversight relative to the teaching staff.)

In the students' experiences at Chrysalis, the influence of teacher leadership is reflected broadly in the school culture, and most specifically in both the morning assembly and the flexibility of placing students in different classes for some of their daily instruction. Such programmatic features could certainly be found in a school with more traditional leadership, with site and district administrators holding the responsibility for the structure of the school day. However, the fact that the teachers have made these decisions and worked out the details on their own means there's complete buy-in. I'm sure we can all think of situations at work or school where the person delivering a presentation or training or lesson is carrying out someone else's directive without entirely agreeing with it, maybe even without fully understanding it. I've been on both sides of that situation. In my time at Chrysalis (and at the other schools coming up in this chapter), I never pick up that feeling. Teachers are completely on board with the unique aspects of the program because they're implementing their own design, based on the staff's consensus.

AJ Johnstone, Humanities
San Francisco Community School, San Francisco

Back in "less-northern" California, I had the opportunity to visit another teacher-led school; San Francisco Community School is a K–8 school within a large, urban, unified school district. Being part of the larger district brings some constraints that aren't present at Chrysalis, but for teachers like AJ Johnstone, the primary appeal of working at a teacher-led school is the same: the opportunity to participate in the design and implementation of a quality academic program. AJ knows the contrast; she taught elsewhere in the district for seven years and is now in her eighth at the Community School. She recalls feeling "under the thumb of the district. We had to be on the same page, have the same bulletin boards, teach out of the teacher's edition"—though she expresses some optimism about the overall direction of the district in improving that teaching climate.

What I learned at Chrysalis is certainly reinforced here: Teacher-led schools demand quite a bit of extra effort and attention from their staffs. As AJ describes it, "A lot of meetings, a lot of conversation about everything. It's always changing. The school is a very flexible, living structure." There are issues about sharing space in a larger school with a wide range of ages; you have the constraints of the building you're in and the numbers of students enrolled, and you have to design a plan that works for kindergartners, eighth graders, and everyone in between. Teachers are the ones setting agendas for full-staff and grade-level meetings, the ones responsible for scheduling and site budgeting. AJ notes that "Spring is really intense, when you're looking ahead to next year" while still dealing with the current year. "You also have to be willing to work in lots of configurations with different people," she says. "Sometimes middle school teachers end up teamed with K–1 teachers. You really have to have trust in your colleagues, because you don't necessarily know their work or their needs, but then you also need to speak up based on your experience too."

In AJ's classes, seventh and eighth graders are grouped together for a humanities curriculum that operates on a two-year loop. It's an appealing strategy, to blend ages and experience levels in the classroom, and one that's found elsewhere as well, in Montessori schools among others. Instead of being constantly surrounded by their age-peers, the younger students have a critical mass of role models who have an extra year of experience, while older students come into a leadership role in the second year. There's also a benefit from having the same teacher two years in a row, with the added comfort of already knowing the teacher's routines, expectations, preferences, and personality. However, due to some program changes a few years ago, and because she has the appropriate credentials to teach multiple subjects and a wider age range, AJ has had many of her current students for four years now, not just two.

On the day of my visit, students are doing research into questions and topics of their choosing, and dedicating some extra time to the development of research skills and critical thinking regarding the results of that research. AJ talks with students about the limitations of the online resources that often come up first in web searches—sites like Yahoo! Answers, Wikipedia, or About.com. She even has them apply some critical thinking to articles on the History Channel website, where they realize there's no information about the author of the content and no indication when it was written or updated. If her push for sophisticated, higher-quality sources seems ambitious for seventh and eighth graders, AJ is certainly not springing this on them out of nowhere. Looking around the classroom, I can see the artifacts of students' prior work in history. Rather than pull information from textbooks about events like the Constitutional Convention and then answer simplistic, factual questions, AJ's students have been creating posters that highlight the differences among various historians' presentations of those events. Howard Zinn's *Young People's History of the United States* is one of the texts they've used in the past.

As students settle into their work for the period, AJ continues to circulate and work with one or two students at a time. I can't say much about the content of those conversations as AJ speaks quietly. However, I can see that she takes her time, looking closely at students' work and the sources they're finding. Occasionally, I infer she must have said something funny because students laugh quietly at her remarks, then resume their research. The atmosphere overall is collegial, among students and between teacher and students. There are occasional moments where AJ has to manage off-task behaviors or confiscate a lollipop. The majority of her time, however, is spent engaging students regarding research methods and sources and collaboratively planning next steps in their learning. When AJ is working with one group of students, the rest of the class stays focused, with students in each group cooperating and supporting each other.

Successful group work in a classroom is not a matter of luck. In fact, AJ has been paying attention to this aspect of her teaching by working with an instructional coach this year, focusing on complex instruction (the technical term for a specific approach to group work in the classroom; the group work I observe is not technically "complex instruction," although students likely carry over some of the skills and habits into this situation). Teachers like AJ understand the importance of planning and structuring group work, carefully considering the nature of the work and the unique combinations of personal traits and strengths students bring to a group. Effective and equitable group work also requires overt and repeated attention to the norms and expectations for group interactions. AJ notes that status issues are part of every group dynamic, so complex group work has assigned roles. Status among peers might correlate to a student's language skills or socioeconomic status, along with other aspects of student identity. When there are assigned roles, a student's opportunity to participate and learn is not diminished by a perception of lower status, and in fact, their status may be enhanced by carrying out their role responsibly in the group.

AJ's support for students extends outside of academics as well. During lunchtime, she advises the school's Gay-Straight Alliance (GSA). These groups are increasingly common in schools, though still controversial in some communities. From conversations with my school's GSA and its advisor, I've learned that students who participate in the club may or may not identify as lesbian, gay, bisexual, transgender, or queer/questioning, commonly abbreviated as LGBTQ. The "alliance" part of the name opens the umbrella to include any student who wants to promote awareness of and campus safety for LGBTQ students. The safety issues are serious, as LGBTQ students (and adults) are at higher risk for bullying, assault, depression, and suicide. (For more information and related resources, see www.pflag.org and www.glsen.org.)

Social Justice Humanitas Academy, San Fernando

My third visit to a teacher-led school finds me in an even larger district—back in Los Angeles Unified. Social Justice Humanitas Academy (SJHA) is a pilot high school within the Los Angeles United School District, though located in the city of San Fernando and among the northernmost campuses in this sprawling district. Dodson Middle School, where Lovelyn Marquez-Preuher teaches (see Chapter 3), is almost fifty miles south in Palos Verdes.

SJHA landed on my itinerary through a combination of factors. One of the school's founding teachers, Jeff Austin, has taken on a leading role in the new Teacher-Powered Schools Initiative, which also includes Alysia Krafel of Chrysalis, Lori Nazareno of MSLA in Denver, and Kim Farris-Berg, co-author of *Trusting Teachers* (see www.teacherpowered.org). Another reason I'm excited about seeing the school because I know and admire the principal, Jose Luis Navarro, a one-time California Teacher of the Year I've met twice before. But as it turns out, Jeff has a number of bureaucratic duties to attend to, and Jose has been temporarily pressed into a support role at a neighboring school with some urgent administrative needs.

The school is housed in a relatively new, multistory building on the Cesar Chavez Learning Academies campus. Walking up to the school on a clear, sunny morning, passing cars lined up to drop students off, I think this would be a great campus for one school, but the buildings house three pilot schools and one charter. I learn later that there is some collaboration among the schools for athletics and facilities, but some tension as well. Students have unflattering nicknames for their counterparts on other campuses, and the schools don't always have the same views about shared costs or managing common spaces. Still, within the halls of SJHA, there's a comfortable and familial atmosphere. There are murals on the walls featuring multicultural imagery and significant historical figures, and the seniors' lockers are decorated with college names and logos. In between classes, the corridors are jam-packed, and though it requires some patience to navigate the waves of students moving this way or that, everyone seems friendly and in a good mood. It's a Friday, and students will be released early so the teachers can have an extended meeting—maybe that helps the mood in the hallways.

The classroom interiors are similarly pleasant, with relatively new (unscratched) desks and long lighting fixtures suspended from the ceiling to provide both direct and indirect lighting. Of course, the atmosphere in the room depends mostly on the people. Over the course of the day, I spend time in four classrooms and consistently find students and teachers who are relaxed, welcoming, and going about their work with a certain seriousness and intentionality. That's not to say that every child is an angel and that these high schoolers are immune to the distraction of a pending early dismissal on a springtime Friday afternoon.

It's an unusual situation for me to be going into classes where I'm spending relatively little time and have had little contact with the teachers beforehand. However, the teachers I observe—Marike Aguilar, Tim Knipe, Sasha Guzman, and Roberto Vega—are all friendly and accommodating. I think their comfort level with visits is partially because their school has already drawn a number of interested visitors ahead of me and partially because of the confidence that comes with every teacher being a school leader. At SJHA, teachers review student and school performance together on a regular basis; they share responsibility for improving the school's overall effectiveness and creating its reputation. Knowing each other's work is valuable for helping students make connections as well. In Marike Aguilar's ninth-grade social studies class, human geography, students are studying the Middle East. As a starting point, there's the question of who came up with the name "Middle East." East of what, and why the middle? Whose perspective is reflected, and who had the power to come up with the name that has been used widely and for so long? Then the question of identity arises and how names reflect identities. At this point, Marike is able to help students make a connection to one of their other classes where this concept has come up, and where students tried an experiment involving the creation and adoption of new names for themselves.

In Tim Knipe's AP English language arts class, I see more clearly how the teacher-led ethos of the school filters through the organization and into the classroom. The students own their learning in much the same way that the teachers own their instruction, taking responsibility for the atmosphere in the room and mastery of the content without the teacher exerting overt control. The evidence of students' intrinsic motivation is somewhat indirect—it's in everything the teacher *doesn't* have to do. Student note-taking is automatic and not in response to any teacher instruction. Constructive and specific peer feedback for essays is offered and received easily and comfortably. When students sing "Happy Birthday" to a classmate, everyone's voice is heard. Tim sends them off with the wish, "Have a good 'Humanitas' weekend—be kind to each other"—which would seem to be a natural extension of how they interact in Tim's class.

My next observations take place in Sasha Guzman's US history class. Like her principal, Jose Navarro, Sasha has deep ties to Facing History and Ourselves, and serves on the organization's teacher advisory board. (Facing History and Ourselves is an international organization providing curricular support and professional development for teachers on historical periods and concepts relating to identity and exclusion in societies. Chapter 12 has more information). Coincidentally, I'm also observing Sasha on the morning after the United Way has honored her as a local inspiring educator. What I find important about her teaching, and not surprising, is that the inspiration she provides seems to come less from her charismatic presence in the classroom and more from the way she relates so well to her students and uses that relationship to push them toward stronger academic performance and a scholarly disposition.

The lesson for the day involves analysis of World War II-era advertisements and propaganda relating to women in the American workforce. While students are making connections to some of their recent learning about the current gender imbalances in scientific and technical careers, Sasha pushes them to make specific observations from their primary source documents, offering analysis and multiple interpretations. Instead of moving from one item to the next when students seem to have a consensus interpretation, Sasha continues to question students to see if alternative interpretations might gain traction; she's not trying to achieve closure or certainty in this exercise, but rather, to teach students to think like historians. In their small-group discussions, students are also wrestling with seventy years' worth of evolution in attitudes about gender and debating the degree of sexism in the material they're studying. Extending the conversation allows more questions to arise about the sources and the intended audience. Does it matter that the source of the material is the US Women's Bureau? What *is* a women's bureau? Is the intended audience mainly women or American adults in general? Does our interpretation change if we understand the intended audience differently?

In Roberto Vega's world history class, I arrive when students are less focused on learning new content but instead are planning for student-led conferences, in which the students will review their coursework, accomplishments, and goals with their parent(s) and teacher. The student-led conference is something I would associate more with elementary school, having attended a few myself and knowing that many of my elementary school colleagues use the same idea. Going through a student-led conference at the high school level seems more serious; the stakes and complexity of the work has increased, and for the teacher, the student load has multiplied significantly. But the overall goal remains the same—for the student to take ownership of the learning process while building a stronger school-home connection. Some students ask Roberto about their current grades and prospects for raising them, and he defers the question, suggesting that his office hours are a more appropriate time for that discussion. "Office hours" sounds more like a college program, but SJHA teachers have created a weekly schedule that includes teacher office hours, allowing students to receive extra help and guidance. Though I don't get to see much history instruction in this particular period, I can see how committed SJHA teachers are to their students. It takes considerable time and effort to organize and run student-led conferences, when conferences are not the high school norm, and it takes more time to hold weekly office hours, when office hours are not the high school norm.

My visit to Social Justice Humanitas Academy is shorter than I would have liked, but my only option was to visit on one of the days when students leave school a bit early so the entire staff can meet together to engage in the intensive work of sharing responsibility for every student's success and participating in the leadership decisions that shape the campus experience for children and adults alike.

There may not be a large sample size to work with, but the teacher-led schools I observed have something essential in common. They demonstrate that when teachers have the authority to make foundational decisions about the academic program and structure of a school, they will respond with innovations that elevate the quality of teaching and learning, based on a clear vision and a strong work ethic. It's ironic that so many contentious stakeholder relationships in education policy involve administrators and school boards engaged in top-down actions that are framed as efforts to *make* teachers work harder, make us more "accountable," and compel our implementation of various plans and programs with "fidelity" to the design. Teachers at these three schools have the least pressure from outside stakeholders, but they hold themselves to the highest standards, taking on the hard work and constant struggle to fulfill their mission a little better every year.

There's a variety of models for teacher-led schools within and beyond

California, though the overall number of teacher-led schools remains a miniscule percentage. Can we take this idea to a larger scale? AJ Johnstone, from San Francisco Community School, sounds skeptical:

> *These teacher-driven models must have the material support to make them happen. We cannot expect to see the expansion of these sorts of models when they require that teachers spend their summer breaks working without getting paid, working overtime, taking work home every weekend, and doing the job of art teachers, music teachers, social workers, PE teachers, college advisors, and therapists. [There must be] support in the form of money—lots of it—and the hiring of many additional teachers to provide classes for students [while other] teachers have time built into the day to do deep, collaborative, reflective work with their colleagues. Until that happens, these types of models will continue to be anomalies and outliers.*

Alysia Krafel, co-founder of Chrysalis Charter School and now working with the Teacher-Powered Schools Initiative, focuses on the positives:

> *Teacher-powered schools require extra work from teachers, but in return, they have academic freedom in the classroom. Their voices are not only heard loud and clear, but listened to and acted on. What is not found in a teacher-powered school are the laments you hear across the country, of frustrated, de-professionalized teachers who have no say in what, how, and when they teach topics to their students. Since our turnover [at Chrysalis] is very low, our teachers think the trade-off is worth it.*

Looking ahead not just a few years but a generation, I wonder: What if the concept of teacher leadership evolves from being a portion of the work carried out by a subset of teachers within a school or district, and instead, becomes the entire *basis* of operating schools and districts? What if nearly every teacher had some leadership responsibility and nearly all school leaders had some teaching responsibility? The main factor preventing such a change from occurring is the assumption that it can't. We create and modify our systems and policies based on what we imagine they should be and will be. If we imagine, and expect more teacher-led schools and school systems, it is certainly possible to make them a common alternative, if not the new norm for education.

CHAPTER 9

Unions and Education:
Working Together to Improve Teaching and Learning

Merced High School librarian Sarah Morgan explains how grants from the California Teachers Association Institute for Teaching provided funding for interdisciplinary student research projects. Students later partnered with a program at the University of California, Berkeley, to improve their research, and later shared the results with the local community.

THINK OF VARIOUS WAYS, LARGE AND SMALL, that we might improve education. *Innovative school design reforms. Partnerships with community organizations. District, community, university partnerships for historical study. Parent outreach and education. Robust teacher evaluations and peer evaluations, with support for new or struggling teachers. Mathematics competitions. Global education initiatives. Outdoor education. Arts in the community. Union activity.*

If you're thinking "union activity" doesn't seem to fit in that list, consider this: Every other item on the list describes one or more initiatives endorsed, fiscally supported, or carried out by state or local teacher unions in California.

If that fact surprises you, then this chapter deserves your closest attention. I learned about many of these activities through my involvement with a state-level union organization, the Institute for Teaching (IFT), a nonprofit branch of the California Teachers Association (CTA) dedicated to strength-based, teacher-driven change in public education. IFT grants, totaling close to $1 million from 2014–16, funded many of the projects referred to above, some of which are described in this chapter. IFT also supports several teacher think tanks in various regions of the state, work I've been involved in for several years. (As noted at the outset of this book, IFT contributed funding to support my work.)

Other references in the list above, to be covered in this chapter, relate to the work going on in districts affiliated with the California Teacher Union Reform Network (CalTURN). At the national level, TURN brings together progressive and innovative associations that are using the union as a framework not only for labor issues, but also for improving professional practices and advocating for social justice. TURN has organized conferences and meetings dedicated to labor-management collaboration, improving assessment practices, and a "whole child" approach to education that includes social-emotional learning. I was part of the steering committee for CalTURN for a couple years and also served as their virtual community organizer while I was working on this book.

So, between CalTURN and IFT, I've had many opportunities to meet teachers whose union leadership involved designing or supporting programs that have a clear positive impact on their schools and students. (And it wouldn't hurt to note at this point that nearly every teacher in this book is also a union member. Most teachers in public schools join their union. Union membership is optional, though even nonmembers must pay a "fair share" fee to the union in return for representation in collective bargaining. At charter schools, union membership is more variable.) Some education policy makers and their allies recklessly stereotype unions as intractable obstacles to reform, which only exist to protect jobs. Unfortunately, the stereotyping works, and popular conceptions of unions have a negative tinge as well. That's another example of "the danger of a single story." The toxicity around this issue is often a byproduct of scarcity. When budgets and personnel are spread too thin for anyone to work to their highest potential, it's predictable, if unfortunate, that relationships become frayed. Everyone is under intense pressure, and the stakes are high.

Labor relations can turn problematic not because unions are inherently flawed, or because management is inherently antiunion, but rather because districts and unions together struggle to maintain positive relationships under trying conditions. Anxiety over public education and the economy exists in the broader community as well, giving "bad teacher" stories a long shelf-life, even as the great majority of teachers make a positive difference for students every day—usually in obscurity and relative anonymity. That's the situation I'm trying to mitigate with this book. The teachers and schools profiled in this chapter demonstrate how unions can provide the collective influence and resources to improve teaching and expand offerings in schools.

Adam Ebrahim, Social Studies
Fresno High School, Fresno

Adam Ebrahim has a busy day ahead, but then again, most of his days are busy, involving a combination of teaching, professional development work, and being the vice president of the Fresno Teachers Association. The day begins with his ninth-grade human geography class at Fresno High School; it's a uniquely structured course, with classes meeting only once a week, for two hours. The course content blends history and current events, with elements of economics and environmental science. Students examine the ways that humans and societies act and interact based on the combination of all these factors. Teaching what is essentially a "half" class (meeting only two hours per week, with students earning two and a half credits rather than the usual five for a semester-long high school course) means that Adam has considerably more students to teach. Such an arrangement would scare off many potential teachers. Adam makes it work in part by being a masterful user of Schoology, an online learning management system (LMS) used in many schools. Effective use of an LMS can keep large amounts of curricular material and student work well organized and help students and teachers exchange information during the interval between weekly meetings.

Adam's other advantage is that he just transferred to Fresno High School this year, so he taught eighth-grade social studies to many of these same students last year at their middle school. This "looping" strategy has been mentioned earlier; see Chapter 7, regarding Dave Berk, and Chapter 8, regarding AJ Johnstone). However, I've never heard of an eighth-grade teacher volunteering to try to stay with his students by following them to high school.

Teachers know that building a good relationship with students is essential and that it's a process that takes time. Ask around and you might hear some teachers say that it takes a week or two, maybe a month, with many variables, of course, based on the age of the students, the numbers of teachers and students, the stability of the school, language barriers, and others that are hard to pinpoint. So, what's remarkable in Adam's situation is that he's achieved a positive working relationship with the classes I observe, even though he sees them much less frequently and has many more students than typical teacher arrangements.

The quality of the relationship shows in the way that students respond to Adam, even when he's pushing them to regain or improve their focus or revise work that he knows could be better. Adam is an Army veteran (and still looks the part with a haircut that would meet regulations), but he conveys his authority in the room by appealing to students' better selves rather than by adopting a commanding tone. As small groups are working on presentations about different triggers for migration (conflict, economics, climate change), Adam is circulating mainly to provide help and occasional redirection. One student's internet search has yielded an interesting article about the effects of climate change on bird migration, and he wants to talk about what he's read. Adam listens briefly, but then says, "Remember: human geography, not bird geography." If there's an open seat in a group he's helping, he'll sit with them for a while not only to listen to their presentation ideas, but also to observe how they work together. The pace is relaxed, as a two-hour class removes the need to rush about.

I began this account by noting that Adam's day is a busy one, continuing hours beyond the school day. As his union's vice president, Adam has much to share with school site union representatives at their rep council meeting. Fresno is the state's fourth largest district, so I'm interested to see what a rep council meeting looks like for the Fresno Teachers Association (FTA). In the year that I was a site representative in my district, I attended meetings that could be held in a classroom or an elementary school library; FTA rents out a hotel banquet room. They observe parliamentary rules and protocols quite carefully, while I was accustomed to a more relaxed atmosphere. My visit runs less than an hour, but the most interesting part for me is seeing Adam's presentation relating to website improvements and an evolving association collaboration with the district to improve the professional growth of Fresno teachers.

More than any other teacher observed as part of this book, Adam practices a brand of unionism that emphasizes the development and continual improvement of teaching, alongside the usual labor issues that unions negotiate and advocate, such as salaries, benefits, and working conditions. I first met Adam at a summer TURN conference in Chicago, where he was presenting on effective use of an LMS to increase student access to a wide variety of information and to facilitate student communication and collaboration in their coursework. I participated in that training, and my visit to Adam's classroom has been a validation of what he presented. Working through a union framework has given Adam a national reach, and he's also a leader at the state level: Adam is among the teacher leaders in California's Instructional Leadership Corps (ILC), a joint project of CTA, the National Board Resource Center, and others to promote Common Core training by teachers for teachers. While the Common Core adoption remains controversial among some educators, Adam suggests that when the Common Core fades or evolves, as educational reforms invariably do, his hope is that models like the ILC will have taken hold, demonstrating that teacher leadership builds the capacity of districts and schools to meet the needs of their teachers and students and that it is more effective and more economical than having outside consultants and publishing representatives deliver training. Such leadership opportunities also meet a clear need felt by many teachers who seek new challenges and responsibilities that don't require them to give up classroom teaching.

The success of a union initiative requires both leadership and the active support of other dedicated teachers in the association. There are many here at the FTA meeting, and by chance, I manage to sit next to Hilary Levine. It's a serendipitous way to meet the teacher whose classroom is next on my itinerary.

Hilary Levine, Fifth Grade
Manchester GATE Elementary School, Fresno

The next day, I'm at Manchester GATE Elementary School (GATE stands for "gifted and talented education"). While it's common for schools to provide some special services and programs for gifted students, it's less common to concentrate those students in one school. Manchester serves grades two through five, with students diverted here from other schools in the district if they're identified as gifted.

Hilary provides a fine example of a union rep in the classroom, precisely because you can't tell she's a union rep in the classroom. She's simply a hard-working, dedicated, skilled teacher. Those of us who have entered that role are drawn to advocate for policies that protect and enhance our ability to do our best work in the classroom, for the long term.

Hilary's classroom stands out among all those I entered in my year of classroom visits, and that's quite a feat—considering how much time and energy elementary school teachers, in particular, dedicate to their classroom decor and organization. The organization of various materials and resources is not unusual, but there's an impressive quality in the student-created work, poetry, and posters on the walls—sophisticated in both presentation and content. The most eye-catching part of the classroom is nearer to the ceiling than the floor, where models of theme parks built on cardboard platforms are suspended with fishing lines. These theme parks have names like Holiday Land, Hotdog Planet, Soccer World, and themes include cars and space ships, mythology and Pokémon. Modeled thrill rides and attractions are constructed with every imaginable material and household item: construction paper, cardboard, pipe cleaners, straws, toothpicks, popsicle sticks, string, feathers, plastic flowers, small plastic toys (soldiers and other figurines, animals, cars, etc.), cotton balls, aluminum foil, thread spools, cardboard tubes from bathroom tissue or paper towels, egg cartons, modeling clay, balsa wood, Legos, and more.

Though the theme parks are not attached to any other work, I infer that the assignment involved a variety of academic skills, based on the clear interdisciplinary tendency in student work posted on the walls. One piece of work blends art, environmental science, and geometry, as students explore naturally occurring shapes and patterns through drawing. Another piece of student work combines the study of poetry and history, with students responding to a poem based on a famous World

War II photograph of a little Jewish boy with his hands up, exiting a building at gunpoint during the Nazi liquidation of the Warsaw ghetto. This class has also been on a field trip to the Museum of Tolerance in Los Angeles, and they are continuing to incorporate that learning in new presentations they're preparing during my visit. Hilary suggests that I listen to one student rehearsing her presentation so I get an idea of what they are all about and the student gets an audience while practicing. Her eventual audience is going to be outside of school at her father's law firm. The broad topics are bullying and leadership, and she runs through an impressive ten-minute presentation with twenty PowerPoint slides. She's refers to the slides without reading the contents word for word, avoiding a common trap students fall into when they're learning to present. More than a few adults still make the same mistake.

The motivation to produce such great work is mostly intrinsic in this group. While work may be graded, the students relish challenges and help set the tone for the classroom. They're deeply engaged with their work and their conversations, whether they're being monitored and graded or not. Many of them stay in the class to read during recess, and even *Shhhh!* each other to maintain a quiet reading atmosphere. Though staying indoors at recess might not be entirely about love of the classroom; at one point, I overhear a girl asking her peers, "What's the point of going outside for fresh air if it's so polluted?" Then she asks Hilary the same question. Given the frequency of Fresno's air quality advisories and warnings, that question requires no answer, unfortunately. At least the students are making good use of their time.

Even if they are intrinsically motivated, and deemed gifted and talented, students don't reach this quality of work by intuition or independent experimentation. The level they're rising to reflects the expectations of their teacher, and Hilary has to work quite hard to keep the class challenging and engaging for these students. No complaints though. If I couldn't have inferred from observation that it's all a labor of love for Hilary, she uses the word frequently in our conversations. Her classroom is one of several in the district piloting what's called a 1:1 program, with one Chromebook computer for every student, and she loves the instructional technology staff that has helped make that happen. Hilary loves the work her students are producing with the constant availability of the technology. She loves the parent community at the school, the teachers she works with, and, of course, the students. In total, "I'm blessed to be at this school. It keeps me going."

The union activist side of Hilary is all about building on these strengths, seeking the balance between institutional stability and dynamism, making the school and district into thriving learning communities. It's an interesting duality that I've observed in many schools: a stable foundation that allows for the most productive growth and change. School instability may bring about change, but it often lacks intentionality and introduces tension or fear. Hilary recognizes the need for constant growth and learning for staff because it infuses the same spirit of inquiry in the classroom. "If we're not changing every year, it would be a pretty monotonous job, wouldn't it?" In an ideal world, we could count on administrators and school boards to act in the best interests of both students and teachers, with legislators and voters ensuring both ample resources and minimal political intrusions on instruction. Reality is far from ideal. Education leaders grapple with difficult decisions about the allocation of inadequate resources, face considerable political pressure, and tend not to last long in their jobs, relative to the most experienced teachers. Unions provide the means for teachers like Hilary to advocate collectively and effectively in this environment.

Encina Preparatory High School, Sacramento

While the Fresno Teachers Association has leaders like Adam Ebrahim and Hilary Levine helping bring the union and district to a clearer focus on improving teaching and schools, there are associations and districts that are even further along in that regard. San Juan Unified School District is comprised of about seventy schools serving roughly 40,000 students in parts of Sacramento and several other communities north and east of the capital. The San Juan Teachers Association (SJTA) has had a leadership role in CalTURN for many years, and it has been leading by example in the work of promoting quality teaching and learning through labor-management collaboration.

As much as I've focused on a strength-based positive approach to this book, I think it's fair and appropriate to note here that almost everyone I talked to about Encina Preparatory High School described it as needing major changes when it entered a redesign process in the 2010–11 school year. That process was supported and structured through the federal school improvement grant (SIG) program. The teachers I talked to at Encina, as well as other teacher leaders in the district, all agreed that Encina has shown significant improvement, predicated on three key elements: teachers had genuine leadership roles in the school's redesign, they continue to have genuine leadership opportunities in the ongoing work at the school, and there's a focus on community partnerships. Union engagement at each step reflects a strong labor-management relationship; for contrast, teachers noted that Encina had been through a top-down redesign effort about ten years earlier, and it had failed to take hold. Teacher Barry Roth explains the difference in part by noting that both excellent and poor administrators tend to leave quickly; "teachers are the glue" holding a school together. The teacher-driven, union-supported model has Encina headed the right direction.

Understanding the improvement at Encina requires some understanding of the student body. The high school absorbed a neighboring middle school and now serves grades six through twelve. Most sixth graders enter the school reading at a second-grade level or below. The school includes high percentages of families in poverty, English-language learners, and special educational needs; on top of that, roughly a third of the students do not have stable, permanent housing. By the time a given class reaches its senior year in high school, teachers tell me, there's roughly 80 percent turnover in students.

Though I did observe some classes at Encina, I learned so much from talking with teachers and principal Richard Judge, that I've focused on those conversations rather than the classroom time.

Brandon Wells was hired to teach at Encina on the Friday before school started in the 2010–11 school year. It was the first year of having grades six through twelve together on campus, and the year before the main reforms in school governance and leadership went into effect. Looking back on it now, Brandon describes the campus atmosphere as

> dark, and chaotic. There was a lot of anger among kids, among the adults, and between them as well. The culture change has been so significant. Watching kids at lunch the first year, I don't think it seemed safe for anyone. Now when you see them at lunch, they're kids. They play, they relax. It felt like I was probably separating kids from fighting every week, especially on Fridays. Now I don't think I've seen a fight in a year and a half.

Brandon suggests that the teachers' ability to craft the academic program and the student supports at Encina have helped change the culture. He sums up the difference with an observation about language; instead of teachers talking about school in terms of what *they* do (administrators, other teachers, and students), now he hears more about what *we* do as a school: how we teach, learn, and help kids. The work of leading the school, designing the academic program, and strengthening the community partnerships all relies on teachers working alongside administrators on various leadership teams, each with a different focus. Brandon suggests that the experience has a significant impact on staff culture and cohesion:

> *If you're part of leadership, you're sympathetic and more effective [at implementation]. There's buy-in. After a while, you might have most of the staff currently or recently in leadership. You trust in each other's intentions and understand the challenges others face. The implications for the kids are also fascinating. If the adults have ownership and involvement, the sense of ownership spreads to the kids more easily. If the adults work together and know how to try new things, it becomes part of the culture. You say it explicitly, but also live it and know it implicitly.*

On a continuum of teacher vs. administrative leadership, Encina is more teacher-led than most schools in its district, and San Juan Unified has more teacher leadership than most districts. SJTA president Shannan Brown was one of the 2011 California Teachers of the Year, and she is an effective advocate for teacher leadership at the local and state level. During her leadership of SJTA, the union and district have negotiated for the creation of school leadership teams at each school site, ensuring that teachers have a guaranteed voice and role in leading each school. To extend this idea even further at Encina, the union and district worked out a memorandum of understanding that added flexibility for the school and expanded responsibilities for teachers.

Two teachers I'm visiting came to Encina from other schools in the district, opting into the school at a time when most of the staff members were seeking transfers out. Dan DeJaeger relished the challenge of helping turn around a school and create a new physical education program to meet the unique needs of Encina students. Dan is a National Board Certified Teacher and has served in a peer support and evaluation role in San Juan Unified. (Their peer-evaluation program is another unique product of the district's labor-management collaboration; more details follow). Dan's approach to PE impresses me with its focus on healthy living and positive peer interactions. Classes are organized into three-week units that emphasize setting and meeting goals for physical activity and skill and building positive relationships along the way. With students of widely varying ages in the class, competition is de-emphasized, and Dan tells me that the older students actually look out for the younger ones most of the time, in a sibling-like way. Dan's personal competitiveness might be more evident in his goals for the PE department at Encina. Noting that PE is sometimes marginalized in the overall academic program, Dan determined early on that this department would be a school leader, early adopter, and enthusiastic supporter of every effort to improve school culture and support students.

English teacher Ed Burgess is the other teacher who chose to come to Encina during its redesign. I've known Ed for a couple years through CalTURN, and his interest in teacher leadership extends beyond his own school and association work, to such an extent that he recently completed a PhD focusing on teacher leadership. As a result of his own research and experience as a site rep in his union, he knows the ins and outs of labor-management collaboration and brings a wealth of understanding to Encina's leadership team.

Barry Roth, mentioned above observing that teachers are the glue holding a school together, also teaches English at Encina, and his time at the school dates back to before the redesign. However, his primary job at Encina has evolved away from classroom teaching and toward community partnerships, which help needy students and families with access to food, clothing, health care, and necessary social services. He has even reached out to some of the local landlords, ensuring that the larger apartment complexes have binders full of helpful information about the school and other community resources. Barry now spends most of his time focused on this community work and credits the teacher leadership of the school with prioritizing this allocation of resources. The area of Sacramento the school is located in, Arden Arcade, is not one with many long-term residents or a strong sense of neighborhood identity. With so many challenges facing Encina students, Barry's work with the community strengthens student and parent connections with the school.

Encina's redesign took place under federal rules and SIG guidelines. The detailed workings and broader politics of SIGs are beyond the scope of this chapter, though I'll note that my praise for the work at Encina is absolutely *not* an endorsement of the SIG program writ large. Readers interested in SIGs, and the broader context of Encina's redesign, might look up Greg Anrig's 2015 report for the Century Foundation, "Lessons from School Improvement Grants That Worked." Anrig's review of the data from the program suggests that the most effective and lasting changes occur at schools that have five strategies in common. Not surprisingly, they put an intense focus on improved teaching, school climate, and more time to work with students needing the most support. The other two findings are those most relevant to my observations: successful SIG implementation includes community involvement and building the capacity of school staff to create and sustain positive changes. Anrig notes that this capacity-building often begins with training and consulting from outside organizations; for Encina, such services were provided by a company called Dialogos, though the school is now on its own.

Richard Gahr High School, Cerritos

In Southern California, there has been a similar, exemplary labor-management partnership in the ABC Unified School District for many years. ABC stands for Artesia, Bloomfield, and Carmenita—districts in southeast Los Angeles County that joined together as a single school district in 1965. As in San Juan Unified, the labor-management partnership in ABC Unified has proved beneficial to students and schools. A significant factor in that relationship is the organizational stability in the district, which has been led for the past decade by two superintendents, Gary Smuts and Mary Sieu, who both came up through the district. The district has been recognized for its instructional quality and its labor-management relations. I first heard about the district at a CalTURN conference in 2013, where their union and district leaders described how they worked together to identify and train teacher leaders to improve instruction in the district and address the shifts inherent in the Common Core standards. While there are persistent and legitimate concerns to address regarding the Common Core standards, I'm encouraged to see unions partnering with district leadership to strengthen academic programs and professional learning. Standards and assessment will come and go over time; hopefully, these structures and expectations will endure.

Laura Lacar was the union vice president when the ABC District team shared its work with CalTURN, and though she's no longer in that position, she helped me plan a highly informative visit to her school, Richard Gahr High School (usually just called Gahr) in Cerritos. Like my visit to Encina, this one ends up including multiple teachers, subjects, and classrooms; fortunately, it's a great day to observe some excellent teaching as well. Laura has some time in the morning before her math classes start, so we talk in the staff room near the front office. She shares with me some of the finer points of the labor-management relations in the district, little things such as a union liaison to provide teacher and union perspectives to district leaders as they plan programs and communications. Another initiative Laura finds useful is a math teaching partnership involving the district, union, and Center for Math and Science Teaching (CMAST) at Loyola Marymount University in Los Angeles. The program identified teacher leaders to receive training and support to improve their teaching through CMAST, and then these teachers serve as trainers at their schools. Laura says that the opportunity to work with university partners and fellow teacher leaders around the district has helped all of them gain a better understanding of the new standards and their own teaching practices. It's largely the quality of the labor-management relationships that leads to the district entrusting teachers with instructional leadership.

Since Laura was my initial contact at Gahr, it seems fitting that we move from our early-morning conversation into an observation of her class. She starts the day with AP statistics and has a variety of interesting real-life situations for students to examine mathematically: What is a statistically significant difference in the performance data generated by potential draft picks entering a professional sports league? How do you compare the relative problem-solving skills of people solving different puzzles? If a chair in a restaurant breaks when an obese customer sits down, how could one use data and statistics to evaluate the potential negligence of the chair manufacturer, restaurant, or customer? That last example takes the class off-task for a moment with thoughts of food, culture, and family. Laura gently redirects them, though noting the shared role of rice in multiple cultures and culinary traditions. Though they come from different cultural backgrounds, Laura and some of her students discover a shared experience, not only based on food, but also food cooked with love by the grandparents in trigenerational households. It's a humanizing moment that costs little in terms of "time on task" (a frequent metric in lesson evaluation) but adds immensely to the sense of community and connectivity on a campus.

For that day, I feel part of the community as well. Laura is eager for me to see other classes and teachers at the school. There are specialized academies at Gahr, similar to those at La Quinta High School (see Chapter 4) and Abraham Lincoln High School (see Chapter 6), and when I enter Kerry Grover's art classroom, I can see why students might want to be part of the Arts Technology Academy. The room is sort of a double-sized, L-shaped studio, with one part of the room dedicated to work space for traditional art media (painting and sketching, for example) while the other part of the room has thirty-four iMac computers for digital design and media. Today, Kerry's students are creating cover art for their portfolios, rendering their names in combinations of images and themes that speak to their interests. A beach-lover might use surfboards for the straight lines in her name, umbrellas or waves for the curved elements, and so on. These freshmen have some fine illustrating skills, and I walk around asking about their work, ending up slightly embarrassed when I can't always make out the letters perfectly. The students joke around with each other, though, chiding, "See? I *told* you that didn't look like R!"

My next stop this morning is an engineering classroom. I observe two classes at different levels, with two different teachers. The introductory-level class is working on 3-D modeling, and the advanced class, taught by Laura Lacar, works on a project centered around an imaginary bridge designed to fit into a specific environment and community. I ask students about their interests and learn that some of them have definitely refined their career goals as a result of having an engineering academy pathway open to them in high school. These types of classes also have some significant logistical and technical demands, and when staffing is short, it means that teachers like Laura end up using way too much of their time installing software on laptops computers, troubleshooting 3-D printers, and managing other materials.

The last teacher I visit at Gahr is Miguel Canales; residents of the city of Artesia know him better as Mayor Miguel Canales. I think it would be an excellent learning opportunity to have an economics and government teacher who is also a city council member and mayor. He's also a site representative for the union and part of the labor-management team his district sent to CalTURN. Miguel grew up in downtown Los Angeles and has been living in Artesia for much of his adult life. I only see him with students for the last few minutes of a class, but that means we have more opportunity for conversation. Of particular interest to me is the way he describes turnover in union leadership, which he views as a strength rather than a sign of instability. The rotation of different people into various roles provides more teachers with greater awareness of what's happening around the school and the district, which is beneficial in discussing and implementing various school improvement efforts.

Rika Hirata, Art
Menlo-Atherton High School, Atherton

This chapter opened with mention of two primary networks through which I've observed unions and their leaders improving schools and classrooms. The remaining examples arise from my interactions with the Institute for Teaching (IFT), a nonprofit, nonpolitical branch of the California Teachers Association focused on improving teaching and schools. As noted earlier, IFT provided monetary support for my travels; the funding was provided without strings attached, and it had been my intent, regardless of that support, to visit and write about teachers I had either worked with or learned about through IFT.

My experience with IFT's regional think tanks has been instructive and inspirational. Our mission as participants in IFT think tanks is to promote strength-based, teacher-driven change in education. IFT leadership empowers each of these groups around the state to devise unique ways to advance that mission. Looking back at my notes from think tank meetings several years ago, I see the origins of a central idea in this book: the need to focus education reform efforts on cultivating the right conditions for improvement, rather than trying to simply import and replicate best practices.

Rika Hirata has been a consistent part of this enterprise in the San Francisco Bay Area; she and I have been through multiple configurations of the think tanks in our region. Because she has also worked at multiple schools and districts in that time, I've been able to learn through her about important similarities and differences among schools. In our conversations, she contributed great insights about school culture and the ways individual teachers find themselves trusted and accepted or excluded in some way. It was interesting for me to visit her classroom and school soon after she joined the staff of Menlo-Atherton High School after several years of teaching in the city of San Jose.

If you're familiar with the town of Atherton, you likely know it is among the most affluent communities in the Bay Area. However, the school draws students mostly from culturally and economically diverse neighboring communities: Redwood City, Menlo Park, and East Palo Alto. (East Palo Alto is not the eastern portion of the city of Palo Alto; it is a separate city in a different county, though it is directly east of Palo Alto.) Menlo-Atherton High School is well-resourced compared to Rika's prior school, which has made a difference for her professional development opportunities. She also makes an important observation regarding fundraising. To make up for shortages of various supplies and materials, students in underfunded schools are sometimes pressed into fundraising duties—selling candy, gift wrap, or other items. It's an approach that's inequitable, taking up student time to raise relatively small amounts of money while students elsewhere enjoy superior resources without sacrificing their time and energy. Rika sees not just a material advantage in her new school, but also a resulting benefit in the school climate.

The climate in Rika's art classes are serious and focused, overall. I observe students finishing up a variety of ceramic projects, mostly hand-sculpted and painted. The subjects and styles of the projects vary; my favorites are the imaginary creatures: some nearly recognizable variations of tortoises or pandas, others entirely fanciful. Occasionally a student opts to work on the pottery wheel instead, spinning lumps of clay into perfectly formed bowls. Cultivating student independence in the art studio is important for the artists and the teacher, though it's not without challenges. During one class, Rika deals with a careless slip by a student who spills $30 worth of ceramic glaze on the classroom floor. She treads a fine line in trying to convey concerns about safety and conserving class resources without blowing the issue out of proportion. Ultimately, the class is more about the students than the art, she points out. "We teach kids, not subjects. They come to our classrooms, and sometimes we think of them as someone we're supposed to start delivering content and information to. But they have their own lives and perspectives; they experience their own lives intensely."

James Workman Middle School, Cathedral City

While Rika Hirata is providing valuable insights that contribute to the work of IFT, teachers elsewhere are the beneficiaries of IFT's contributions to their work. One campus with an interesting program supported by an IFT grant has already been described in Chapter 6. James Workman Middle School in the Palm Springs area, the professional home of Teacher of the Year Jessica Pack, is also the site of a marvelous outdoor education project run through the PE department. Teachers Phil Sanchez and Bridgette Kennedy have created an Adventure PE program for their school. The Adventure program is one of three PE options; the other two focus on sports or fitness training. With the monetary help of the IFT grant and the blessing of a supportive administration, they've made a significant investment in camping equipment and taught students how to use it. After learning how to use everything in the camping kit, students are encouraged to borrow the equipment for family camping trips. And we're not just talking about tents and sleeping bags. The standard set of items also includes a stove, pots, pans, utensils, flint, a compass, guide book, camping cookbook, a tarp/fly system for shelter, a first aid kit, water bottles, a hand-pump water filter, and rope—all bundled together in a bucket that can also be used for various other purposes. Students learn to use all of these starting in seventh grade; by eighth grade, they are able to teach these skills to their families and to their younger peers at school, and even help with planning trips.

With multiple field trips, hikes, and camping experiences in their seventh- and eighth-grade years, students learn about a healthy lifestyle that combines exercise and an appreciation of the natural world. They learn about geography, environmental science, and the local history of indigenous cultures. Phil points out that their new skills and knowledge even have potential career applications for students who might work in wilderness conservation, outdoor recreation, and tourism. I can't imagine a better example of why schools need the flexibility to take advantage of the unique skills and passions of their teachers. Not every middle school has teachers like Phil and Bridgette, with strong backgrounds in outdoor education and wilderness recreation, and not every middle school has the same access to the wilderness. When all these factors align, however, something wonderful happens. The teachers' vision and passion, the administration's trust and support, and IFT's resources combine to make a positive difference not only for these students, but also for their families.

Moreno Valley Unified School District, Moreno Valley

From James Workman Middle School, you can drive fifty miles west on I-10 and CA-60 and—without leaving Riverside County—arrive at Moreno Valley Unified School District. There, another IFT grant has improved education and family engagement and also spurred a district to support teacher-driven innovation. In this case, the subject matter is mathematics, and the program is district-wide. I didn't have a chance to schedule a visit with teacher Deepika Srivastava during the school day, but she agrees to meet me after school to talk about the Moreno Valley Math League and Family Math Night. Unlike some mathematics competitions that might aim only at certain students, the Moreno

Valley approach is to provide fun and challenging problems to every middle school student. The competition eventually focuses on the top 25 percent, but even at that point, the goal is to emphasize fun and collaboration, as teams are formed with students across grade levels. Deepika's eyes light up when she relates the enthusiasm and intrinsic drive among students engaged in these challenges. She recalls a competition in which a scoring error required the second- and first-place teams to switch places—and trophies—something that was achieved without dispute or negative feelings. The district-wide effort to celebrate mathematics has also led to a family event that brings a huge turnout, where parents and students enjoy math games and challenges together. While these programs began with teacher initiative and IFT support, the district leadership recognizes the value in these efforts and has provided additional resources.

Tara Nuth Kajtaniak, English
Fortuna High School, Fortuna

About 700 miles northwest of Moreno Valley, I had an opportunity to visit a teacher who has both the IFT think tank and grant recipient experiences: Tara Nuth Kajtaniak teaches English and global studies in the small Humboldt County town of Fortuna, a bit south of Eureka. This visit brings me further north than I've ever been by car, about six hours from home in Palo Alto. I'm glad to have Tara pick me up at my motel to ride with her from Arcata to Fortuna High School the next day. The drive turns out to be quite educational, too, as Tara fills me in on some of the key differences in understanding small towns, their schools, and their people. I would have anticipated the advantages of having a tight-knit community, but there are disadvantages as well, including a degree of skepticism about change that can slow down innovation. Tara is the kind of teacher who welcomes a challenge, and she has equipped herself to meet those challenges in part through her IFT think tank involvement. (She drives or flies 250 miles or more to participate in these meetings.) Not only does this kind of engagement inspire and fuel her efforts to improve, but the IFT connection has also helped Tara and multiple colleagues land multiple IFT grants. Tens of thousands of dollars have helped her create a vibrant global studies course, helped a PE teacher develop a new fitness education program, and helped another colleague initiate a school-community partnership in which graduating seniors create projects that "change the world" (in a "think globally, act locally" kind of way).

Tara's commitment to global education reflects her own global experience and how that plays out in a community that might be described as provincial. Branches of Tara's family tree extend as far as Norway and Indonesia, and she has extensive travel experience. Meanwhile, many of her students are approaching adulthood and significant choices about their future with limited exposure to the world. Many of them haven't given much thought to college, and if they are considering higher education, it's usually College of the Redwoods (the nearest community college) or Humboldt State University in nearby Arcata. There's nothing wrong with attending college close to home, of course, but Tara considers it essential to expand students' options and their awareness of the world.

As students arrive at Tara's room for their global studies (English) class, they hear some Ethiopian jazz, the music of Mulatu Astatke playing, and see information about him projected on the screen in the front of the room. It's not part of the curriculum per se, but it's certainly part of the mind-set and outlook of the course. With homecoming and Halloween converging soon on campus, there are students and teachers in disguise today. One student arrives with very convincing fangs, actual (temporary) caps on her teeth rather than the typical plastic set of teeth. Tara seems genuinely taken aback for a moment, then shares a laugh. The students are currently in groups, preparing research presentations on global issues. Tara reviews some tips for effective presentations, putting the emphasis on people over materials. "*You* are the presentation. The slides are a tool," she advises them. Research continues in the computer lab today, and Tara moves throughout the room helping groups, at ease with all her students and warmly enthusiastic about helping them. They're looking at organizations working for peace in the Middle East, and Tara seems to have done her own homework, showing familiarity with everything her students find.

This global studies program grew in part with the support of an IFT grant, and Tara's connection to IFT has reaped great benefits for her school and all of its students. In between observations of Tara's classes, I have time for a conversation with English teacher Amy Conley, whose Change the World project has been supported by an IFT grant. Her innovative leadership has resulted in every graduating senior at Fortuna High School participating in some type of project to improve their community. IFT funds have allowed students to use the Gallup StrengthsFinder tool, used by many professional organizations to improve collaboration and leadership. The project also involved pairing students with mentors in their community and later doing thirty-minute presentations to the community at the project's conclusion. A former student, Chanel, is on campus and tells me that her project, helping redesign Fortuna High School's freshman orientation, also proved valuable in helping her understand what to do to make her own successful transition to college.

Tara's continued involvement with the Institute for Teaching provides her with an opportunity to exert a positive influence on teaching around the state. Her IFT think tank came up with the idea of organizing an IFT Innovation Exposition, organized as one of the preconference options for a California Teachers Association Good Teaching Conference. The union offers multiple education conferences around the state each year, helping thousands of teachers learn from each other and improve their craft. The IFT Expo brought together dozens of grantees to share their work and inspire fellow teachers. After seeing these exciting examples, expo attendees heard from IFT board members and grant application readers, who gave advice designed to help newly inspired teachers craft winning IFT grant applications. For me, attending the expo was like receiving a directory of schools I could have added to my itinerary for the year, options everywhere to see teachers and schools using union support to nurture the sparks of student creativity, inquiry, and community engagement. However, the timing of the expo and my already busy travel plans meant I had to make some difficult choices. I was impressed by an intensive outreach and remediation program to support struggling students, intrigued by students mastering aquaponics and hydroponics, and inspired by multiple parent education programs.

I found two standout presentations so compelling that I simply had to work the schools into my spring itinerary. One was Merced High School, and the other was Murdy Elementary School in Garden Grove (near Anaheim).

Sarah Morgan, Librarian
Rich Sandoval and Joel Sebastian, History
Merced High School, Merced

Merced has actually received multiple grants in the past couple of years, and while they share a historical angle—an oral history project and a summer history institute—school librarian Sarah Morgan is my main contact at the high school.

At the risk of minimizing Sarah's unique qualities and personality, I find her to be typical of the librarians I know: enthusiastic about learning, articulate about the goals of education, and passionate about helping students (and guests) make connections that advance their understanding. Strong advocacy skills are a survival apparatus for librarians, who are, tragically, considered expendable when budgets must be cut.

"We really need to *work* our program," Sarah explains. "English teachers are more 'necessary.' We need to make the argument for our importance. You should think of librarians when you think of schools."

We start the day in her office, where she has many of the artifacts of the IFT grant projects. She hopes to set up a display of the photographs, posters, and writing that students did for their oral history projects. The work had a prior life outside the school when it was on display in a local museum spotlighting "Young Historians at Work." Students benefitted from collaboration among the school, the museum, and the UC Berkeley Oral History Project. Not surprisingly, Sarah tells me, students emerge from this kind of work with a new appreciation of the elders in their families and community as well. Sarah and I are both so enthused about this kind of work that it's hard to resist shifting to personal stories. I end up talking about my own high school experience interviewing my father's uncle about combat in World War II, and Sarah relates what she learned about her grandmother's shipbuilding experiences during the same conflict.

Returning to the purpose of my visit, I also learn from Sarah more about the Summer History Institute, an intensive three-week course funded mainly by the IFT grant, with some additional funding allocated by the principal. Students studied the history of their own town and community and also had the opportunity to travel to various museums in Los Angeles and San Francisco to learn more about the work of historians in these venues. Their own historical investigations were rich and authentic experiences digging through city records and archives, finding out how their town played a part in the broader history of the country: Their county fairgrounds became a staging ground for the processing of Japanese-Americans headed to internment camps during World War II. Sarah tells how the students were given the responsibility of creating three rooms' worth of historical displays in the Merced Courthouse Museum, and how they came up with a variety of artistic, photographic, and interactive digital products. She has photos of the students all dressed up for their grand opening. The words "celebrate" and "outreach" keep popping up in conversation as she relates the experiences of her students and colleagues.

Of course, I haven't come to the school just to sit in the librarian's office. We try to head out, but it's hard for Sarah to make a clean break. "We should go over to Joel's classroom now," she begins, but then each photograph on her desk triggers another story. "Oh! *This* family had a picture of Buffalo Bill. And this one was about a doctor who moved from India to America, a great American success story. Now his daughter has skipped college in the US and went straight to medical school in India."

Joel Sebastian and Rich Sandoval are the history teachers who have led this work, and I have the chance to observe both of them in class and have lunch with them as well. Rich is not only a twenty-year veteran on the Merced High School staff, but also an alumnus and father of four daughters. They estimate that about three-quarters of the staff grew up in the community; Joel is an exception, having moved here from Minnesota in 1998. Their collaboration on IFT grant projects is an outgrowth of their partnership in the classroom. They even co-taught double-sized classes for a while, and though seventy students at a time was a management challenge, they speak warmly of the teamwork and camaraderie this arrangement engendered.

During my time in Joel's classroom, he's using the work of his prior students as part of the history curriculum for his current students, sharing a video interview with a veteran who survived the attack on Pearl Harbor. His manner is enthusiastic as he explicitly tries to make history come alive in a meaningful way for his students, laying out for them the potential for their end-of-semester projects to be genuinely exciting work. Richard, a former football coach, has a powerful voice and physical presence in the classroom. His classroom walls are covered with flags and posters from various nations and time periods, visually immersing the students in world history. On the day of my visit, students are writing about the concepts of personal and social responsibility, with reference to the choices made by average German citizens during the Nazis rise to power.

After visiting Rich's class, I go back to the library, but this time Joel comes along and brings a student named Erika Bricky. It's one of the few times I'm able to speak at length with a student during my project, and it's not surprising that it happens here among educators who have clearly made a point of pushing students to make their learning into a public act and a contribution to the community. Erika is a junior with the confidence and clarity of thought you might expect in someone several years older. Regarding the Summer History Institute, she tells me, "I learned a lot about my city and about how things work for museums—what curation involves. And it wasn't from notes, or PowerPoint, or from classroom instruction. We were learning by doing. A lot of students struggled with the fact that the teacher doesn't necessarily know the answers. They may not even know the process." This kind of struggle is productive, though, and Erika is clearly excited about this kind of learning. In her interactions with Joel, she seems like a peer, a coleader of the project with her own perspectives and sense of ownership. As much as Erika likes her community and cares about it, she sees many problems in Merced and hopes to go to college elsewhere. Her plans are rather specific for a high school junior: study anthropology, social work, or global studies; continue on to law school; and eventually work for the government in a children's advocacy role. Hearing Erika talk about her work, learning, and life, it's easy to believe she'll end up accomplishing whatever she wants.

Camie Walker, Fifth Grade
Murdy Elementary School, Garden Grove

Students in Camie Walker's fifth-grade class at Murdy Elementary School in Garden Grove are learning that there's much they can accomplish, even at their age. Her approach is to take students deep into the topics that interest them while still fitting their studies into the standards she's expected to cover. Her IFT grant helped provide materials for a hands-on study of engineering principles for seismic safety. They tested their designs of model buildings on a platform that used large rubber bands to simulate an earthquake, then redesigned their models repeatedly. To understand the importance of seismically safe engineering, they contrasted the damage done in earthquakes in Haiti and California. After learning about the scale of the damage in Haiti and the ongoing efforts to repair infrastructure, Camie's students undertook fundraising efforts that netted $2,000 to benefit students in Haiti and followed up the research and fundraising by using Skype to make the connection more personal. The combination of math, science, social studies, and language arts is almost seamless when students are energized to work on a project like this. As they write appeals for their fundraising efforts, they don't think of it as a lesson. When they build models, they don't necessarily think, "Now it's time for math; now it's time for science."

When they read articles about earthquakes, they don't think of it as a lesson in English language arts, but rather, the next step in building understanding.

By the time I visit in April, Earth Day is coming and Camie's students are focused on environmental issues. It's a large class in a relatively small room, and there's a near-constant buzz of conversation and energy. Once again, the lines between disciplines and subject areas are blurred. Students have brought in a household object to help review the three Rs: reduce, reuse, recycle. Is this social studies, science, or language arts (which includes public speaking)? Camie doesn't categorize the work, and the students enjoy seeing each other's selections. Later, the class has time designated for PE, but no PE teacher. Camie takes them outside to play a game like tag, though based on environmental science. On one side of the field, students play the roles of animals that need food, water, or shelter. On the other side, each student represents one of those three necessities by using hand signals. Camie sets up different conditions, tilting the ratios one way or another, and then sends the groups toward each other. Sometimes there's balance and the animals survive, and sometimes there's imbalance and animals are "out" due to their inability to meet basic needs. From the street, a passerby would just see kids running around. When it's all over, students return to the classroom and write down the ecological lessons from their "play" time.

The connections continue: Camie's students have previously learned about the endangered monarch butterflies, which can only survive by laying their eggs on milkweed plants. As they did with their earthquake studies, the students are looking for ways to make a difference, not just study content. According to some of their reading, there are efforts under way to plant more milkweed in areas where the butterflies are found or along their migration paths. Naturally, they want to plant milkweed. It turns out you can't just plant the plant; you have to buy the seeds. It also turns out that milkweed is toxic if ingested and is not considered acceptable for schools, so the effort turns to community education, with the hope of convincing people to plant milkweed in their home gardens. By the end of the year, these fifth-graders will be on their way to middle school, but thanks to their teacher (and in part to the support of an IFT grant), they're already thinking far beyond school, recognizing ways that their education empowers them to make positive changes.

While the dominant "single story" of unions is misleading and incomplete, I would be guilty of trying to substitute one single story for another if I were to suggest that everything is wonderful all the time in our unions. Local unions vary, just like local schools and districts, and even within a single organization, opinions diverge and disagreements arise. There have been times when I've disagreed with my local and state associations. Sometimes local unions may be at odds with each other or the state union. In one instance, my local association proposed a bill to our state senator, and our teachers helped advocate for the bill, even though our state association opposed it. (The bill, SB-1381, was passed in 2010 and gradually rolled back the birthday cutoff for students entering kindergarten. While CTA supported the concept, they opposed certain details in the bill.)

California has well over 300,000 teachers working in nearly 1,000 school districts. Local teachers' unions come in all sizes, and with diverse experiences and viewpoints regarding education. However, on balance, union organizing benefits not only teachers, but also our students and schools, as will be further documented in the Epilogue. My view of local- and state-level efforts leaves me proud of our collective work.

CHAPTER 10

Teacher Leaders, Beyond the Classroom:

Instructional Expertise Matters

First graders at Alexander Science Center Elementary School, in Los Angeles, flock around their teacher, Jane Fung, as she leads a song. Outside the classroom, Jane is an accomplished leader of teachers, having served multiple schools, districts, and organizations in a variety of capacities for many years.

THE CENTRAL ARGUMENT OF THIS BOOK IS THAT PUBLIC EDUCATION already has dedicated and talented people in place and that the further improvement of public education depends on capturing the sparks that animate and energize excellence in classrooms and schools. If I were to identify two recommendations to make that goal possible, I would focus on equitable funding and expanded, strategic development of teacher leadership within systems. Budgetary issues will be addressed in the concluding chapter. Teacher leadership has been a thread present in the past several chapters and will be discussed in greater detail in the next two.

As I described in Chapter 1, Teacher Leaders Network, a project of the Center for Teaching Quality (CTQ), was instrumental in helping me find outlets for my interest in educational leadership. With a solid foundation from the Stanford Teacher Education Program (see Chapter 5) and the added benefit of National Board Certification (see Chapter 7), I was eager for opportunities to contribute to education policy and reforms. My semi-frequent letters to the editor just didn't seem to be having much effect on the broader system (surprise!), so I continued to look for more sustainable and substantive means of influencing education policy. While CTQ is a national organization, it proved helpful for me in connecting and collaborating with fellow California teachers. Two of those teachers are Jane Fung and Cheryl Suliteanu, elementary school teachers in Los Angeles and Oceanside.

Jane Fung, First Grade
Dr. T. Alexander Jr. Science Center School, Los Angeles

Jane Fung teaches at a school that is unique among elementary schools in Los Angeles, if not the entire state, nation, and maybe the world. Dr. T. Alexander Jr. Science Center School (often shortened to Alexander Science Center) in on the edge of the broad complex of facilities connected to the University of Southern California, and it operates in partnership with the California Science Center. Technically, the elementary school campus boundaries extend beyond the primary buildings and grounds and include a major botanical garden and multiple world-class museums, including the one that houses the space shuttle Endeavor; in other words, taking students to learn in these facilities is part of school—*not* a field trip. (My own after-school trip to see the shuttle was almost as much fun as spending the day with Jane's class.) One of the museums is even connected to the school via interior hallways. Multiple airplanes are on display outdoors in Exposition Park, and one of them, a Boeing 737, is perched about forty feet above the drop-off circle for the school. It's a bit of a shock to approach the school with no prior knowledge and walk under the wing of a jetliner casting its huge shadow on the driveway and parking lot.

Jane's classroom was the first one mentioned in this book, one of the warmest atmospheres I experienced in my year of school visits. Her first graders enter the classroom en masse after assembling in a designated spot and being escorted to class. I've barely settled into a seat near the back of the room before their arrival, and as soon as they've put their jackets, sweaters, and backpacks in place, about five first graders descend on me with questions. I'm surrounded by pastel-clad children (the school uniform polo shirts come in a variety of blues, pinks, and purples) wanting to know, "What's your name? Are you a science teacher? What's your favorite thing to do? What's your favorite food?" Their complete sense of ease and their eagerness to converse turns out to be typical for Jane's class throughout the day.

When Jane brings the class together for morning songs and talking about the day, it's a relatively quick and easy transition. They sing "God Bless America," and then a song about the water cycle. She provides some feedback about their focus and behavior through a points system, and when they need to move on to reading lessons, they're left with an interesting math problem for the class to solve regarding their points for the morning: $10 - 5 + 10 + 10 + 5 = ?$

Many students are able to solve the problem, but Jane is also interested in hearing how they solve it, what observations they make about the numbers and operations prior to solving the it, and whether they think it's best to proceed straight through the equation as written, or cancel out the minus and plus five first and then add the tens. She goes a step further by asking students to restate or summarize what their classmates have said. It's a fine example of embedding both arithmetic and academic skills into the fabric of daily interactions.

Over the years, Jane has been a mentor teacher for many new teachers coming through the USC teacher education program. At the time of my visit, Jane has a student teacher named Jenn Dou, who takes over the class for a reading lesson shortly after my arrival. I don't know Jenn well enough to say how much direct influence Jane has had on her practice, but Jenn runs the reading lesson smoothly, and later, in smaller groups, students are eager to work with her and show what they know. Jane, meanwhile, works with another group on some spelling exercises, using magnetic letters on a metallic tray.

I can't imagine a greater stroke of luck for a student teacher than being placed in Jane's classroom to learn how to teach. Jane is a National Board Certified Teacher, with an abundance of patience and love for her students. She has a perfect blend of personal warmth, high expectations for behavior and effort, efficient management, clear communication, and a smile that draws people in, young and old. In addition to all her classroom talent, however, Jane has been widely recognized as a leader in the field: Of the many honors she has received, the highest profile is the Milken Educator Award, and she has been appointed to multiple state and national advisory boards. Jane's classroom has at times been a "demonstration classroom" into which other educators are invited to observe exemplary practice, and she has also run various trainings after school, for the benefit of both teachers and parents.

My own observations are going well this morning. There's so much activity in Jane's classroom, and I've been taking quite a few pictures as well. My photography has been noticed by a student, who approaches me with a LeapPad, a frog-themed learning device with reading and numeracy activities. This one is fancier than the one my children used at home about ten years ago, and it has a built-in camera. Since I've been photographing the class all morning, now this student wants to use the LeapPad to take my picture. Seems fair enough, so I listen to the student's instructions to smile, when suddenly, using super-hearing from across the room (and likely knowing the temptations that typically arise in her room), Jane calls out, "We're not taking pictures with LeapPads right now." No harm done, until the next transition, and students are gravitating to me again. I have to admit it's much more fun this way than in classes where I'm ignored, but at the same time I know I'm affecting what I'm observing ("observer effect" is a well-known scientific principle, after all!). Some students share their thoughts or questions with me: "You have a big nose. Like the Grinch." How *old* are you? "You look like you're in *high school*."

One girl comes up to me looking very serious and says, "Hello. How are you?" *Fine,* I reply, then ask her the same question.

"Mmmm, not so good," she replies. "I have a problem." She taps on the desk where I'm sitting.

"Uh oh, am I sitting in your seat?" She nods. I gather my belongings and move to another seat.

As the day progresses, I'm reminded just how much an elementary school teacher needs to know and be able to do. By the end of the day, Jane has not only worked on reading, writing, and math with her students, but she has also taught physical education and science. The day's PE lesson begins with stretching and yoga poses, followed by a short run around the athletic field. Students then move to a shaded area to play catch with bean bags, working on their coordination and having fun with the challenge of increasing distances once they succeed at close range. The afternoon's science lesson is set up in a separate lab adjoining multiple classrooms, including Jane's. Her students are learning about plants, making observations, and generating hypotheses regarding different stages of bamboo growth.

Many of Jane's gifts as a teacher are observable during the school day: the careful planning, the engaging instruction, the way she nurtures every child, the sense of purpose and respect among her students, the atmosphere of warmth, trust, and mutual responsibility. What can't be observed, at least directly in the classroom, is how much time and energy Jane dedicates to leadership activities that benefit her school and district. It's not necessary for a teacher to lead in these ways to excel at teaching, though it helps. The amount of extra time Jane spends learning more about teaching and curriculum, talking about education, conducting action research in the classroom, sharing her insights and experiences—all of that effort leads to intentional planning, stronger decisions, and a better understanding of her own practices.

Cheryl Suliteanu, Fifth Grade
Nichols Elementary School, Oceanside

Cheryl Suliteanu teaches in Oceanside, a small community north of San Diego and bordering the US Marine Corps base at Camp Pendleton. She and I connected through the Center for Teaching Quality, and we first met in person through the Institute for Teaching (see Chapter 9); at the 2014 Teaching & Learning Conference in Washington, DC, we were co-presenters and panelists in a session about formal roles for teacher leaders.

The night before observing her classroom, I meet Cheryl for dinner next to Oceanside Harbor, where we have a chance to catch up. Cheryl's particular interest in leadership concerns parent engagement, a topic she wrote about in her winning entry for Goldman Sachs' 2014 "Innovation in US Education" essay contest. That success gave Cheryl the opportunity to return to Washington,

DC, and as sometimes happens, success at the national or state level opens other doors locally; for Cheryl, that meant an opportunity to work on her district's parent engagement strategies. The main takeaway from our dinner is that we both find it essential to our career satisfaction to work beyond the local level; extended networks validate our experiences, push our learning and thinking forward, and make us more effective as teachers and teacher leaders.

Nichols Elementary sits on the edge of a relatively new housing development and looks about the same age; I later learn that the school opened in 2002. So many California schools built in the 1950s and '60s have the same utilitarian rectangularity, while Nichols shows a Spanish architectural influence, with aesthetically pleasing arches, red-orange ceramic roof tiles, and some neatly maintained landscaping within the campus. Cheryl's classroom of fifth graders is full to the brim, thirty-five energetic students arriving for class on a sunny mid-April morning. Her class has the responsibility of recording the morning announcements for the school, and Cheryl finds a volunteer to read. After she coaches him a bit ahead of time, he uses the telephone handset to record the message and handles it fairly well, though he clearly forgets to take deep breaths at one point. When Cheryl points out what happened afterward, he nods and smiles, realizing that, yes, a person *can* forget to breathe!

It's a busy day for Cheryl's classes as they are working on their regular curriculum and also beginning preparations for a colonial-era simulation. They'll set up a colonial village outdoors and conduct a role-play, portraying American colonists or Native Americans for the benefit of the younger students at Nichols. I'm impressed that Cheryl and her colleagues won't settle for generic information about the colonies, but rather, divide up the fifth-grade classes into regions so student research will lead to an understanding of geographic distinctions among colonies that had different environments, resources, agriculture, and industries. To help her students learn in different modes and develop some sense of connection to history, Cheryl uses young adult fiction. *Blood on the River,* by Elisa Carbone, follows a young boy from the streets of London to the establishment of a colonial settlement in Virginia; Cheryl has also used *Encounter* by Jane Yolen, providing an indigenous person's view of Spanish conquest in the Caribbean.

Engaging curriculum and academic activities are the key to a thriving classroom, but a class this size requires some strong organizational and classroom management skills. Cheryl is a veteran teacher with a variety of strategies at her command,

and she's continuing to try new techniques as well. Recently, she has begun using software called ClassDojo to help her track student work, participation, and other information; two months into her experiment with the program, Cheryl is finding it helpful, and with so much happening in her classroom, with so many students, I can see the benefit too. More important than the program, of course, is the person. Cheryl maintains a positive and encouraging energy; when she does occasionally chide or correct student behavior, it's done with well-received touches of humor, always promoting high expectations for their work and behavior. At the end of the school day, Cheryl keeps her class a minute or two after the dismissal bell, waiting until the full class has fulfilled some responsibilities for keeping the room neat and organized. There's no grumbling or resentment that I can see; the students know what they need to do and why, and I think they know Cheryl's intentions are positive. Just to reinforce the positivity, Cheryl dismisses them with words of affection: "OK! *Now* you can go. Goodbye, I love you, and I'm looking forward working with you tomorrow."

Unsurprisingly, Cheryl can't leave—or at least she can't go home yet. There are always meetings at the school or district. In past years, Cheryl might jump in the car and go work as an adjunct instructor for National University, providing candidate support for others pursuing National Board Certification. Currently, her after-school hours are focused more on leadership efforts for the Colonial Day simulation and an event coming later in the spring, Career Day.

Like Jane Fung, Cheryl regularly extends herself as a teacher, making herself available to her peers and community, providing an example of the power of teacher leadership to improve a school and district. From personal experience and observations and conversations with teacher leaders like Jane and Cheryl, I know we all wrestle with the question of sustainability. Just how much can we take on? How can we make our efforts viable in the long run and not overly reliant on a single individual? We're hopeful that schools and school systems are moving in the right direction on this issue, as the next examples suggest.

Growing Demand for Formal Teacher Leadership

Any student of the history of American education knows that many "new" ideas are, in fact, quite old. The same levers of educational improvement—training, evaluation, test scores, teacher pay—have been pulled this way and that for decades, over a century in some cases. (Dana Goldstein's book *The Teacher Wars* provides a detailed and highly readable history of American educational practice and politics.) So I'm cautious about suggesting that there's anything new in education. Whether it's truly new or a pendular swing dating back further than my experience in education, I do see an increased effort in the past two decades to elevate teacher leadership at every level. Schools are making more use of teachers as specialists (like Kelly Rafferty, whom we'll meet in Chapter 13) or instructional coaches (like Jessica Simpson, Chapter 7). Some teacher leaders like Barry Roth (Chapter 9) and Lovelyn Marquez-Preuher (Chapter 3) take on broader responsibilities to help their schools manage a particular program or help lead during a certain process or transition.

Within the field, there are some lively debates about teacher leadership. Are all teachers also leaders in some way? And if so, what does the term "leader" mean? How important is it for teacher leaders to have formal roles and titles? Do schools and districts really have a fair and objective way to identify teacher leaders? What are the perceived and real limitations on teacher leadership? If it's more responsibility without additional training and compensation, does that really advance the profession?

Part of the push toward teacher leadership, both informal and formal, comes from practical concerns. Demands on school administrators have grown as standards evolve and expectations for staff and student support expand: Who better to provide the support than trusted—and ideally, trained—teachers in the school and district? The typical job descriptions of principals suggest they should be instructional leaders, and yet there are so many variables among teachers, classrooms, and schools that an individual leader is wise to recognize the value of including more people and perspectives in the work of instruction leadership. The teacher's job description is changing as well, expanding as we integrate technology and attend to more of the social-emotional needs of our students. So, the job is becoming more challenging at a time when demand for teachers is growing. There are many steps we can take to attract and retain teachers (see the Epilogue for more on that topic); expanding teacher leadership is one key to support effective teaching. To increase and sustain our leadership capacity, we must be clear about the scope of teacher leadership and treat it as one more professional skill teachers can learn and develop.

Teacher Leader Certification Academy, Riverside County Office of Education

One educational agency that has an excellent plan for expanding teacher leadership is Riverside County. The county office of education created a Teacher Leader Certification Academy (TLCA), a two-year program that provides teachers with training in leadership skills and principles of organizational management and provides guidance as teachers develop and implement projects at their schools around the county. Lanelle Gordin and Wendy Kerr launched the program a few years ago, and we connected at a time when I was still helping to direct Accomplished California Teachers. In the time I've known them, it has been my pleasure to speak with them multiple times in person and by Skype, and to co-present with Gordin on the topic of formal roles for teacher leaders at the 2014 Teaching & Learning Conference (the same panel that featured Cheryl Suliteanu).

The TLCA program consists of monthly meetings, readings, and discussion both in person and online. Teachers study leadership traits, personality types, group dynamics, adult learning, management styles, and strategies—the types of topics an organizational leader or human resources manager would study. In the second year of the program, teachers also collaborate with their school site leadership to design and implement a "capstone" project that incorporates leadership skills and learning in order to meet a need at their school.

Jeff Frieden, Shari Micheli, Greg Mummert, English Hillcrest High School, Riverside

The TLCA has left its imprint all over Hillcrest High School, which opened in 2012, and as of my visit, doesn't yet have its first senior class. Located in the Alvord Unified District in the city of Riverside, Hillcrest occupies a new campus too large for its current student body but ready for growth. It's not quite aptly named, built on the side of a hill rather than at the crest, but it's high enough to offer a view of southern Riverside and the towns of Corona and Norco.

The teacher I originally wanted to visit was Karin Ribaudo, a former member of Accomplished California Teachers who was also part of the TLCA the first time I visited Riverside. Since completing the TLCA program, Karin has decided to put her leadership training to use by taking an assistant principal position at the newly opened Hillcrest High School. So, while I do have a chance to meet up with

Karin, my classroom visits at Hillcrest involve other teachers, all in the English department, and all current or former TLCA participants. It's no coincidence that a new school has attracted teachers interested in leadership; starting a new program offers teachers the opportunity to develop and implement a vision. It's a situation where leadership opportunities are built in to the experience, and I'm excited to see how TLCA-affiliated teachers put their leadership training to use.

I start my day with Shari Micheli, a ninth-grade teacher who also happens to be Karin's sister. Her freshman honors class is huge—thirty-six students—though it's a size that's all too common in California high schools. (There's a significant equity issue here as well, and though it has been noted before, it's worth repeating. Districts with more funding keep class sizes lower, so much lower that for high school teachers, it's the difference between having five classes or six. More affluent districts can lure experienced teachers with higher pay and smaller class sizes, essentially, more money for less work.) Shari has the class working on a project with a juvenile justice theme. Their discussion takes place at a high level: Shari pushes them away from words like *good* and *bad,* and the simple reminder brings out conversation about *idealism* and *malice.*

A tall boy with thick curly hair and glasses is sitting in the back corner of the room. He's trying to be patient, waiting for his chance to jump into the conversation, but his bouncing feet, visible from my angle, show his anxiousness to participate. When his turn comes, he notes that "Society frowns on physical death, but it's OK with emotional death." Other students wonder if it's possible that sometimes there's nothing to live for, if there are punishments worse than death, and when it's acceptable to risk one's life for a principle. One student answers that question with a question of his own: "What's the point of having a belief in right and wrong if you're not going to act on it?" *Heavy stuff.*

Later in the discussion Shari refers to a quote from author William Golding (*Lord of the Flies*), who wrote, "I'd seen enough to realize that every one of us could be a Nazi." Shari wonders if any students make the same connection she does. One student calls out "*The Book Thief!*"—and it turns out that's what Shari is thinking of too. As a former elementary school and middle school teacher, Shari has a strong background for teaching freshmen, understanding the skills and reading that most of her students have been exposed to up to this point.

Later in the morning I observe sophomore and junior classes taught by Jeff Frieden, the department chair, and his colleague Greg Mummert. Both teachers have experience in other high schools in the district and were attracted to the opportunity to start something new at Hillcrest. Changes can be maddeningly incremental in a larger and well-established program. Jeff and Greg don't seem intent on revolutionary transformations of the English curriculum; the appeal of being at Hillcrest is that starting a program offers the chance to arrange the whole rather than rearrange the parts. Over the years that a school exists, adjustments are made to the academic program, teachers and students change, and the vision can become obscured. Hillcrest teachers will be close enough to the creation of the program to implement their own vision.

Jeff's class of sophomores is working on a video project related to the classic Greek tragedy *Antigone*. Much of the focus is on planning and logistics; however, these academic planning and group communication skills are applicable to success in school and work, not just the reading of a play. Jeff moves around the class, helping groups think through their work, conducting what he calls a *pre-mortem*: "Imagine it's the due date, and you totally failed. Why did that happen?" Students easily identify the common pitfalls of projects like this and make plans to avoid such a fate. Meanwhile, in Greg's AP language class, students are discussing fate at a more philosophical level, working through the novel *Sophie's World*, which guides its young protagonist through a review of many significant world philosophers. In the course of one class period, there are references to Socrates, Plato, Aristotle, Descartes, Kierkegaard, and Hegel, with a pivot to discuss the power of ideas, images, and narrative. Suddenly, there's a connection to violence and protests in Ferguson, Missouri, providing an example of how people observe and evaluate the world though different lenses, producing varied understandings of events.

At the end of Greg's class, Jeff comes into the room to teach the same course to a different group of students. In the few minutes between classes, there's a rapid exchange of ideas, as Greg announces, "Hey, I hit on something that worked! After seeing how you presented academic writing as a conversation, I had my students represent the conversation in this format (gesturing to the wall). I went out to Office Depot last night and spent twenty dollars for 2,400 Post-its!" Looking more closely at the squares of paper stuck to the wall, I see how Greg has helped his students create a visual model of how a community of scholars engages in academic discourse. As a fellow high school English teacher, I can appreciate the idea and might even use it myself to help students move from passivity to interaction.

I'm further impressed when I join Karin, Shari, Jeff, and Greg for lunch and hear them continuing to discuss their observations of students' work and attitudes. For example, the Post-it activity has yielded some interesting results, with students showing a surprisingly critical view of their own essays. The teachers are wondering if this pattern reveals a problematic lack of confidence or a healthy recognition of room for improvement. Their curiosity about their practices and their students, and their inclination to discuss these questions over lunch, suggest that they have the beginnings of a strong department.

These teachers are in an enviable position, I think, as the formative years at a new school create an inviting opening to develop new ideas and question everything. Hillcrest has no tradition to lean on, no "way it's always been done." Jeff, Shari, and Greg all knew each other prior to Hillcrest, providing a solid foundation for their work. The relationships, the choices they made to be part of this new school, and the opportunity to be creative all produce a real synergy in their interactions. Greg tells me that prior to Hillcrest, he was teaching at his alma mater, and at the age of forty, was the youngest teacher in his department. Some part of him, however, didn't want to stay in one place so long that his teaching could become stale. He also didn't want to eventually watch his colleagues all retire in quick succession, leaving him behind. The opportunity to start anew beckoned, and he made his move.

Since they work together at Hillcrest and are also both going through the Teacher Leader Certification at the same time, Greg and Jeff are seeing plenty of each other and using their work in each setting to help the other. The daily interactions help them keep each other accountable for progress in the leadership program. The curriculum of TLCA is shaping the way they plan meetings and push each other to be clear and effective in meetings, giving them a common language and framework for their collaboration.

Shari has already completed the TLCA program and says the two years spent learning about and developing leadership skills gave her the confidence to move into high school teaching after years in elementary and middle schools. The TLCA capstone project also gave Shari practical experience in developing a program at her prior school, facilitating staff meetings to promote dialogue and peer support among teachers. She hopes to start a program at Hillcrest, something informal but regular, promoting trust and relationships that are good for interdepartmental work and the quality of the work environment overall. According to her sister, Karin, Shari was always the kind of teacher who could lead by example. Now, she tells Shari over lunch, "You're becoming a new person. I think [TLCA] helped get you out of your own head, to be an intentional leader rather than a leader by default." The idea is that you can *hope* for followers based on the work you take on, or you can act more strategically to *bring* followers to what you're doing.

Greg echoes the idea: "I was taking walks by myself. *Come on everybody!* And then no one follows. Coming to a new school site included an expectation of leading. Part of it is being a model of flexibility and inquiry. But I'm not the only leader here, and I can be a great first follower."

Tiffany Coates, First Grade
Lilly Ellefsen, "Newcomer" Class, Fourth to Sixth Grade
Live Oak Elementary School, Fallbrook

Later in my journey, I have another school visit that connects to TLCA, this time across the county line in San Diego County. Wendy Kerr helped establish TLCA along with Lanelle Gordin, and she has since gone on to complete a doctorate degree in educational leadership while serving as the principal of Live Oak Elementary School in Fallbrook. I was curious to see a school where the principal has not only a commitment to teacher leadership, but also a strong background in building it at the county level.

Fallbrook is a small community in the hills of northern San Diego County, reached via two-lane roads through a chaparral landscape, typical of the coastal mountains of southern California. When I arrive at Live Oak Elementary, the school day is just under way, and with Wendy out on the campus, I end up waiting in the front office. The school already exudes a vibe of comfort and familiarity, as the front office staff makes me feel welcome and juggles all the demands of students, parents, and grandparents coming through the office. Switching effortlessly from Spanish to English as needed, they deal with notes and explanations for late arrivals and upcoming early departures, missing lunches, and lost-and-found items—all with gracious smiles and genuine affection. They know the students by name, ask about their families, activities, and hobbies, and share details of their own families and lives in these brief but important interactions that shape a school culture.

Wendy and I have a few chances for short conversations during the day. After she comes to meet me at the front office, she gives me a quick tour of the campus.

As we're walking, we talk about Wendy's interest in promoting not only teacher leadership, but also extending leadership skills to students as well. In the hallways there are posters and other wall-hangings referring to Franklin Covey's leadership program for students ("The Leader in Me"), and Wendy tells me how teachers are using this material in their classes. I sometimes have doubts about schoolwide mandates to use outside materials and programs, but knowing Wendy's advocacy for teacher leadership, I have confidence that she's working with teachers rather than giving orders.

My short tour concludes with Wendy dropping me off in the first of two classrooms I'll visit today. I'm once again observing teachers I didn't know prior to my visit. In this situation, which is not common during my year of school visits, I'm benefitting from a level of professional courtesy and hospitality that involves an extra layer of trust, something I never want to take for granted. When I arrive in the first-grade classroom of teacher Tiffany Coates, a little girl named Aubree comes up to me right away to welcome me to the class and share information about what they're doing. Her manner is confident and serious for a six- or seven-year old, and I thank her for the orientation using a similar formality. She's done her job well, showing some leadership qualities in the process. It's clear throughout the morning that as Tiffany teaches students skills and curricular content, she's cultivating student awareness of community and leadership. As Aubree was the designated classroom ambassador for the morning, all the students also know they have a job to do. Or more precisely, a series of jobs. It's explicit in Tiffany's instruction, which sometimes embeds a call and response. As they go through their morning, students answer or echo Tiffany based on her cues: "My job right now is: *fractions!*" or more broadly, "My job is to do my best!" There is some irony in cultivating leadership skills through following behaviors; the idea seems to be that leadership flows from understanding and accepting responsibility. Students are more likely to develop actual leadership when they are familiar with expectations, have the respect of their peers, and make positive contributions within their classroom and school community.

This morning's work includes a fun and tasty math lesson: Using graham crackers, students are learning the mathematical language of fractions. Tiffany teaches her students the difference between saying a graham cracker has been "broken in two" versus "divided in half" (if they're careful to break the graham cracker along the dotted line). The use of graham crackers invites a degree of risk into the class of first-graders, though—the risk of eating too soon. Tiffany handles it with humor, saying, "Repeat after me: My graham cracker is a mathematical tool!" She also reminds them to clean up after themselves out of respect for the school custodian, Mr. Snow. On the way out to lunch, Tiffany asks students to debrief the morning's work, and they're using Covey's language (*"synergize!"*) to talk about how they worked together. I'm not sure they could parse out the connotations of that word, though what matters most is that the students are developing the vocabulary and awareness to connect their behaviors to ideas like responsibility, priorities, and goals.

As Tiffany's students head out to lunch, I have another chance to check in with Wendy. I share some observations from my morning, and the conversation veers toward broader issues: how the shape and dimensions of teacher leadership vary across schools and districts. Every school has a unique history and culture, and a unique combination of people involved as staff, students, parents, and community. The various elements of teacher leadership might be envisioned as overlapping circles, with the needs of different schools located within one or more of those circles. Needs will even vary from year to year. An influx of new staff calls for more attention to induction and mentorship. New standards and curriculum will motivate some teacher leaders, while others might be drawn to school redesign efforts, parent engagement programs, professional development, or union leadership roles. The dynamic and fluid nature of teacher leadership should lead us to cultivate leadership skills in as many teachers as possible.

After lunch I have a chance to meet and observe a teacher who understands well the necessity of professional flexibility in different settings. When I arrive at Lilly Ellefsen's classroom, I find some students spending their lunchtime working on an invention—a remote control vacuum cleaner—as part of a kind of engineering club or competition. They're quite self-sufficient, giving me a chance to talk to Lilly, a fifteen-year veteran in the district, now in her first year at Live Oak Elementary, where she teaches a mixed-grade class for "newcomers," students who are new to the country and need intensive language support.

Teaching fourth through sixth graders in one class requires considerable organization and management skill: At any given moment, Lilly is most likely working directly with smaller groups of students, yet she must ensure that all students are productively engaged in learning activities. The multiage classroom with students working independently bears some similarities to a Montessori educational model, as

I understand it (though I haven't observed Montessori classes or schools). However, I infer that Lilly exerts more influence and direction over her students' activities, even when she's not working with them directly. In an otherwise traditional school and district, this newcomer class is an outlier. Lilly accepted the challenge of teaching this type of class several years ago, at another school in Fallbrook. Looking for a change after teaching second grade for a number of years, Lilly was offered a multi-grade classroom instead of a move to another grade level. She took the plunge and says it completely changed her teaching paradigm, making her more responsive to students' specific developmental needs and less focused on following a set curriculum.

Since making that decision, Lilly has done research on this pedagogical model and developed a program that the district superintendent wanted to replicate. The model didn't catch on, however, perhaps because it requires such a shift for teachers not trained in this model. Although teachers might find the model intriguing, few would be prepared for the challenge of teaching multiple subjects to multiple grades of language learners, working directly with only a few students at a time. Lilly continued with this type of class for seven years prior to joining the staff at Live Oak. In addition to developing the skill to teach mixed-grade classes, she learned a valuable lesson about school design and leadership: Sometimes the key to success is the person rather than the program. In the long run, we'd likely prefer to see pedagogy based on what's best for students, and then see teachers and schools adapt accordingly. In the meantime, however, there are teachers who can excel using methods that differ from the typical practices in their school or district. These individuals may be the sparks that ignite positive changes in the future, when they are supported accordingly. To better understand the organizational dynamics and constraints that affect teachers and schools, Lilly has also pursued a master's degree and administrative credential.

As I experienced in Tiffany Coates' class this morning, Lilly's class has student leaders who have the responsibility of orienting me to the class. Maria takes charge. She points out key features of the classroom setup that indicate what they do and how they work, and directs me to her own writing posted on the wall. Using the language of her school's leadership curriculum, Maria has written about wanting to become a teacher or a doctor, because she's good at helping people. She has certainly helped me!

Class time begins with a visit from older students who come over regularly from a nearby middle school to help Lilly's class with math skills. They're practicing the multiplication of fractions, using chalk on the blacktop outside classrooms. I always enjoy hearing about or seeing these types of arrangements, where older students come from other classes or schools to work with their younger peers. I recall how my own children have told me about what they valued in these relationships, as both the younger and older students. For the younger students, they not only receive some help with their skills, but they also see the older students as friendlier and more approachable. The older students have the chance to review some skills and also learn the challenge of trying to explain and model what you know, sometimes repeatedly in various ways, in order to help others understand. Lilly's students face the challenge of learning new mathematical concepts and a new language at the same time, but their middle-school buddies are patient and friendly. Talking to both teachers about this weekly get-together, I mention, "It's a win-win!" Then, a moment later, I realize I'm using some of the "Leader in Me" mindset and terminology that's infused throughout Live Oak Elementary, and they're putting it into practice.

Back in the classroom, Lilly's fourth and sixth graders are working independently on math skills through various computer lessons, math puzzles, and games. The fifth-graders are working directly with Lilly, learning about multiplying fractions by using Play-Doh. It's a challenging concept, since multiplication of numbers greater than one always produces larger numbers, while multiplying by fractions between zero and one generates products less than their factors. They're getting into some fractions with larger denominators like one-fifteenth and one-eighteenth and discovering that large denominators represent smaller pieces: a fifteenth is smaller than a third, even though fifteen is greater than three. The students working throughout the room are completely focused and on task, and those working with Lilly are wrestling with the math and language at the same time, without any signs of frustration. Lilly tells me after class that this is typical of their effort, and the work has paid off: "These kids are so quick, they have so much enthusiasm, love, excitement. It's a like a big family in here."

Teacher leadership can improve a school or district because teachers like Jane Fung and Cheryl Suliteanu bring a passion for the work and manage to find ways to make a difference—or many differences. If we want to capture that spark, protect and nurture it, we must take more systematic approaches. The intentional and strategic cultivation of leadership can do wonders for teachers and academic programs, as I saw at Hillcrest High School, and can even filter through directly to students, as I observed with Tiffany Coates and Lilly Ellefsen at Live Oak Elementary.

Even those steps are not enough. Teacher leadership, as we'll see in the next chapter, needs to extend to our local school boards and our state and federal departments of education.

CHAPTER 11

Teacher Leaders, Beyond the School:

The Intersection of Policy and Practice

Sarah Kirby-Gonzalez discusses a student's work in her fifth-grade class at Mather Heights Elementary School. Sarah is also a school board trustee for the Washington Unified School District in West Sacramento.

AT THE SITE AND DISTRICT LEVEL, THERE ARE SO MANY REASONS to embrace and expand teacher leadership, yet we must also recognize the limits of our individual contributions when they come up against broader systemic conditions. If you ask the typical teacher about education budgets, policies, and politics, the answers are likely to come back in generalizations and with a negative tinge. Our district and site budget allocations usually seem inadequate to match our aspirations. Many times, policy decisions reflect an awareness of what should happen broadly, but the implementation of those decisions saddles professional opportunities with bureaucratic constraints. It's not surprising then that so many teachers are turned off by the word "policy."

And yet there are some outstanding educators in California who embrace policy discussions, taking their teacher leadership into policy work at a variety of levels. Their efforts ensure that school boards, state commissions, and the education department in Washington, DC, will hear from accomplished teachers, even if we can't count on those bodies to craft excellent policies in every case. As expected, I saw quality teaching when I visited these teachers, and it was reassuring to know that skilled practitioners are stepping up to represent our work and advocate on our behalf.

The most challenging aspect of this examination of teacher leadership is determining whether participation in high-level policy work makes someone a better teacher. I contend that it does—not that these teachers are collectively superior to those who don't engage in policy—but that these engaged teachers are better than they would otherwise be. As I suggested in the previous chapter, part of the value of teacher leadership is providing a better understanding of your own practices. If Jane Fung spends hours training other teachers to use new science curriculum and materials, she ends up making even better use of them herself. Cheryl Suliteanu's dedication to family engagement at the district level improves her engagement strategies with her own students' families. In this chapter, the leadership question shifts to different levels. Does participation in the crafting of state policies on teacher licensure make someone more effective at teaching reading or math to second graders? I can't say. It's certainly a harder line to draw.

However, I will argue that policy-level teacher leadership improves the way teachers feel about their work, and it's not much of a leap to suggest that people do better work when they feel valued, respected, effective, influential, and fully engaged. Conversely, no one will thrive in conditions where they feel voiceless, powerless, ignored, or manipulated. While directing a state-level task force won't improve a teacher's lesson planning, it probably makes that teacher more motivated to continue planning lessons—for years. This chapter will also offer more direct observations that high-level policy experience makes teachers into greater resources for their peers and affects the way teacher leaders advocate for their own students.

I rely somewhat on my own experience here as well. During the years I helped direct the advocacy organization Accomplished California Teachers, I was still teaching high school English. I collaborated with teachers around the state to research, write, and disseminate policy recommendations relating to teacher evaluation, professional pathways, and compensation. That work didn't improve my skills in teaching literature and writing, but it energized and renewed my commitment to every aspect of my engagement at school, in my union and other professional organizations, and in the broader educational community.

Alicia Hinde, Second Grade
Bagby Elementary School, San Jose

I met Alicia Hinde a few years ago when I learned about the community outreach work she initiated as the president of her local union. One creative strategy she described was having the union give away children's books at the local farmer's market, a fun way to promote family literacy that also made union leaders more approachable and accessible to parents and the community. Since then, Alicia has moved from union leadership to a position of broader responsibility, serving on the state's Commission on Teacher Credentialing. (Haydee Rodriguez, profiled in Chapter 5, also serves on this commission.) In this role, Alicia has direct influence over professional licensing policies that affect every public school teacher in California.

An impressive resume is no guarantee of pedagogical skill, so there was always an element of optimism behind my choices to spend days observing a teacher based on their nonteaching accomplishments. In Alicia's case, that optimism was richly rewarded when I spent a day in her second-grade classroom at Bagby Elementary School in San Jose.

Alicia orchestrates her students' school day to maximize learning. Like a skilled conductor, she sets the tempo, anticipates the movements, and observes closely to ensure everyone's collective success. While a morning lesson has students making

Venn diagrams to compare and contrast different oceanic wildlife, students are also learning to navigate peer relationships in the classroom. Most of the time the groups are running smoothly, with Alicia moving about the room, checking in with a few students at a time, yet keeping an eye on the class as a whole. One girl leaves her group and comes to Alicia to complain about someone else's behavior. Alicia quietly summons the second girl to join the conversation, and without disrupting any other students in the room, the girls negotiate a plan to get back to productive collaboration. All Alicia had to do was facilitate the dialogue. The girls walk back to their group, pull out their chairs, and resume working together. Minutes later, in another group, a boy has thrown something small at one of his classmates. Instead of simply chastising the boy, Alicia asks the affected student to articulate how she feels when the boy throws things at her. By encouraging communication and empathy, Alicia has helped them continue working while also practicing skills that will help them avoid or resolve future interpersonal conflicts.

Effective teachers (and wise parents) know that one of the keys to communicating with children is to take a sincere interest in their ideas and speak to them at their level without condescension. Alicia manages all this and more; her manner is consistently warm without being overly effusive and humorous without being comical. While circulating to check on student progress, she offers, "Here's a free strategy I'll teach you. I'm not even going to charge you for it." The kids smile. Later, as students put away their materials after making Venn diagrams, she tells one group, "I'm having a *heartbreak moment!* Something terrible is happening right now." She has everyone's attention for sure. "There's a marker on the floor—with no cap on it! Just drying out. Right over there." Who wouldn't want to help their second-grade teacher escape from a heartbreak moment?

The next segment of the lesson continues with the oceanic theme, building on the scientific observations students already attempted with Venn diagrams about wildlife, and now blending language, math, and art skills. Alicia reads from a book titled *How Many Snails?* by Paul Giganti Jr., in which each page features drawings of items that have multiple shared or distinguishing characteristics. The questions that follow require some careful attention: How many snails are there? How many have stripes on their shells? How many are on top of a rock? It can be challenging to keep everyone's focus, so Alicia has to employ some strong observational skills and class management. At one point, a boy is absentmindedly tapping his foot against a desk leg, which in turn, is causing some distracting noises from a metallic water bottle on the desk. Instead of focusing on the problem directly, Alicia calls the boy to the front of the room to help with the next part of the book. As he comes up, Alicia asks a girl sitting near the desk to move the water bottle elsewhere. Problem solved, without any interruption or calling attention to the distractions.

Alicia's students enjoy *How Many Snails?* and now have a chance to apply the same concept on their own, drawing an underwater scene with groups and subgroups to count (how many fish? how many fish with spots?). Eventually their pages will be compiled to form a class book. The boy who was throwing items a little while ago is thoroughly engaged in this activity, and while most of his classmates are drawing sharks and seahorses, coral, and seaweed, this second-grader has drawn a sunken ship with pirate skeletons. And I have to look very closely, because one of his questions is "how many skeletons with ghosts?" I lean in closer and squint to see a faint, watery ghost hovering above a skeleton with an eyepatch still on the skull.

The highlight of the day for me is watching the science experiment. Alicia introduces the concept of buoyancy, relying partially on students' experiences in water, but also showing the buoyancy control device from her personal scuba diving gear. The question of the day emerges: Does buoyancy differ between fresh water and salt water?

The experiment begins. Students have plastic containers holding an egg in two cups of water, a paper plate with a large scoop of table salt, and a plastic spoon. If they change the fresh water into salt water, will the submerged egg start to float? As you might anticipate from an adult perspective, the answer is yes, the egg is going to float, eventually. Alicia's students are careful with their procedures at first yet hope to see quick results; there's disappointment when adding a few spoonfuls of salt produces no effect. Of course, if they keep going and stir the water enough to dissolve salt sitting on the bottom, the egg floats. Students are elated. "It's floating! It's floating!" Some jaws drop. One boy claps his partner on the back, and that's not enough to express his excitement, so he pairs it with claps on his partner's chest as well. When some students see other groups' eggs floating, they abandon careful and deliberate additions of salt one teaspoon at time and start dumping. The room is becoming messy and noisy, but Alicia simply moves around to make sure every group has managed to make the egg float. She tells me later that tomorrow's lesson is to start figuring out *why* the egg floats in salt water, so the priority for the moment is not quiet and order, but simply to make certain every student has directly observed this phenomenon.

I'm not only impressed by Alicia's teaching, but also by the fact that such a skilled teacher has a key role in state-level teacher leadership. It speaks well of the Commission on Teacher Credentialing, and its selection process, to have identified and commissioned people like Alicia Hinde (and Haydee Rodriguez). It's reassuring on multiple levels: We all benefit from having policy leaders with a deep knowledge of the work and the people affected by their policies, and it's affirming to see that participation in leadership opportunities can be compatible with classroom teaching.

Martha Infante, Social Studies
Los Angeles Academy Middle School, Los Angeles

Months later and hundreds of miles away, I have a chance to spend a day with Martha Infante, a middle school social studies teacher who also manages to take on state-level leadership opportunities while teaching full time. In her subject area and on state-level policy initiatives, Martha has been a powerful advocate for quality public education and for teachers. She's a National Board Certified Teacher, has served multiple times as the president of the California Commission on Social Studies, and was the Commission's middle-level Teacher of the Year for 2009. We first connected through Twitter a little while after she won the award, when we were both relatively new to education blogging. Based on her writing and advocacy for students and schools in South Central Los Angeles, I invited Martha to write for InterACT, a multiauthor blog I managed for Accomplished California Teachers, and she remained a contributor for a year and a half. In 2011, we both received an invitation to address members of the federal Equity and Excellence Commission. The following year, Martha was appointed by the State Superintendent of Public Instruction, Tom Torlakson, to help produce our state's "Greatness by Design" education policy framework for strengthening teaching; she served as the cochair for a group studying teacher evaluation and, in 2015, codirected the update of the entire report.

Arriving before school starts, I enter the Los Angeles Academy Middle School (LAAMS) campus through a side parking lot and find my way to Martha's room. To check in more properly, I accompany Martha to the front entrance of the school, where I meet assistant principal Ernesto Guerrero. He offers a smiling welcome along with a friendly handshake and he asks about my visit. When I tell him about my year-long project, he expresses gratitude for the fact that *someone* is taking a positive approach in examining education. He shares his admiration for Martha and teachers like her who have options but stay at high-needs schools like LAAMS. He says, "We love the school and the community. I wish some of the policy makers would come spend a day here." Guerrero's next question is how long I'm staying; I answer that I'm staying all day, and he laughs. "Well, I'll come find you at the end of the day and see what you think!" (Six hours later, he does.) The implication is that I might not emerge with positive views if I spend a full day there. It's said as a joke—a revealing one: There's some question about how I might view the school as an outsider, whether or not its better qualities will shine through once I've been exposed to its challenges.

Of course, my mindset throughout this work has been to focus on the positive. There are occasionally moments that require a more conscious effort to maintain that lens, as might be expected when spending full days at over sixty campuses. Perhaps because of Guerrero's comment, and also because LAAMS really does have more than its share of challenges, this day turns out to be unique among my school visits.

Walking back to her classroom, Martha provides me with some context for understanding her school and her classes. Like many schools in Los Angeles, LAAMS must find ways to serve students who are new immigrants or long-time residents with limited English, many of whom are in foster care, contend with housing or food insecurity, learning differences, and various undiagnosed or undertreated conditions. The school and district lack the resources to do this effectively for all students, and at this point, LAUSD schools are contending with a new mandate to sharply reduce suspensions and introduce restorative justice practices that aim for understanding and reconciliation in place of punishment. Not just at LAAMS, but throughout the district, most teachers are overwhelmed by the demands of the job. And somehow, they keep going. Martha, at least, has some outlet beyond the district level: As a leader in the state organization for social studies education and in her work with the California Department of Education, she has opportunities to speak out about what teachers and schools need to better serve students.

Her teaching day begins with a seventh-grade social studies class, with students drawn from the LAAMS honors program. Before they come in, she tells me, "This class is heaven. It's heaven." For their current unit of study, Martha blends a combination of discussion, reading, and writing to guide them through a fairly standard lesson on a rather heavy topic, the "Black Death." Beyond some of the simple who-what-when kinds of information, Martha is challenging them to think about more complex issues, such as the economic effects of a sharp reduction in the European labor force during and after the Plague. The class meets in "block" period, which is eighty-eight minutes long; and though she's not sure the powers-that-be would sanction unstructured break time in the middle, Martha allows a five-minute intermission. The moment it begins, many students practically jump out of their seats for a chance to stretch and converse with classmates. Some students pull out their own reading and just enjoy a few minutes to escape into the fantasy world of *Eragon* or one of Rick Riordan's books from the Percy Jackson series. Using a chime to regain the students' attention after five minutes, Martha has them transitioned back into classwork and completely focused in under thirty seconds.

Her later classes are not composed of honors students, and that means Martha needs a broader array of teaching methods and strategies. As I would expect of a National Board Certified Teacher, Martha is adept at adjusting to meet students' needs. The overall curriculum goals seem to be the same, but during the rest of the day, I observe Martha mixing up her approach. She makes more regular efforts to forge connections for students, using bits of Spanish here and there, as well as religious and cultural references that she knows most of her students can understand. At select points in the lesson, she dramatizes the content more, emphasizing the Plague's symptoms and how misunderstandings of the causes of disease led to horribly misguided attempts at cures.

At lunchtime, Martha's room is full of kids—mostly girls—who prefer to eat in her class rather than outside; many of them hustled in early to score seats on the couch or desks together. Martha spends much of lunch coordinating with student leaders who are trying to raise money for a class trip to Washington, DC. Then, amidst all the lunchtime noise, one of the girls offers to sing a song. It turns out she's a contestant on a Spanish version of *The Voice* for kids and teens. I don't understand the Spanish lyrics, but her classmates are quiet and respectful, listening attentively before applauding at the song's end. The overall atmosphere, if you know middle schools, would seem typically energetic; if you don't know middle schools, it might seem loud and chaotic. Around the room some are playing a game, others are braiding each other's hair, and many are checking their phones. Martha sits at her desk on the side of the room, with kids coming over constantly. They simply call her "Miss."

One girl turns to talk to me for a moment, and tells me, "Lunch in Miss Infante's room is the best thing about this school!"

When I relate the comment to Martha a few minutes later, she laughs. "I don't even know all of them," Martha tells me, "but they're quintessential South Central [LA] students. Smart, no filter, inappropriate, interesting. I'm glad to have them come in since I'm here anyway, but I don't know exactly why they want to be here." From an outsider's perspective, I find it obvious: Martha provides a space that's comfortable and safe, where students know they'll be accepted and understood, where they can relax a bit and remain assured that someone is watching out for them.

Martha's most challenging class is coming through the door for the last class period of the day. She tells me this class overall has a lower average skill level and more behavioral issues to address. There's one pair of boys in particular who have been annoying each other, exchanging comments back and forth. Martha's injunctions work temporarily, but when the class has a midperiod break, one boy approaches the other, who is still seated, and tries to provoke a response. On the surface it's sarcastic, with a tone that might suggest humor, if the other person seemed responsive. The provocation escalates, with the one wrapping his arms around the shoulders of his seated classmate. It still isn't really fighting, but it's also neither friendly nor wanted. Martha reacts immediately and calmly, demanding an end to the physical contact, to no avail. The boy who's seated is not being hurt and isn't even reacting. Taking the discipline to the next level, Martha manages to write up a disciplinary referral while giving instructions to the rest of the class to continue their work. I don't know how she keeps such an even-keeled manner, but it works. She diverts the potential spectators and keeps them focused on academics and has the troublemaking student on his way out. He's angry about the situation and wants to argue, but Martha makes it clear there's no debate to be had at the moment, and she sends him out to the office.

Examining the situation superficially, some observers might attribute these interactions to the character of the students or the practices of the teacher. The underlying causes likely run much deeper in both the school and the school system and in the unique story of this particular boy, glimpsed here in a mere half hour of his life. What I choose to focus on is this: Most students in the class reacted perfectly to the situation, showing their self-control, self-respect, and respect for their teacher. What I choose to celebrate in this moment is the way Martha approached the other student at the end of the class, and lauded his earlier restraint and self-control at a crucial moment. "You did the right thing. What helped you do that today? What was working for you?" Recall that before being wrapped up by his classmate, this boy was also struggling with focus and appropriate behavior. Martha's patience with him has paid off, and she has the opportunity now to positively engage with him. I infer from the questions that he hasn't always done "the right thing." Martha is now in a position to help him recognize his strengths and perhaps put them to use in the future.

Some of the other students on their way out for the day veer in my direction before heading toward the door, saying, "Goodbye, Mister. It was nice meeting you."

No sooner than the last student exits, assistant principal Ernesto Guerrero steps through the door. He remembered. "So how was it?" he asks me, grinning. "Did you get the full experience?"

Martha answers for me, "Oh, he got the *full* experience today!" It's a quick interaction, as Guerrero moves on after chatting for a minute or two, and I do appreciate his interest in checking in with me again. For a moment, I almost feel like an initiate, a member of the family. It's fleeting, though. Taking Martha at her word, I may have had the complete experience for a day, but I know how much the challenges multiply over time and how little time there is to meet those challenges.

Martha starts to talk about the day, thinking about ways to improve lessons—a reflective habit typical of accomplished teachers generally and National Board Certified Teachers in particular (see Chapter 7). In her place I'd likely do the same—partly because we're rarely satisfied, and partly in recognition that the observer may have picked up on some elements that I want to improve. With some teachers, I might indulge in some of that reflection with them, though it's not my purpose in this project to evaluate anyone or suggest improvements. In Martha's case, I respond that, while her teaching situation is far from ideal, I think she may be the ideal person for the situation. In a blog post the next day, I put it slightly differently: "the perfect person for imperfect circumstances."

Linda Yaron, English
University High School, Los Angeles

During the Obama administration, the US Department of Education created a program to bring more teachers into direct contact with those who create and implement federal policy. The Teaching Ambassador Fellowship (TAF) allows teachers from all over the country to spend a year engaged in policy discussions with the federal government. Some of the Fellows remain in the classroom while receiving compensation and release time to participate in the program. Others move to Washington, DC, for a year and work full time in their TAF role. All are engaged in offering opinions and insights regarding the school and classroom-level effects of current or proposed federal policies.

Linda Yaron, a National Board Certified English teacher at University High School in Los Angeles, had the opportunity to spend a year in Washington advising the education department. (Marciano Gutierrez, Chapter 5, held the same position). I imagine that Linda was able to offer valuable insights and perspective during her TAF experience, and during my visit to her school, I hope to observe how the TAF experience has shaped Linda's teaching.

My visit to University High School brings me once again near my old elementary school (Brentwood Science Magnet, Chapter 2). Though I've never set foot on the campus before, it feels familiar. Several of my friends attended "Uni," and I drove past it many times in my adulthood. Linda's classroom is a bungalow-style building, the ubiquitous one- or two-classroom concrete blocks found on so many LAUSD campuses. Stepping into Linda Yaron's bungalow classroom feels much like entering my fifth- and sixth-grade classrooms. The interior is in serious need of renovation, from the floor to the ceiling, including all of the furniture. The floor isn't even level, but instead tilts slightly to my left as I face the front of the room. The good news is that help is arriving—and soon. Linda has secured a grant to modernize the classroom, and the upgrades begin in a matter of days. She shows me some of the letters students wrote in support of the grant application, describing what they want to change and how it would help them. Were I reading such letters in another setting, I might expect to see references to computers and tablets, internet connection speeds, interactive whiteboards, or 3-D printers. And while they do write about technology, these high schoolers also let readers know that their classroom lacks bookshelves, desks that aren't scratched up and rusty, and chairs that aren't mismatched or in disrepair. They want color in the classroom instead of white walls, a white ceiling, and a gray linoleum floor. They try to reassure their readers that they will take good care of whatever they receive and even cite their perfect record with returning school books and not adding to the graffiti already on the desks.

Despite the deficiencies and defects of the room, Linda and her students have established a positive and productive atmosphere. Her teaching assignment includes three English courses: one for English language development (ELD), and one each for grades nine and eleven. In all of her classes, Linda balances full-group conversation and instruction with plenty of time for students to work while she checks in with them. Despite an overall student load of roughly 150 students, Linda usually seems to be resuming a conversation with a student rather than starting from scratch. As ELD students write about their lives in the style of a news article, Linda checks in and recognizes connections: "Oh, that reminds me of your mother's story," or "That makes sense. It really fits with your move from Saudi Arabia."

Knowing students well is essential for a teacher, and it also paves the way for students to share even more and surprise the teacher, their classmates, or themselves. Linda has asked her juniors to bring in an object, or "artifact," that they can present to the class as a symbol of the American dream. One student has decided to write a poem instead, an unexpected response that Linda receives with enthusiasm. Later, a student's explanation of his apartment key provides unexpected insights, as he reveals to his classmates that he has moved into his own apartment and is paying the rent with money he earns. After class, I chat with him briefly and learn more: With one parent who passed away and another who couldn't care for him, the young man's sister took care of him for the past few years. But now that he's eighteen, he's on his own, trying to ease the burden on his sister's family. He has hopes of attending college and says University High is helping him toward that goal. He mentions an attendance clerk who has known him since he was in eighth grade, and I'm reminded that children often connect with nonteaching staff at schools. It's an important dynamic I've observed at my own school and reminds me of the supportive front office staff at Live Oak Elementary (see Chapter 10).

Not surprisingly, making sure that students are known and heard was part of Linda's focus during her Teaching Ambassador Fellowship. One of her favorite contributions in that role was helping to create a Student Voices discussion series between students and the education department, including then-Secretary of Education Arne Duncan. The program has grown since Linda's fellowship ended and still continues today. As she explains, "Schools work best when authentic teacher and student voices are part of the decision-making process. Creating spaces for this increases investment, ownership, and better alignment of policy decisions with the pulse of current classroom realities."

Linda has a gift for connecting her school and students with outside resources, a vision and skill set that was enhanced by her time in Washington, DC. Regarding her experience as a TAF, Linda tells me she gained "a wider perspective on education by talking to educators and stakeholders from across the country. Visiting schools and learning about a diverse cross-section of educational practices enriched my vision for what was possible for my classroom and school." What's possible? In addition to obtaining the classroom makeover grant already mentioned, since returning from her TAF experience, Linda helped arrange for her classes to be part of a multiorganizational research project to raise student awareness and promote mental health. The work now continues across the wider campus, thanks to another grant. Linda also finds ways to bring the arts into her teaching. One project led to student art being displayed at the Department of Education. Another involved a combination of photography and writing, with the support of community partnerships with The Getty Museum and an organization called 826LA. The latter organization is a regional branch of 826 National, which got its start at 826 Valencia Street in San Francisco.[3]

Connecting students with outside agencies and opportunities often spurs greater interest and engagement. There's something energizing about getting out of the classroom and school setting or changing the routine by bringing in guests. Focusing on writing with 826LA, in a project that also involved the Getty Museum, Linda's students have had some transformative learning experiences. Linda shared the following student reflections with me:

- "It allowed me to find my identity, and it helped me find what really represents me."
- "It inspired me to work hard so I can have a great future. It impacted me by finding my inner self and focusing on what doors to open for my future."
- "It helped me find and understand my identity. The experience helped me look deeper inside myself and be vulnerable enough to let myself and others in to help me figure it out. It impacted me to be open with myself."

Linda has also arranged for her students to participate in the August Wilson Monologue Competition, a national (eight-city) effort to bring arts to high schools and engage students in drama and literature. On the day of my visit to her class, Linda's ninth graders are studying August Wilson with a guest teacher, a professional actor named Tony. He has a strong rapport with Linda's class (this is not his first visit) and, just as important, from an academic standpoint, he continually guides the students to link their personal reactions to concrete details from the text. He models what he wants by opening up about his own life—how he connects to Wilson's characters as an African American, a male, a son, and a brother. At points in his story, heads around the room are nodding with recognition of their own lives as well, and one girl begins to respond aloud, "Mmm hmm . . . Mmm hmm . . . Me too . . . My mom too . . ." The discourse is complex and lively as students disagree about whether or not the son in the play still loves his father, a debate that necessitates differentiating between love and respect. When the conversation veers to intergenerational family expectations within the play, a few African American boys speak up, relating their own experiences. Then the topic shifts to the idea of personal sacrifice—what some characters sacrifice for others. Another boy in the class says he can relate because he's responsible for taking care of his seven-year-old brother.

Later, students perform a scene or two from the play, and their work would be impressive for a drama class. I can't quite believe that I'm actually watching such sincere, unrehearsed performances in a ninth-grade English class. The reading is smooth, conveying some real feeling, and even includes the embraces called for in the stage directions. Two boys improvise a gesture portraying their shared grief: facing each other with hands on the other's shoulders, they bow their heads until their foreheads touch, and they pause for a moment. As the emotional tone of the scene shifts, one young man exclaims, "I don't want to be Troy Maxwell. I wanna be *me!*"—punctuated with three loud slaps to his own chest. Then there's a part of the script that requires singing a song—something about the family dog—and the boy reading the part is game, trying to improvise a little melody to accompany the words. His peers in the audience provide a beat, and he begins singing something closer to the blues, but he then changes the tune again, turning the text into a rap. As a former drama teacher myself, and as a freshman English teacher of many years, I'm in awe of the work accomplished in this classroom. It's the confluence of Linda's broader vision, Tony's charisma and talent, and the depth and emotion of August Wilson's writing that have combined to bring out excellent work in these students.

When the students are gone for the day, Linda's teacher leadership continues. She has experience as a union representative, serves on her school's instructional leadership team, and has led various professional learning activities. She tries to stay active in educational leadership and policy discussions through writing and participation with organizations like the Center for Teaching Quality. Clearly, Linda's voice is one we need to hear in education policy conversations, and her inclination to bring in the voices of more teachers, and students, will serve us well.

Sarah Kirby-Gonzalez, Fifth Grade
Mather Heights Elementary School, Mather

Of course, there's always the possibility of something being lost in translation, something the teacher leader tries to communicate to the policy maker in a situation where there is no substitute for experience. The best way to mitigate this problem is to ensure that we have some teachers who not only assist policy makers, but also *become* policy makers. In Chapter 9, I described my brief meeting with Gahr High School teacher and Artesia mayor Miguel Canales, but he is an anomaly—mayors in most towns have little influence on education. I know two Bay Area teachers who are former school board trustees, and for my book research, I spent one day with a teacher who is a sitting school board trustee.

Teachers can't serve on their own school board, as it creates a conflict of interest; living in West Sacramento while teaching in the Folsom Cordova Unified School District, Sarah Kirby-Gonzalez avoids that conflict and is able to combine her interest in classroom teaching and policy leadership. Her initial election (she has since been re-elected) to the Washington Unified School District Board of Education garnered some national attention in education circles, as her main rival was employed by the education policy lobbying organization Students First. (Founded in 2010 by Michelle Rhee, the controversial former superintendent of Washington, DC, public schools, the Students First reform agenda focused on weakening unions, increasing focus on test scores, and expanding charter schools. The organization was established with lofty goals for fundraising and sweeping national reforms; they had offices in about ten states before merging with another education reform organization, 50CAN, in 2016.) While Sarah had less funding than her opponent, she benefitted from a solid reputation in the community and a commitment to strong grassroots organizing, with plenty of door-to-door campaigning. Having a father who's been a city councilman and mayor probably helped Sarah as well.

Going back a few more years, one of my first interactions with Sarah was political in nature, as we teamed up to visit California legislators to share the Accomplished California Teachers report on teacher evaluation. Sarah reinforced our message about improving teacher evaluation by bringing her most recent evaluation to our meetings, showing the single sheet of paper with a few check marks and comments that essentially said, "Keep up the good work!" We were advocating a shift to evaluation processes and outcomes that are more meaningful and robust, but only one of the three senators in the room was receptive to our teacher-led efforts. On the way out of the meeting, Sarah and I chatted with different staff members; when we reconnected, Sarah told me that a male senator had said goodbye that day with a dismissive, "Stay perky!" Essentially, her efforts at policy engagement had been reduced to a comment on her demeanor and personality.

Sarah has done much more than stay perky. As a former Sacramento County Teacher of the Year and National Board Certified Teacher, Sarah has a platform to advocate for teachers generally and for National Board Certification specifically in the district where she works. As a school board trustee, she naturally works on a broader variety of issues, all of which she approaches with the complementary viewpoints of an active community leader, parent, and teacher.

My visit to her school, Mather Heights Elementary, comes in mid-February, and her fifth-grade classroom is running quite smoothly at this point in the year. It almost seems like a classroom you'd pick if you wanted to represent our state. It's a highly diverse group of students from a wide range of ethnic, cultural, and religious backgrounds; some are immigrants, while others have multigenerational roots in the community.

If you were to set up a camera in the corner of Sarah's classroom and use time-lapse photography, you'd see a classroom that strikes a productive balance between stillness and motion, allowing students time to work individually, in small groups, and as a whole class. At the start of the day, students are working with partners on research and writing, coming up with topics of interest and determining good directions for their research prior to writing an article on the topic. Some students want to research video games, while others are taking a more local and investigative approach to find out why their school's athletic field has been closed for renovation as long as it has. The research methods might include looking up information and news articles online and also conducting interviews with people who have firsthand knowledge of the topics. Sarah moves from group to group, always kneeling or sitting at the same level as the students, and doing more listening than talking. The activity concludes with student groups sharing with the whole class some of their challenges and seeking the advice of their peers. When Sarah interjects some advice, the conversation becomes momentarily silly, but with a serious point. Sarah suggests, "If your story is about a man who fell through a window, maybe you should interview the window! If the story is about a horse that had an operation, interview other horses." As the giggles subside, Sarah clarifies the point: Students tend to think first about the perspective of the central figure in the story, but there are other interesting and relevant points of view.

Her other main piece of advice to her fifth-grade writers is to give themselves permission to write first drafts that contain errors. She encourages them to see writing as a process with multiple opportunities to improve the work through revision and editing. "First drafts aren't *supposed* to be great. But after it's done, you need to review it and improve it. That's the time to bump it up." This last phrase turns out to be a favorite of Sarah's during the day, as she encourages students to revisit their first answers, review their first attempts, and improve through a process of analysis and reflection. For the moment, students have taken her advice, and they immerse themselves in quiet, independent writing.

It's no accident that Sarah encourages her students to elevate their work using the same habits she uses to grow as a teacher. She even models this kind of thinking for the students later in the day, after a history lesson. Students are learning about the colonial era in American history, and today's activity involves some "artifacts" from the colonies—facsimiles of the objects that might be found in a colonial home: eyeglasses, toothbrushes, playing cards, soap. Each artifact comes in a box, and small groups of students read hints about the content of each box prior to opening it. Once they have the artifact in hand, the idea is for them to generate questions about the design or characteristics of the object to see what they might infer about the lives of the people who used it. Sarah tells me ahead of time how much she and her past students have enjoyed this lesson, but after it wraps up today, Sarah asks the class what could make the activity better in the future. She listens, validates their input, and also shares her own observations about how she could have improved the flow and efficiency.

Later in the day, it's time for math, and I see some hallmarks of Common Core math standards here, as students articulate the different approaches that can be used to solve a problem. Some students are also working on a probability game that involves rolling large foam dice. I know that Sarah has mixed feelings about the Common

Core implementation, partially based on concerns about the standards themselves, and even more because of issues relating to the assessments—their costs, timing, instructional impact, and equity issues. As a teacher leader in her district, Sarah brings the unique perspective of a school board trustee with a greater understanding of the policy landscape and the legal mandates involved. She understands the constraints on her district leadership and focuses her energy on great teaching instead of complaints. At the same time, being an elected leader gives Sarah a stronger sense of agency, a willingness to speak out and take her concerns public, as she did in 2016 when there were flaws in the state's technical support for testing; her Facebook post about the issues led to an appearance on the local evening news. Back in West Sacramento, as a school board trustee, Sarah brings practical teaching experience to bear in the realm of policy, making her an effective advocate for students and teachers.

It is a source of constant frustration for many teachers, and many other education observers and stakeholders, to know that there are legislators, education departments, superintendents, school boards, and others making education policy without the partnership of teacher leaders like those profiled in this chapter. With only the faintest understanding of the complexity of our work and the challenges we face, even well-intentioned leaders tend to focus on the most basic data, such as test scores, and accept oversimplified theories of change. The most common and damaging policy misconception in the past twenty years has been that if the government exerts more pressure on schools through the creation of punitive consequences, school leaders and teachers will respond by working harder to raise test scores, and that will mean our students will learn more. This theory simply doesn't prove true, as it fails to recognize what drives *and sustains* improvement in teaching and schools, and assumes too much about the meaning of test scores. And that's why we need outstanding teachers playing a direct role in crafting education policy at every level. In the final chapter of this book, I'll offer some more specific policy suggestions.

CHAPTER 12

Supporting the Whole Child:

Hearts and Minds Connected
for Better Learning

At Duveneck Elementary School in Palo Alto, fifth-grade teacher Mangla Oza shows her delight in a student's success building a "scribble-bot.

IN SCHOOLS AND IN VARIOUS ORGANIZATIONS PARTNERING WITH SCHOOLS, I see people paying more attention in recent years to the idea that we must meet the needs of "the whole child." This focus has become a cause and a mantra of sorts within the Association for Supervision and Curriculum Development (ASCD), for example. Schools are increasingly aware that learning depends on certain nonacademic factors, and they are increasingly *acting on* that awareness. Part of this trend toward social-emotional considerations and wraparound services, which allow schools to provide a variety of social and health services, results from a recognition that such approaches benefit all children. The shift is also a response to the unfortunate fact that so many American children live in poverty, face housing and food insecurity, and cope with undiagnosed post-traumatic stress disorder.[4] As the benefits of these nonacademic activities become clearer, they are gaining in popularity in more affluent areas as well.

I imagine that discussion of social-emotional learning, yoga, meditation, and mindfulness practices might lead some people to question whether schools are straying from their academic purpose, embracing what appears to be the opposite of a back-to-basics approach. However, many educators are coming around to the idea that attending to a student's sense of self and well-being might be the *most basic* of basics to get back to. Supporting the child's core emotional and mental needs facilitates better learning. What used to be the touchy-feely fringe of academia is becoming mainstream, and emerging research from major universities shows why: These practices have tangible learning-related benefits for students, including improved focus and stamina, decreased stress, better self-regulation and attendance, and improvements in the overall school environment. Health care organizations and schools are expanding their offerings in response to these findings and to increased interest among families.

Jennifer Harvey
Barron Park Elementary School, Palo Alto

In my school district, a number of teachers have begun using some mindfulness practices with students of all ages. I had my first introduction to mindfulness in the classroom by observing Jennifer Harvey's summer school class, called Mindful Education. Jennifer is a first-grade teacher whose work in mindfulness has become part of her regular practice during the school year as well. There are many ways for a teacher to establish norms and routines that make students feel safe and comfortable, but for some students, that's not enough. Mindfulness offers metacognitive strategies that can make children more aware of themselves, their feelings, and their choices, as well as how they respond to people and situations in the classroom.

Meeting with Jennifer Harvey before my class visits, I'm struck by her openness and interest in sharing. Her personality seem conducive to mindful teaching and learning. She's generous with her time and attention as we talk after school one day. Mindfulness is a subject and set of strategies that she has studied at length, even contributing to a book on the topic. As students arrive, I notice immediately how Jennifer models and reinforces mindfulness in every interaction, putting words to her feelings, observing her students and surroundings, and expressing appreciation for the little things, like a student's friendly smile or good manners.

Jennifer uses my presence as an opportunity to review past lessons. "Let's tell David what we've been learning," she says. It's always helpful to students to refresh memories and contextualize learning; by incorporating me into the conversation, the review becomes more authentic, with the additional purpose of informing me about the class. My favorite new learning from their review is the idea of–*ish*. The suffix represents the acceptance of imperfection, of work in progress, giving ourselves permission to struggle with challenges, to attempt and revise without expecting perfection to come quickly or easily. Sometimes there are right answers: eight minus two is six, not five-*ish*. Still, it's a liberating concept if it can internalized, as many learners—children and adults—wrestle with the fear of failure, or even the fear of imperfection. Looking at student artwork around the classroom and thinking back to my early years, I wonder what a difference it might have made if I'd been willing to attempt more drawings and paintings that were picture-*ish;* instead, I focused on my lack of artistic skill and gave up trying. In Jennifer's classroom, the students' artwork is clipped to strings crossing from wall to wall, creating a vibrant space above us that is saturated with flower-*ish*, rocket-*ish*, monster-*ish* and rainbow-*ish* color, which feels especially warm as the early morning light comes through the windows.

After telling me what they've learned, the students have a chance to show me some mindfulness in action to begin their day. Following Jennifer's lead, they're sitting cross-legged and straight-backed, eyes closed. She directs them to pay close attention to their bodies, and especially their breathing. "Now put a hand on your

chest. Think about what's in your heart. Let's remember what we're grateful for."
It's tricky for me to observe without participating; I don't want to distract the kids
by watching them in an obvious way, but I want to see how it's going. I squint now
and then, sneaking a peek, although our eyes are supposed to be closed, and I can
see that I'm not the only one faking it a bit. I'm sure Jennifer is well aware of this,
but she's letting it go. These students are around seven or eight years old, and this
is a practice that takes time to master, even for adults. So, they're mindful-*ish* in
their morning routine. As the minutes pass, some of the children are catching on
a bit more. You can see the process happen: One girl, hair in a long ponytail and
slouching over her sparkly sneakers, looks around the circle at the other kids and at
me sitting just outside the circle, then notices Jennifer as if for the first time. Now
she straightens her spine, looks down to make sure she's completely cross-legged,
closes her eyes, opens them again to sneak a quick confirming glance at Jennifer,
then keeps her eyes closed. It's all quiet, no disruptions.

The next activity is bringing a bit of science and anatomy to mindfulness.
Students have learned about the brain and how there are many types of thoughts
and ways of thinking, associated with different regions of the brain. I'm enjoying
watching Jimmy working on his diagram; he's got this brain stuff down cold! As
he colors in different sections and writes captions, he's reading aloud in sing-song
voice, "Amygdala pro*tects* us . . . prefrontal *cor*tex helps us *think* . . . hippo*cam*pus
holds our *memory* . . . Yay! I did it!" Jennifer gives the students metaphors and an
easy-to-model kinesthetic way to understand the brain. Like a snow-globe, your
thoughts can be scrambled in your mind if you're upset, but if you can wait, the
feelings settle and clarity returns. She talks to them about triggers and reactions.
"Hold your index fingers in front of you, pointing at the ceiling. Then bring them
together, touching lengthwise, making lines pointing upwards." Side-by-side, these
fingers represent a trigger event and a hasty reaction. Jennifer wants the students
to separate their fingers now, putting the hands at shoulder-width, representing the
pause, the time between the trigger and the reaction. "That space is mindful space.
That's what we're practicing. So you can think about what happened."

For reading time on the carpet, there's mindfulness presented in a story form.
Visiting Feelings is a short illustrated story in which a child's feelings are represented
by little creatures and monsters; imagine some combination of Muppets and Gremlins
and *Where the Wild Things Are*. The idea is that your feelings come to visit you, but

they're not permanent, and even if some of them are less pleasant or more difficult to handle, "Your feelings are really OK." As the child in the story realizes, it's possible to figure out your feelings: "Treat your feelings like friends talking to you. They might even tell you why they are there."

Jennifer has only a few weeks to teach this class, so efforts to help the students process and internalize the lessons are essential. One strategy she uses is to have the students keep a record of their learning using a couple of easy tech tools. With iPads, students take pictures of their work, and at the end of the day they create a blog post about the lesson using Kidblog. Some of the students show me pictures of their prior work as well. One of the girls asks me to be in a picture with her and Jennifer, and soon, I'm smiling for many of the pictures reflecting today's Mindfulness Class.

Roni Habib, Social Studies
Henry Gunn High School, Palo Alto

Nearly a year later, I'm reminded of these observations when I see mindfulness practices in use at the high school level. Roni Habib has been part of the social studies department at Palo Alto's Henry Gunn High School for many years, teaching courses in psychology, economics, and history. The class I'm visiting is called positive psychology, which is a semester-long course offering students the opportunity to blend academic and personal growth by studying some basics of psychology and neurology, along with topics like interpersonal communication, emotional literacy, and cognitive distortions. The intended outcome is for students to better understand psychology, enabling them to use theory and practice to improve their mental and physical health, well-being, and personal satisfaction. Roni's training and experience in the field are quite academic, and although the subject might sound like some kind of group therapy, the course requires academic work and mastery of essential theory and concepts. The course has been popular at Gunn not only because it speaks to students' needs, but also because Roni is an effective ambassador for the centrality of social-emotional learning (SEL) in the future of education. In his TEDx talk about the topic, he cites research evidence that SEL improves academic performance and school climate, discusses various ways that major companies try to identify social-emotional competencies in job applicants, and points out that some companies include SEL in their professional learning opportunities for employees.

Today's school observation is the only one I didn't arrive for by car, choosing instead to bicycle from home. The last half mile of the trip turns into a walk instead of a ride, as my bike pedal falls off the crankshaft after nearly twenty years of service. It's not a disaster, but by the time enter Roni's classroom, I'm certainly in need of a little positive psychology.

The use of mindfulness techniques looks similar in high school and elementary school, with a blend of meditative exercises and journaling to help with focus, calmness, self-awareness, and gratitude. The high school students, not surprisingly, are better able to move in and out of these activities with minimal direction or correction from the teacher. The rest of the period finds students engaged in more academic and analytical work, though the concepts are still applied in a personally relevant way, whether through completing online surveys or writing about personal experience. As it's the start of a new week, Roni introduces a focal question for the week, regarding the power of beliefs, and in particular, what we believe about ourselves. Roni models the kind of reflection he's seeking from students and shares some of the ways that his self-concept is multifaceted, with dimensions and complexities that vary in different areas of his life. He shares how he might feel strong and confident in one area of his life but then hear the voice of his "inner critic" at other times.

It's clear that Roni has established a level of trust that is essential in a course like this. His personal openness has certainly been a key part of that effort, and I infer that the students trust each other as well. It's evident when they share personal information from their journals and when Roni tells them about an assignment that they show no hesitation about completing. In the coming days, they will write three-page letters to themselves in the voice of their internal critic, print copies of the letter, and bring it to class to read aloud to a partner, repeatedly. The idea is that the student actually takes control of that internal critic, owning its words, repeating them, making them familiar, even banal. That negative voice gradually loses its power, the words and the criticisms no longer impactful after several iterations. Drawing upon his own learning and his use of this exercise with prior classes, Roni makes a persuasive argument that briefly adopting a negative voice can provide a positive outcome, and the students seem ready to give it a try.

On a typical day during a typical school year, while Roni teaches at Gunn High School, I would be a few miles away at our district's other high school. We don't have a positive psychology class at Palo Alto High School, but there's one teacher whose class comes nearest to providing similar benefits, and my work on this project gave me a good excuse to spend an entire day with one of my favorite colleagues.

Letitia Burton, Living Skills, Read 180
Palo Alto High School, Palo Alto

Letitia Burton is a veteran teacher and at times has been essentially a one-woman department at Palo Alto High School. She has taught the Living Skills class here for about sixteen years, helping students navigate a curriculum that covers health, sexuality, identity, and social justice. The one-semester class is a graduation requirement in the district, ensuring there are always several sections of the course running. While Letitia isn't the only Living Skills teacher, she has been the only one teaching the class consistently for many years.

She has also been a leader on our staff throughout my time at the school, a voice for equity and inclusion, an advocate for all students and an instigator of hard, yet necessary, conversations. You could say Letitia specializes in hard conversations since so much of her time with students is spent addressing challenging topics they rarely discuss—but doing it in a structured manner with an adult to facilitate discussion and provide accurate information. I ask her at the end of the day what she enjoys about this work, and her answer is both predictable and surprising. Like most teachers, she's energized by her students' learning. The surprising part is that she's energized by her students' partial success at discussing sexual harassment, assault, and rape. To some adults, it might be maddening to listen to a conversation in which teenagers make some insensitive and ill-advised remarks about these topics. And yet when do most teens have an opportunity to have these conversations in a safe space, under the guidance of a skilled, professional educator? Letitia knows it's necessary to let teens speak without fear or condemnation if we want to know what they've heard, seen, and really think. The educational piece follows, often with students questioning and correcting each other respectfully; other times, Letitia provides the necessary facts or balancing perspective to help students be better informed and prepared to act responsibly in the future.

Succeeding with these essential yet difficult topics requires someone who knows how to relate to students without trying to be one of them. Letitia is calm, even-keeled, and consistently easygoing on the surface, yet her expectations are clear and high. She can gently correct a student's behavior without appearing to be threatening or shaming. I see a young man losing focus, veering off track when he should be working, beginning to disrupt class. Without any apparent haste, Letitia makes her way over to the student, and I can see him start to relax and quiet down just seeing her coming. A moment earlier, he seemed poised to jump up, but he leans back against the seat as Letitia places a gentle hand on his shoulder. I can't hear her exact words, but the tone is simultaneously gentle and firm. There's no doubt about her expectations, which are conveyed with love rather than anger.

In another class, students are working on social justice projects, finding creative ways to express a personal plan to incorporate their learning into actions that help the community. Their mutual interest in each other's work keeps the class focused and positive, and they welcome Letitia's interest as she moves among them. In one instance, some girls are talking about a choral performance they'll be part of during an upcoming school function; as Letitia walks nearby, they say, "Ms. Burton, you should sing with us on Friday!" It's a sign of how well they know her; Letitia sings professionally now and then in local jazz venues. And she knows her students' activities and plans, because she starts singing the chorus of the song her students will perform—Cyndi Lauper's "True Colors"—audibly but not disruptively. I may be biased, as both a friend of Letitia's and as someone who believes strongly in the power of music to unite people, but I find the moment touching, an affirmation of sorts that connects the class on multiple levels: academic and personal.

Harriet Garcia, English
Independence High School, San Jose

In addition to welcoming me to her classroom, Letitia helped me with this project by guiding me to visit Harriet Garcia, an English teacher at Independence High School in San Jose. You might recall I described the enthusiasm and passion I observed in the teaching of Martin Brandt (see Chapter 6), also at Independence. It was a pleasant surprise to discover that my plans to visit the school would bring me into contact with someone Letitia admires and respects as well. Letitia and Harriet know each other through a program called Camp Everytown, which invites diverse teens with leadership potential to spend a few days in an intensive educational experience focused on identity and diversity. Harriet's classes are less overtly focused on identity and social-emotional learning, but her teaching still seems informed by an awareness of those issues and their relevance to students' learning.

I observe three of Harriet's classes at Independence, all of them different in content yet similar in atmosphere. The pace of each class feels relaxed, and yet, by the end of the period, students have proceeded through a variety of reading, writing, and speaking opportunities. As Harriet moves among student groups or leads full class discussions, I can tell that students trust her from the way they accept her pushback on their thinking. Every student answer, comment, or assertion is met with a follow-up question or counterargument. With her seniors, working through a nonfiction unit of study focused on education, Harriet manages to acknowledge and respect the students' observations about the inequities that negatively affect them and their school and, then a moment later, push them to consider whether circumstances trump individual determination to succeed. Comparing schools with better or inferior funding, she questions them: "Why should it make a difference? They have books, you have books. They have desks, you have desks. They have brains, you have brains." She's not dismissing their prior observations, but rather, expecting them to sharpen their arguments and analysis.

On questions of systemic educational inequity and the individual's response, Harriet can speak to her students from shared experience, since she grew up in San Jose herself, attended San Jose State University, and taught her entire career in the city. I'm not certain that Harriet's students know all of that, but it wouldn't surprise me. Throughout the morning, I can see that Harriet has built relationships with her students: They can maintain their focus on small-group work and still make a quick joke with Harriet when she checks in with them. When the conversation shifts momentarily to the topic of elementary school education, students make connections to Harriet's children. The overall effect of these small interactions is that Harriet's classes are not only academically robust, but they also have a familial atmosphere. It's that kind of awareness of each other, that kind of caring, that makes it possible for Harriet to lean on her students to think harder, work harder, and trust in the process.

Mangla Oza, Fifth Grade
Duveneck Elementary School, Palo Alto

In a classroom like Harriet's, we can see the importance of a concept called *identity safety*. The term means that students of all skills, interests, and backgrounds are not only welcomed and accepted, but valued because of who they are and what they bring to the group. The idea of identity safety is detailed in the book *Identity Safe Classrooms: Places to Belong and Learn* by Becki Cohn Vargas and Dorothy Steele. Cohn Vargas is a former administrator in my district, so I was able to seek her input regarding other teachers I should observe. She directed me to a fifth-grade classroom at Duveneck Elementary School, in Palo Alto, where teacher Mangla Oza invests considerable time and effort in the cultivation of identity safety among her students. Her methods not only create a peaceful and positive atmosphere, but also help students develop metacognitive awareness of themselves as learners and empathy for others as well.

Every day starts with a morning meeting that lasts about twenty minutes. On the day of my visit, Mangla shares a schedule with her students, who are disappointed when she tells them today will be the last day to build "scribble-bots," an engineering and design challenge involving small motors, plastic cups, magic markers, and lots of tape. Attaching the markers to the upside-down cup in a tripod-type of arrangement, and then attaching the small motor, students can make the scribble-bot move across a sheet of paper, leaving an interesting ink pattern. Shifting the location or angles will produce different patterns, but some combinations will not produce any movement at all. Mangla is particularly interested in the fact that no one ended up with the robot they planned on. She calls attention to the tendency of designs to evolve with time and experimentation, both for the experienced "bot" engineer and the novice. This kind of identity-safe framing of the work puts the focus on the process, rather than labeling any people or work as successes or failures.

The morning meeting proceeds with a theme for the day: respect. Mangla asks a series of questions about the meaning of respect, what it looks like in the classroom and at home, and why it's important. Students go around the circle to share something about their day or life, add a compliment to classmates, and then add something about respect. After each student shares, they all say, "Thank you." They clearly know the routine and demonstrate great patience. Investing this time each day in reflection, conversation, and community building helps make each student feel known and appreciated. At different times of year, such routines provide time and space to incorporate family, life cycle events, and holidays and traditions from various faiths and nationalities without favoring any one in particular.

When the regular academic work of the day commences, Mangla demonstrates some problem-solving involving the calculation of area. In one problem, she writes the wrong percentage in a particular space, and students point out the error. Mangla says, "Yes, I make mistakes sometimes. Is that OK to make mistakes?" Yes, the students reply. "Why?" Because we can learn from them. Later in the exercise, a student makes a similar mistake and Mangla refers back to her own mistake: "It happens to all of us."

The safe atmosphere ensures that learning continues and respect is maintained even when students disagree with each other. I observe small-group conversations in which students share reactions to their reading and ideas in their personal journals; everyone talks, and I hear students asking each other follow-up questions and even expressing respectful disagreement. I see smiles throughout. When it comes to full-class discussions, Mangla doesn't talk about right or wrong answers to questions but instead asks follow-up questions constantly: How do you know? What is the evidence? What does that connect to? What do other people think? The conversation about a book leads to issues of racism and stereotypes. These fifth graders define racism and manage to include not only ideas of prejudice, bias, and judgment, but also the idea that racism is learned. It's a sophisticated and mature conversation, one that I recognize is the byproduct of identity-safe teaching occurring consistently over a long period.

Identity safety goes beyond awareness of ethnic, racial, or cultural identity; gender and sexuality; nontraditional families; and neurodiversity. It's a way of thinking and teaching that not only values the sense of identity that students bring to the classroom, but also helps them build a sense of identity that includes respect, kindness, and curiosity, while preventing students from allowing their deficits to define them. I'm observing Mangla helping her students as they move on to the much-anticipated scribble-bot activity. While many students' creations are up and running quite independently, Mangla pays close attention to the kids whose bots are barely moving, and she talks about failure as part of the design and experimentation process. She speaks of perseverance and what students learn while trying.

For one girl, I hope the talk is having some impact because there seems to be minimal effect in each of her adjustments to the markers, motor, and plastic cup. Around the room there have been many laughs and cheers in the past half hour, and some students are beginning to clean up their materials as time is running out.

Then, *eureka!* It's working! The final scribble bot begins to loop and spiral around on a large piece of paper, creating a colorful pattern and producing huge smiles from Mangla and her student, whose classmates swarm to her table to celebrate. Though they've seen many others today, they summon enthusiasm and tell the girl, *"Oooh! That's a cool pattern!"* Mangla seems the most delighted of all: "See? I told you if you persevere, you'll succeed!" Later on, Mangla confides in me with some relief: "I'm so glad that worked. I *really* wanted her to have that experience."

This moment could become the kind that a student looks back on years later, recalling how it felt to try, fail, try again, fail again, and finally succeed. She might remember what it meant to her to have a teacher who stood by confidently and patiently, without taking over the process, without pressure, ready to celebrate the effort whether the experiment worked or not, and then thrilling at eventual success.

Then again, looking back at my own experiences as a student, and having spoken to many former students about their memories of my class, I know that learning and memory are unpredictable. It's almost inexplicable why I remember some particular class period or assignment, or a single comment from a teacher, and forget most of the others. We pour so much time and effort into our teaching, so much intention, yet we never know what will stick or whether students will receive the lessons we hope to impart. Will they remember at all, and if they seem to recall, will they remember correctly? Memory plays tricks on us: I once had a former student describe how inspiring I was teaching a lesson I'd never taught, focused on a novel I hadn't used. There have been times I was sure students connected with my curriculum on some profound level, only to have the students' later words and actions suggest otherwise.

From the classroom and school perspective, we know that when students connect with their curriculum, their teachers, and their schools, that provides a foundation that can help them reach their full academic potential. There's a justifiable concern, however, if the pursuit of connectivity and engagement becomes an end in itself; instead, we address the whole child as a means of optimizing learning and the learning environment, in the pursuit of more specific and observable learning and skill acquisition.

Facing History and Ourselves

Fostering learning experiences that help students feel directly connected to content while also developing robust academic skills is the ultimate goal in teaching. My ability to achieve that goal took a significant leap forward in 1999 when I found out about Facing History and Ourselves (FHAO). With its origins on the East Coast, focusing on Holocaust education, FHAO is now an international organization providing curricular resources and professional development to help teachers address difficult historical and current events that relate to identity and membership in society. With regards to the Holocaust, FHAO founder Margot Stern Strom realized that genuine learning, the kind that would positively affect students' participation in their own democratic society, required more than simply showing students horrific pictures of concentration camps and preaching "Never again!" From 1976 to the present, FHAO has gradually expanded its focus, with abundant resources and training on a variety of historical case studies, and topics related to race and religion, immigration and discrimination, justice and human rights. The organization has also expanded its geographic reach by opening new regional offices and using web-based platforms to support teachers regardless of location. It has now served many thousands of teachers and, in turn, helped millions of students on multiple continents. It has been the most valuable and sustained professional affiliation of my teaching career and has enriched my own learning immeasurably.

FHAO's success comes from having figured out how to do what their name suggests, though more accurately, the usual approach is to "face" ourselves, and then history. Starting with the learner involves helping students develop an age-appropriate understanding of the concept of identity. From there, we can analyze the dynamics of group relationships, which are shaped by the ways that we identify with some people but not others. Historical and social events and phenomena become more accessible when understood as the consequences of individual choices often grounded in individual and group identification.

After the Rwandan genocide, the country's schools suspended the teaching of Rwandan history for years. How do you teach that history while you have the perpetrators and survivors of genocide in school together, among the students and the adults? When it was time to develop a curriculum and methodology that would allow Rwanda to move forward, their educational leaders turned to two US-based organizations, including FHAO. I can't imagine a stronger endorsement of what the organization does, or a greater responsibility to bear as educators.

The FHAO regional director for the San Francisco Bay Area from its opening until 2015 was Jack Weinstein, a former history teacher and parent of one of my students at the time we first met. In those sixteen years, I learned from Jack and his colleagues through workshops and events that lasted from a couple hours to a full week. He visited my classroom many times over the years, mostly as a guest teacher, and also during planning time to help me design units and curriculum. However, I had never seen Jack at work in another school until I visited Santa Clara County's EDGE program.

Stephanie Boulianne, English
Santa Clara County EDGE Program, San Jose

It was a unique visit, not only because Jack Weinstein was part of it, but also because it was the only school I visited where I found a class size in single digits. EDGE stands for Encouraging Diversity, Growth and Education, and students in the program attend by court order only, as a condition of parole. When I first arrived at EDGE, I found teacher Stephanie Boulianne working with two high-school-age students; a later class had eight students, and a number of other adults around as well (counselors, social workers, and parole officers come and go throughout the morning).

EDGE might sound like a place most teachers wouldn't want to work, but Stephanie Boulianne was drawn to this placement. She's an experienced and dedicated educator whose background includes working at traditional comprehensive schools where she found less sense of purpose in her work. I understand the appeal. In schools like mine, most students have ample support at home and a clear path they intend to follow through high school, to higher education, and then a career that makes some use of their formal education. In a setting like EDGE, the students often lack a clear vision of a viable future, or if they have that vision, they're also facing considerable obstacles. At the same time, many of them have already overcome significant challenges, and they are often more appreciative of those who can help them make positive changes in their lives.

As I arrive in Stephanie's English class, a young man is talking about visiting his mom at work. She's a mortician, and he has become comfortable in that setting, despite how grim it might seem to outsiders. One of the adults in the room talks to the student about what it takes to do that job well—how professional and empathetic you must be and how you must be able to deal with the intensity of other people's sadness without letting it weaken you.

The transition from this conversation to class time is ambiguous, as there are only two students present. Stephanie is never alone in the classroom with her students, so my presence means the adults outnumber the students at the moment. Otherwise, the room looks and feels like a regular high school classroom. I'm offered the chance to introduce myself and explain my work. Stephanie's two students are interested and ask a few questions about what I've seen and learned along the way. I ask about EDGE, and they say they like the school, their classes, and the support they receive from caring teachers and probation counselors.

As the lesson begins in earnest, Stephanie's manner is gentle, friendly, energetic, and sincere. The morning's lesson concerns a poem titled "The Hangman," by Maurice Ogden. The poem is an allegory about the dangers of bystander behavior; people in a village fail to challenge a hangman as long as the victim is always someone "different." Stephanie's students recently had a visit from a Holocaust survivor, arranged through FHAO.

The poem involves some challenging vocabulary, and Stephanie discusses the poem while working in some key academic vocabulary as well: irony, stanza, upstander, bystander, metaphor, simile, personification, and theme. The terms are the same ones that would come up in almost any English class. When the language and imagery of the poem steer them toward the concept of justice (and the role of judges), Stephanie's students are open to discussing their experiences of being locked up in the past, being on the receiving end of judgment. They disagree about whether or not judges and courts are all about fairness and justice (and in today's climate of concern about police misconduct, their ambivalence about the justice system is more than understandable). There's an interesting conversation about the word "dread" and an attempt to explain why people often feel afraid or nervous in the presence of authority, even when they haven't done anything wrong. This conversation is entirely relevant to the students' personal lives, not limited to an academic discussion.

As if on cue, a probation officer stops by the class to give them a heads-up about police sweeps in the neighborhood and advises them to avoid potential trouble. Students in EDGE generally have court orders to stay away from gangs, but there's so much gang activity around their neighborhoods that it can be difficult even to go outside. One student notes that the nearest place he'd be able to go for a walk and buy a soft drink is a liquor store where gang members hang out. He concludes,

"I'm going to stay home. I want you to see me on Monday." The conversation starts to veer off track, and there are hints of some more disturbing stories that could be told, but Stephanie says, "not now," and that's the end of it.

Students have been arriving now and then during the morning, and by the conclusion of a mid-morning break, there are eight students in the room (one girl), with an age range of approximately fifteen to seventeen. Jack Weinstein, from FHAO, has also arrived. He's been here before and clearly knows the kids, calling them by name. As prologue to his lesson, he tells a story. He was driving late at night on a remote road, with his niece asleep in the car, when he saw a large man stranded on the side of the road dealing with a flat tire. There was no cell phone coverage in the area, so the man might be stranded for a while if Jack didn't help him somehow. Discussion of what to do in this situation involves some analysis of risk factors and safety considerations, and raises issues of stereotypes and assumptions relating to race, gender, age, and other traits. Jack and the students try out some hypothetical changes in the variables: What if the person on the side of the road seems more threatening? What if the driver is the one who seems more threatening on the surface and the person on the side of the road feels more vulnerable? Should you help? How should you help? Students eagerly respond to each question and variable, speculating about what might happen.

Jack's point is that social situations like this, with moral dimensions complicated by cultural assumptions and biases, are not clear-cut. Our ability to think about our lives in a complicated way, using moral concepts and a moral vocabulary, increases our chances of making good decisions. He moves from this discussion to a short film, and then another discussion, all developing the same themes. Overall, it's a successful lesson and a good day. I find out later that I lucked out with my visit. Some days are smooth and peaceful, but there had been a fight in the classroom the day before.

Jack heads out, and I take a moment to visit with him before he leaves. His work with county programs like EDGE has provided him with some valuable insights. "This kind of program needs teachers who *want* to be here and have exceptional social-emotional understanding. Otherwise, you have instability and lots of turnover. Stephanie is one of the best."

As students have lunch, Stephanie and I have a chance to talk. I relate Jack's comments, and she agrees that it's important to want to do this work, while acknowledging it's difficult to want to do the work all the time. There are frustrations for students and teachers, and they all need to work through those together. She says the key to success is in relationships: "How do you get to the point where they'll listen to you when you're upset with them?"

At EDGE, it helps that the students have been ordered here by the courts as part of their probation; when they know there are consequences, they do better, Stephanie says.

> *In other programs, they'll just say fuck you and walk out. Here, we have a chance to crack through and deal with things. You're getting them to talk about things they may not be ready to address.* Why are you the way you are? Why do you do the things you do? *If you [as a teacher] care, you can say things more directly. And you have to care. This isn't about school, none of this is about school. And if you heard their stories, you'd be like,* How do you get out of bed to come to school? *Any adult would be broken down. [The students] have post-trauma issues, ongoing trauma . . . they might be living in a garage, with no personal space.*

Stephanie imagines her students in a regular school setting, being assessed by standardized tests. "We sit there and tell them *This test is really important.* Really? *Just focus, do your best.*" It's sad, because we both know that the trauma and the effects of poverty are undercutting so many students in our mainstream comprehensive schools, and they are facing a system that can seem uninterested in more than the scores.

Students come back into the classroom as Stephanie and I are chatting, and one starts to interrupt. Stephanie points that out and he apologizes, sweetening the apology by offering her a Klondike bar from his lunch, and all is forgiven.

Another boy has a Klondike bar he seems intent on taking home for later, and it becomes a serious conversation with Stephanie about whether it will melt and how to get it home without a mess. For a split second it strikes me as humorous, then I wonder how important it might be for him to share this treat with someone at home—how much food there might be at home—and then it's not funny at all. The swirling contradictions of childhood and adulthood, of ice cream and probation, are rather poignant in this otherwise innocuous conversation.

The issues are complicated at dismissal time at the end of the day. The students are not all dismissed at the same time, and they don't all receive their cell phones at the same time. One student becomes frustrated and agitated, and the tension level escalates quickly. With some calming guidance from Stephanie and one of the counselors in the room, the young man calms down a bit and can explain his situation: He's in a hurry to help his brother repair the brake lights on his car because driving with broken tail lights could lead to being pulled over by the police. Stephanie can't let him leave because he has a court-ordered support program right after school. There's no option here, but Stephanie can at least help him put words to his problems and show him that she understands. "What can I do to help you *right now?* You're disappointed? You had plans?" She acknowledges the importance of his commitments outside of EDGE, then brings him back to the priority of compliance with court orders.

When all the students are gone for the day, I have many questions for Stephanie, wanting to understand better how she succeeds here. She explains:

You learn by doing. You think to yourself, How do I get the *response I need? If you're dealing with tough kids and you want to win, you'll lose. If you want to be right and make the kid wrong, you might have some short-term success, but lose in the long run. Kids don't want to be bad. They don't want to misbehave. It's usually a visceral reaction. No book will help you handle every situation. Some kids need it straight:* You will do this now, or else. *Other kids need you to back down. Even when they try to piss you off, even if they say they don't like you, and they don't want you to like them, they want you to like them.*

Again, the idea of relationships is the key, and dealing with young adults on probation bears some similarity to dealing with any children in any school.

Stephanie also tries to help students learn about themselves and how to improve relationships with other people. "A lot of my kids look a little scary. When people see them and react, it's usually out of fear. It helps my students to understand what impression they make and recognize that they *have* done things that *should* make people afraid of them," she says. "And yet they need to understand why it bothers them that people are afraid of them. *So, what can you do? What is your responsibility for changing the dynamic in these situations?*"

Maybe it sounds more like therapy than teaching. That doesn't bother Stephanie. "There are a lot of teachers who don't want to be the life-coach, the ally. They signed on to be instructors." In settings like EDGE, that's not enough; Stephanie accepts the importance and recognizes the value of being more attuned to her students' full range of needs. Sometimes, even the little things that are easy to do will make a difference. As we wrap up our lengthy conversation after school on a Friday afternoon, Stephanie adds one more important note about her students. "They don't get smiled at a lot, you know? *Is someone happy to see you?* It makes a difference. I try to show them *I'm glad you're here.*"

What if the key to a person's ultimate success in life has more to do with social-emotional learning than with academics? Knowledge and skills are certainly essential; in the long run, however, our ability to put knowledge and skills to effective use in a sustained, satisfying, and productive career might depend on our self-knowledge, self-regulation, and empathy. While most teachers understand the need to support students as people and not merely as learners of discrete skills and knowledge, some teachers take a more proactive approach, putting issues of identity and social-emotional learning into a central position in their teaching.

CHAPTER 13

Connectivity and Networking:

Expanding Horizons for Teachers and Classrooms

Genein Letford is an award-winning music teacher at NEW Academy in Canoga Park. She's also an effective advocate for arts education, financial literacy, and higher education affordability. We met through Twitter.

I ALWAYS FIND IT INTERESTING TO TRACE ORIGINS, CONNECTIONS, and patterns in learning and relationships, trying to understand how I reached a certain point in my own education and life experience. In earlier chapters, I observed how much of who I am as a teacher and what I do in education has its roots in the Stanford Teacher Education Program (see Chapter 5) and in National Board Certification (see Chapter 7). But there are other important threads that run through this project. One that might be surprising for some readers (and completely obvious to others) is Twitter. By now, tweets have become rather ubiquitous in our culture, with politicians, athletes, journalists, and all sorts of celebrities using this "microblogging" format to share links and short messages with a (potentially) broad audience. Twitter has played a notable role in social movements abroad and domestically, with activists using tweets to organize people, coordinate actions, and disseminate information. For teachers using Twitter, the ability to find and follow fellow educators with similar interests has greatly expanded our world.

I should qualify that statement by noting that Twitter users must have some intention and strategy to get that value. If used primarily to share funny videos, celebrate pumpkin-spiced lattés, or comment on Super Bowl commercials, Twitter has no advantage over other social media, and relatively little value. My use of Twitter, like that of many other teachers, is almost entirely focused on education. I follow thousands of people with education-related careers—teachers, administrators, union leaders, writers, trainers, researchers, consultants, policy makers, activists—and most of my Twitter followers come from those same groups. I also follow publications and organizations that work in education, and the solid majority of my tweets, retweets (sharing), and interactions on Twitter are education-related. As a result of being active on Twitter, I've been able to share teaching information and perspectives with people around the world and have made a number of important personal connections "in real life."

Genein Letford, Music
NEW Academy, Canoga Park

I wish I'd had the time and opportunity to visit more arts classes and teachers during my travels. Rika Hirata (see Chapter 9) was the only art teacher, and Genein Letford the only music teacher. Rika is a friend and colleague from our work together in the California Teachers Association Institute for Teaching, while I found Genein through Twitter. Her engagement online is consistently positive and productive, and as I began planning this book, she was one of the first teachers I contacted from my personal/professional learning network (PLN).

Genein has been honored and recognized for her work as a music educator, and that would be reason enough to sing her praises. However, she also works as a teacher educator at California State University at Northridge and in various ways to help teachers find grants and funding for innovative programs. She also promotes financial literacy and debt avoidance for post-secondary students, seeing it as part of her extended commitment to former students and their peers.

On the day I visit, Genein first shows me around the campus; she seems like a combination tour guide and spokesperson. NEW Academy is a charter school run by a nonprofit organization called New Economics for Women. NEW operates an affordable housing complex next door to the school, and about 40 percent of the students live there. NEW focuses on economic empowerment for women, especially immigrants. In addition to the school, NEW supports families with adult classes in language and finance and runs a community center. Genein knows the overall program well because she has helped design and update the school's website and contributed photos and videos for the site.

Genein takes pride in the school's facilities and programs and wants me to see the school's library as part of my tour, though it's empty at the moment. I can see many creative touches in the library's decor—painted characters on the walls, posters and pictures, color all around—and as Genein tells me about the librarian's various outreach efforts and engagement strategies, it becomes clear that I need to return later. Meeting Kelly Spector turns out to be an unexpected bonus of my visit. Like most librarians I know, she's a connector and innovator, looking to support student learning in ways that not only make books exciting, but also to promote curiosity and a sense of connection within and beyond the school. She schedules regular author visits, via Skype and in person. Kelly and Genein have also collaborated in projects that integrate literature, music, and other arts.

In her classroom, Genein makes music fun and challenging at the same time. The fun comes from plenty of hands-on activities, sound, and movement, with the complexity changing a bit depending on the grade level of the class. The challenge includes exposing students to complexities in music and approaching music literacy as a pathway to reading literacy and linguistic fluency. So, in addition to listening to and playing music, Genein's students read or hear short stories and poems with musical themes. When discussing families of musical instruments, like strings and brass, the students encounter the word "woodwind." Genein asks, "What kind of word is that? Listen to it: wood, wind. Woodwind." Ah, a compound word! In addition to helping students develop a vocabulary to talk and think about words, Genein expertly incorporates synonyms as she speaks, introducing advanced vocabulary in a natural way. She wants students to sort the instruments in the classroom and asks, "What's another word for 'sort'? 'Arrange,' right? When we arrange the instruments, we're going to classify them. Say that with me: 'classify.'" And later, when they describe one of the percussion instruments, she asks, "What's the name for that shape? Mmm, not a circle . . . it's a . . . cylinder."

The discussion of instruments is balanced with time for play, whether it's playing the instruments themselves and practicing various rhythms or playing through singing and dancing. I also have a chance to see Genein as a conductor of a small student band. They come in at lunchtime to practice, and as you can see in the photograph at the start of this chapter, she rewards their dedication by conducting with warmth and smiles, even as she pushes for improvements in their performance.

Kelly Eveleth, Fifth Grade
Design39Campus, Poway

One of the unique experiences I had in this project was visiting a new school. Poway Unified School District opened its Design39Campus (D39) in fall 2014, occupying a new campus and offering an innovative academic program. After a transitional opening, the plan is for D39 to serve students from transitional kindergarten through eighth grade. The name of the school reflects its focus on design thinking and the fact that it's the thirty-ninth school in the district. Design thinking is a growing trend in schools. The Institute of Design (d.school at Stanford University) and the international design and consulting company IDEO have been encouraging schools and educators to help students create their own learning opportunities rather than simply study facts and practice skills in a predictable, linear, teacher-directed way. Design thinking emphasizes real-world applicability and a deep, empathetic understanding of others beyond our organizations. A process of brainstorming, modeling, trial and error, and gradual improvement allows designers, or students, to generate creative solutions to problems and novel products or experiences.

I found out about D39 through Twitter, months before the school opened. It's not surprising that educators interested in this kind of school would find and share relevant information via Twitter. I likely could have arranged a visit simply through email or a phone call: Plenty of people were interested in visiting D39 during its first year, and it garnered additional attention because author and blogger Grant Lichtman (author of the book *#EdJourney: A Roadmap to the Future of Education*) was involved in the school's inception and design. Instead of cold-calling the school, however, I sought a facilitated introduction through Candy Smiley, the president of the Poway Federation of Teachers, whom I know through her leadership in the CalTURN (see Chapter 9).

I couldn't have asked for a more perfect day to visit D39, which shows quite well on a sunny and breezy springtime morning. The buildings are shiny and new, metal and glass, with generous splashes of blues, greens, oranges, and browns that complement the school's foothills setting north of San Diego. Checking in as a visitor is a quiet and professional procedure, not unlike arriving at a corporate campus. I have my picture taken through a webcam as my time of arrival and destination are recorded, and my personalized name badge emerges from a printer. Fifth-grade teacher Kelly Eveleth meets me at the front office and walks me to her classroom.

I can tell at a glance that this building was designed for a different kind of learning. Instead of seeing a hallway with classrooms up and down both sides, I note that the interior corridor connects classrooms, open learning spaces, small conference rooms, and even a small library of books that students can borrow on an honor system. The classrooms are unique as well. There's much less emphasis on decorations and displays. The furniture includes rolling desks with whiteboard surfaces, allowing students at a table together to brainstorm and collaborate, solve problems, create diagrams, whatever they need. If they want to share their work with classmates, the tabletop can be flipped to a vertical position for display purposes—a rolling white board, if you will. Place the board between groups, and you have makeshift dividers that allow groups to focus on their own work while blocking distractions.

When they aren't in the classroom, D39 students enjoy a flexible, relaxed, and trusting atmosphere. Recess arrives at midmorning, not according to a schedule, but rather by Kelly's checking in with her students to see if they want to take a break in ten minutes. If they had been losing focus or anxious to get to get out, they could have started recess earlier. They won't be watching the clock waiting for recess to come, because there's not only no set time for recess, but no clock on the wall. Recess ends when the teachers outside with their classes all look at each other and agree it's time to go in. No whistles, no bells. They just start calling kids in, and those out of earshot see what's happening. During a free-reading time, students find a comfortable space somewhere in the building, not just in the classroom. There's an open area called the loft that's quite popular. Other students find a spot in the amphitheater-style benches in a tall open space at the end of the building, while some prefer the cozy, nest-like holes built into the adjacent walls, resembling a tree-hollow with a book-reading owl inside.

Kids will be kids, of course. It's not as if Kelly's students remain perfectly on task at all times. But then again, students sitting in perfect rows all day long never stay perfectly on task either. Compared to the rules-and-authority orientation we associate with traditional schooling, the approach at D39 seems healthier and more likely to foster self-regulation in students.

The idea of trust extends beyond staying on task and managing transitions without bells; there's also an inherent acceptance of moderate risks. Students who aren't monitored every minute could slip on the stairs, drop a laptop computer, cut themselves with scissors. I first recognize that aspect of the school culture when asking permission to do something daring. As Kelly's students are working in small groups to prepare for an informational writing assignment, I ask her if I might stand on some chairs to achieve a better angle for photography; I don't want to be a bad role model. Her answer catches me by surprise for a moment, as she says, "Sure! Kids do it all the time."

Later in the day, I see students in a mask-making activity using a small electric drill independently, boring holes into a papier-mâché mask. Students down the hall in an electronics and robotics lab are experimenting with the equipment, trying out various configurations of devices connected through different circuits and hooked up to a laptop computer. In front of the school, students are maintaining the school's edible garden, with rows and planter boxes sprouting a variety of fruits and vegetables. These activity times are called "deep dives"—student-selected, multigrade activities allowing students to explore their interests for a few hours per week, twelve weeks at a time. In each setting at D39, there's some equipment that could be misused or damaged, some chance of bump, bruise, cut or scrape; there's also a sense that the value of student exploration and initiative outweighs the minimal risks incurred from not overplanning and approving every step in children's inquiry. Not every deep dive is high risk, however; there are decidedly lower-risk options, like chess and debate.

Kelly is part of the team that designed the school, along with Brett Fitzpatrick, the teacher in the electronics and robotics deep-dive class. The principal and a team of teachers had one year to work together on the academic plan, school policies, campus design, building and classroom architecture and furnishings, and technology plans—everything that goes into a school. They were also interested in learning from other types of organizations, to see what might be applicable to their program design and their students' needs. Kelly explained the rationale and value of this approach:

> *There is a big wide world out there that we are preparing students for, with jobs in fields and places that I know little about. This makes my connections and networks with people outside of education so much more important. Some of my favorite professional development days have involved leaving the school site and visiting companies and businesses in the local area. Conversations with HR departments, design teams, and employees help me keep my eye on the future for my students. It helps validate the work we do with our kids every day on our campus.*

It's also worth noting that D39 is a district school. Too many casual observers associate innovation with private schools and charter schools. D39 offers evidence that districts can innovate, and unions are not obstacles to change. (To the extent that unions are obstacles to some changes, I think they're usually raising important questions about equity and sustainability that some "innovators" would prefer not to address in their zeal to "disrupt" the field of education.) The teachers and students at D39 have all come from other schools in Poway, through selection processes that had some accompanying conflicts and disagreements within the district. I don't know the situation well enough to weigh in or make predictions about the future. I do hope that D39 will be around for a long time, providing a useful model for school design and student agency in education.

New Technology High School, Napa

While D39 was exciting in its newness, I also visited a more established and similarly unique model for innovative, noncharter schools. New Technology High

School in Napa opened in 1996 and is the flagship school in what has become the New Technology Network, now comprising nearly 200 schools around the nation, including elementary and secondary schools, public, charter, and independent schools. New Tech High is part of the Napa Valley Unified School District and open to all students in the district.

My visit to the school has come about through informal networking and social media. Riley Johnson is the school's principal (assistant principal when I first encountered him), and we connected via Twitter before meeting in person at Edcamp San Francisco Bay Area. "Edcamp" is a professional learning and networking event that runs as an "unconference," meaning that when educators come together to talk and learn, there's no predetermined agenda. Participants generate topics on arrival, throw together a schedule, and spend the day moving in and out of conversations that reflect the needs and interests of the people who attend. There's an Edcamp Foundation that offers guidance and support to those who seek it, but otherwise, each of hundreds of Edcamps around the world operates independently with volunteer organizers. Edcamp participants often open their experience to others who can't be there by using shared files, Twitter, and sometimes even live-streaming video. Conversations that begin face-to-face with everyone in the same room continue afterward, as each participant's PLN expands.

I already knew about New Tech High, so upon meeting Riley, I was eager to seize the opportunity to arrange a visit. Riley crafted a schedule for my day that put me in a variety of subjects with nearly every grade level at the school. Like D39, New Tech's facility is more modern and professional than is typical for a school campus. High ceilings, open spaces, and lots of glass are typical not only in the common area outside of the classrooms, but also the classrooms themselves. I'm a bit taken aback when I enter the classroom for an American studies course (combining American literature and US history), and find that it feels only half full, although there are about fifty to sixty students in the room. It's a huge room, furnished more like an office than a school: Students sit in rolling chairs that are cushioned and adjustable for comfort and ergonomics, and their tables and desks can roll as well, facilitating different set-ups of the room for different purposes. Even though its setup is professional in style, the room feels homey as well, with couches in a corner alcove overlooking a grass lawn. There's also a collection of guitars in the front of the room and a piano in the back. Over the years, I've sometimes kept a guitar in my classroom, picking it up now and then, or letting students play it outside of class time. It's a great conversation starter and a way to make the room more inviting, but there are so many instruments here that I wonder if they've been put to some academic use as well.

When I arrive, students are wrapping up a live character tableau, using key quotes from *The Great Gatsby* to create a visual and aural representation of Gatsby's evolution as a character. This large class has two teachers: Andre Baldauf, a history teacher, and Nancy Hale, an English teacher. However, in the time that I observe the class, I wouldn't be able to distinguish their roles or expertise as both interact with the students, offering feedback and guidance.

The activity I see on arrival is a mere warm-up. The main activity for the period involves students creating newsreel-style films that blend original and archival material. The original material involves staging and filming scenes based on plot and characters in *The Great Gatsby,* imagining the surviving characters five years later. Students have a variety of props and costumes to help suggest an opulent, 1920's setting. The archival footage consists of newsreels, now online, capturing the reality of that era. Some groups opt for newsreels that convey the "Roaring Twenties" mood, while others select contrasting stories of struggling immigrants and child laborers. The tech component in New Tech, for this lesson, involves videography and video editing, and Andre reminds students that there's a green screen available for their use, suggesting to me that they already know how to use it, though no one does for this particular task. They haven't all mastered the use of the video-editing software, but they help each other troubleshoot; it's an organic way to learn to use a tool purposefully, rather than isolating it in a separate video or computer class.

Again, as I observed at D39, technology is present and significant at New Tech, but the schools are defined by their student-driven approach, breaking down subject-area divisions and allowing students to be more active and creative with their work. Technology is also used to organize and streamline tasks that might otherwise involve volumes of paper. Nancy wraps up the class by reminding students that they need to complete a digital "exit ticket" before leaving. The exit ticket is a common teaching technique allowing teachers to check in with students regarding the day's work. Students seem to know the routine and expectations, and Nancy and Andre will end up with a paperless, searchable record of what students accomplished today or what they need help with next time.

Elsewhere at New Tech, I observe a lively debate activity for seniors in a political studies course. One pair of groups debates making body cameras mandatory for police officers. Another debate addresses the possible repeal of the Affordable Care Act. Groups participating in today's debates are attired in suits and dresses and will present not only to their peers, but also to an audience of invited guests who will provide feedback about the debates. The inclusion of adults from the community provides an authentic audience for the students and is also a good way for the school to showcase student learning. As Riley Johnson puts it, "At New Tech High, we focus on creating authentic connections for our students. Whether it be with peers, the staff, or the community, we don't want to simulate the real-world, we want to live in it and change it."

The blending of English and history classes is not so unusual, but New Tech ninth graders have a unique course that integrates health, physical education, and biology into a biofitness class. Again, the large class size is mitigated by the team-teaching approach, this time with a husband-and-wife team, Tom and Christie Wolf. Their freshmen are about to start a new unit of study and will work with a new group within the class. Today's lesson focuses on the idea of community and how to ensure that a community adopts and abides by positive norms. Students watch a short video, engage in some journal writing, then enter into a full class discussion, which is certainly a challenge with a group this size. Tom and Christie not only navigate that challenge, but also manage to make the class a safe space to express dissenting views. One student questions the premise of the video, claiming that it's overly optimistic regarding people's natural tendencies. Tom pushes back gently, asking who determines what's normal for any given group. I don't know if the student is satisfied with Tom's answer, but if I were participating, I'd offer that the experience this class is having right now is good evidence that norms are situational and contextual. While technology is at the core of the school's name, New Technology High School's most important norms have more to do with student voice, inquiry, creativity, purpose, and engagement.

Union Middle School, San Jose

A couple hours south of Napa, Union Middle School in San Jose is another campus I visited as a result of connecting with a principal at an Edcamp. Twitter played less of a role in this visit, as Todd Feinberg was once my assistant principal at Palo Alto High School. Todd is an energetic leader with a clear vision of how to improve learning experiences for students, making school engaging, relevant, and more effective. He sums it up this way: "As educators, we need to connect with our students through their lens and on their terms. Building the teacher-student relationship is paramount in ensuring student success." His enthusiasm for the school and the work teachers do in the classrooms comes across in conversation and in the way he supported my visit to his campus.

Todd was glad to extend an invitation when I told him about my project, though we left the date open for quite a while. When we finally settled on a date, it was only two days ahead; yet by the time I arrived at Union, Todd had worked out a schedule that would allow me to see almost every subject and grade level and had seemingly alerted every teacher on campus that I'd be visiting. It's a great feeling, not only as a sort of personal validation, but also as a reflection on the school. Who wouldn't want to spend a day among people who are so welcoming and eager to share their work?

In fact, the moment I enter Susan Peers sixth-grade English language arts classroom, I see "Welcome, David Cohen!" written on the board. Susan also offers me a scone, just because, and a school pen, telling me, "Hope it works!" Aside from the personal touch, Susan provides a great starting point for my visit because she so thoroughly embodies the kind of connected practice that I'm interested in here. Susan is quite active in CUE (Computer Using Educators), received training from Apple and Google, and also trains other teachers in various technological approaches and solutions. You don't have to meet her in person to benefit from her teaching wisdom, as Susan uses social media to share resources and student work, along with information about new and potentially useful hardware and software.

Since I'm here to see the school and more than just one teacher, I have limited time in Susan's classroom. In terms of technology, I observe how students use Chromebooks to read articles, write speeches, and collaborate with classmates. At various points in the class period, Susan points out resources or models procedures using a large-screen monitor in one corner of the room and a SmartBoard projector in the front of the room. I can't always keep track of what's coming from where and what's hooked up to what, but Susan has it all under control. Technology skeptics might point out that all these tasks can be accomplished without going online, but the fact is that such tech-enabled sharing will be the norm for these students in high school and beyond. One other advantage is that the articles they read are curated and filtered through a service called Newsela, a popular way for teachers to guide students to the same content while offering "leveled" texts: The teacher can have everyone read the same environmental issue article, for example, but the vocabulary and sentence complexity is adjusted to suit each student's language skills.

Still, Susan's class is not without simple, old-fashioned pleasures, including a class read-aloud of Natalie Babbitt's *Tuck Everlasting*. The activity is off to a fine start, then Susan playfully "catches" me not reading along. She hands me a book so I can take a turn reading for the class as well. It may seem like a minor gesture, though I think Susan has made a veteran move, taking advantage of my presence to mix up a routine, add a touch of humor, and make a connection among people.

Connectivity is a perfect word to describe the rest of my visit to Union Middle School. There's a consistency among the principal and the teachers and classrooms I observed, a sense of community, inquiry, and learning through doing, that pervades the campus. My next stop is Mary Martin's eighth-grade science class. The students are using Chromebooks to answer questions about atoms and molecules, though sometimes they find it easier to produce a diagram or solve equations using pencil and paper. When they need help with a problem, they're able to consult not only their peers in the room, but also access a web page Mary has set up for her classes, with a section called Students Helping Students. It's an approach that's consistent with Mary's work as a technology trainer for Google, a technology coach among her colleagues, and a union president. In our brief conversation before I move on to the next classroom, Mary shows just how connected she is to her colleagues' work of by describing what I'm going to see in other classrooms on the schedule Todd has provided.

After lunch, I see even more hands-on learning at Union Middle School. Students in a design class, one of several interesting electives, are preparing TED-style talks about creative projects they've undertaken in the class. In another class, students are using the popular game *Minecraft* to design virtual buildings and villages, incorporating a variety of engineering, mathematical, and aesthetic principles in the process, though they probably think it's just play. An engineering class in another room is experimenting with designs for mini-windmills, using a variety of pieces of precut metallic elements, hardware, and gears. And back in another science lab, I observe seventh graders extracting DNA from wheat germ. At least, that's what everyone agrees is happening; it's a bit beyond my own scientific experience.

Kathy Day-Bobb, Fifth Grade
Kelly Rafferty, Science
Santa Rita Elementary School, Los Altos

The theme of connectivity fits Santa Rita Elementary School in Los Altos particularly well. Part of the sense of connection comes from geographic proximity: the school and district are close to my home and school, so as I talk with Santa Rita teachers I find that some of them know colleagues in my district, and others know people at Union Middle School not too much further away. It also turns out that members of the D39 team came from Poway to Santa Rita to observe the school as they were planning to open their own campus. My initial contacts in the school and district came through social media, and then a series of emails led to a plan involving two other teachers, Kathy Day-Bobb and Kelly Rafferty, who had some particularly interesting lessons and activities planned for the day of my visit.

I start off in Kathy's fifth-grade classroom, where the highlight of the morning is student oral presentations. These oral presentations are more precisely "elevator pitches"—short speeches to convince the audience to invest in or buy a product, invention, or service. Students have written and practiced their speeches, based on the results of a design process that has led to prototypes of all sorts of inventions. I like the doormat that can be connected to a vacuum cleaner, which sucks the dust and debris away from underneath, through the mat's fibers. Another student has redesigned the traffic flow for the front of the school and designed a pedestrian bridge to protect students from cars. There are a couple of apps in the works, of course—this is Silicon Valley. "Lunchify" would allow students to provide feedback to improve school lunches, while another unnamed app would help monitor the cleanliness of student bathrooms. Speaking of such functions, another youngster has a prototype of a doggie diaper. The sales pitch is summarized in the tag line "Pet your dog, not the poop!" No word on whether any dogs would cooperate with that revolutionary approach.

Considering this activity from an academic standpoint, the students' work does align with core skills in the language arts: They're writing specialized content that requires keen awareness of their audience and involves stylistic adjustments to optimize the text for listeners, as opposed to readers. The speaking itself is also part of the language arts standards. The design part of the activity is not so easy to categorize in our traditional subjects; it's not social studies or math, and it's not quite art, but that's part of the point. Teachers in schools like Santa Rita are connecting with peers and with the broader community to understand new ways of thinking and teaching, and in the process, helping students learn in ways that are more holistic, integrated, and experiential. Kathy has ensured a high degree of extramural connectivity in this project by enlisting a parent volunteer, a business consultant specializing in innovation strategy.

The same learn-by-doing approach is especially apparent in Santa Rita's science lab. The school has a dedicated STEM teacher (science, technology, engineering, mathematics). Kelly Rafferty is a graduate of the same elementary school where she now teaches, having arrived at her current position after starting her career as a classroom teacher in upper elementary grades. She enjoys supporting the entire student body at Santa Rita, and in a way, she supports her colleagues as well, as they pick up skills and ideas to improve science instruction they can use later. It's not a drop-off program—when a class comes to study science with Kelly, the primary teacher stays as well.

The afternoon's activity is a cow's heart dissection lab. The timing of this particular lab is somewhat of a joke—today is the Friday before Valentine's Day. That's Kelly's sense of humor at work. Many students are also wearing t-shirts that evoke Valentine's Day—lots of red and pink, and many heart shapes. The students are mostly eager to try the dissection, and even those who look momentarily squeamish are finding that curiosity wins out. If needed, an alternative assignment with no cutting required could be provided: The science lab has some sophisticated 3-D modeling computers and displays, with special glasses to wear and unique hand-held tools that can be used to manipulate virtual 3-D images in a digital dissection. Instead, everyone has opted to do the real thing. If you're recalling dissections from your own school days, and the smell of formaldehyde comes to mind, this situation is slightly different, as Kelly has purchased the cow hearts from a butcher or slaughterhouse, rather than a biological supply company. Well refrigerated in the interim, they give off only a faint scent of raw meat instead of any chemical.

Kelly alternates between instructions to the whole class and moving around the room to help pairs of students with each step in the process. When speaking from the front of the room, she holds up a cow's heart and carefully explains and demonstrates each step she wants students to follow. They gradually understand the relationship of various parts of the heart, relative sizes, proximity, even differences in texture that help illustrate differences in function for chambers, valves, and arteries. The students would probably manage quite well just working with partners to follow Kelly's example, but they also have Kathy here to help and a cadre of five parent volunteers assisting in today's lab work. Yes, five. I don't think I saw many more than five parent volunteers total in the other sixty-plus schools I visited. It's not only indicative of the affluence in the community, but also the sense of commitment and connectedness that the school cultivates. (That observation isn't meant to suggest that parents who can't spend time in schools are less committed or connected; their jobs, family commitments, and various other circumstances may render them less visible on campus.)

Nancy Ureña Reid, Math and Computer Science
Abraham Lincoln High School, San Jose

More important, of course, than my connections to teachers is their connectivity in supporting student learning. One of the teachers I visited who is less active in social media and building a virtual PLN is also perhaps the most gifted at providing students with real-world connections that advance their college and career opportunities. It's late spring by the time I visit Nancy Ureña Reid's math and computer science classes at Abraham Lincoln High School in San Jose (not to be confused with the school of the same name in San Francisco, where Valerie Ziegler teaches; see Chapter 6). At this time of year, much of Nancy's effort in the classroom involves circulating among students, helping individuals and small groups with various end-of-course projects. As an English teacher who doesn't regularly engage with these subjects at this point in my career, I don't have a great grasp of advanced mathematics or computer science, so while Nancy is helping students with their projects, I find myself gravitating toward having conversations with students rather than listening in on Nancy's conferences around the room.

One student shares his plans for next year, to attend nearby San Jose State University on a track and field scholarship. Another student confirms my inference about her destination next year, as I comment on her 3-D printing design for a Cornell University logo key ring. Most of the students in the class are seniors, but my longest conversation of the day occurs with a junior named Caitlyn. She's a young, eager computer programmer and a natural spokesperson for the value of science and technology education. It turns out she has quite a bit of recent experience talking about this topic, as she has a long list of events and contests she's been involved in. She lists projects like Girls Who Code, experiences that have brought her into contact with Microsoft, MTV, the San Jose Sharks, and Congresswoman Zoe Lofgren. These various activities and names come up not in a boastful way, but just in a sort of one-thing-leads-to-another conversation about Caitlyn's passion for tech education.

I find out later from Nancy that Caitlyn shouldn't even have been in AP computer science as a junior. She talked her way into the class, persuading Nancy that she'd work hard to compensate for concurrent rather than prerequisite enrollment in Algebra II. I wonder if Nancy sees something of herself in Caitlyn. Nancy also attended high school in San Jose, and was also a female student of color interested in math and computer courses, even though they tend to attract mostly male students. Now at the end of the course, it's clear that Caitlyn has thrived; she lists a variety of programming languages she's learning (Java, Python, Ruby, Scratch, HTML), and she talks about learning Swift next, in order to write applications for the Apple operating system. This amount of learning extends beyond Lincoln High School and involves quite a bit of travel around the Bay Area, with Caitlyn's dad serving as her chauffeur.

"Ms. Reid is one of the best teachers I ever had," Caitlyn tells me, unsolicited. "She puts in so much time writing grants and raising money, taking us places, getting us opportunities. She helps us at lunch or after school. A lot of teachers are dedicated, but not like her. A lot of what I've done this year is thanks to Ms. Reid."

In her postgraduate career, Nancy started as a programmer for a government contractor. In her eventual transition to teaching, she completed a master's degree in education, and as part of that work, she crafted a project developing computer education pathways for minority students and English language learners. Nancy is keenly aware of inequity in technology education and access for poor and minority students. The inadequate tech infrastructure and educational access is particularly ironic and troubling in San Jose. "We're here in Silicon Valley. Why don't my kids have what they have at other districts, private schools?"

Nancy does what she can to advocate for change and address the deficits, plus she takes on a mentorship role for students with strong interest and desire. Her efforts have resulted in media attention from the *San Jose Mercury News,* along with local radio and television stations. Connectivity for Nancy means drawing on personal knowledge of the tech industry, advocating for equity and fostering awareness in both her students and the community. Thanks to Nancy's efforts, her students are finding inspiration and opportunity, and the community is better informed about the need to support such capable students in reaching their full potential, especially when they're starting out with less privilege and access.

The word "innovation" is thrown about quite frequently in education. It is typically associated with technology and project-based learning, where students are afforded more opportunities to be creative and to connect their learning with the local or global community. Innovation can also mean that we shift our paradigms about schools, teaching, and learning. We must look at different ways to organize learning time, educational spaces, and the people in them. When teachers, school leaders, and community members hope to make schools more innovative, it's worth looking at programs and teachers like those profiled in this chapter while keeping in mind that the real drivers of education are not technological or programmatic. It's the educators who make innovation work, when they're connected, empowered, and inspired to make learning come alive for students.

CHAPTER 14

Teacher-Authors:

Practicing What They Publish

Jennifer Roberts, co-author (with Diana Neebe) of the book Power Up: Making the Shift to 1:1 Teaching and Learning, *confers with her students at Point Loma High School in San Diego.*

SEVERAL OF THE TEACHERS I VISITED WITH ARE FELLOW AUTHORS. When visiting a teacher-author's classroom, I had a chance to match my observations with my host's writing. Their books, articles, and blogs provide a frame—a set of expectations and an understanding of the teacher's views and strengths. The results were mostly predictable, in the best way possible. But in one case the results were surprising: There was a visit, however, where the results were surprising, as the teaching didn't match the book—and in that case, I emerged even more impressed.

For me, writing a book about teaching and schools has been a passion project, one that's relatively low-risk because I've focused on other teachers. The educators profiled in this chapter have done something bolder, asserting their pedagogical expertise and publicizing their practice. That kind of writing raises the stakes for the teacher-author, as students, peers, and administrators have something to refer to as they examine classroom practice. For that reason, I was grateful for the opportunity to watch these educators at work, though not surprised that they welcomed me.

Two of the teachers described in prior chapters are also authors. I profiled Heather Wolpert-Gawron in Chapter 3, when I wrote about middle schools. Her authorial and online persona, "Tweenteacher," made that chapter the natural place to write about Heather, whose several books have focused on teaching tweens, along with highlighting best practices in technology and internet usage. Leslee Milch was featured in Chapter 7, as her book about National Board Certification aligned perfectly with a chapter about National Board Certified Teachers. The other teacher-authors I visited are all high school teachers, authors of at least one book and with at least some experience in blogging as well.

Most of the teacher-authors profiled in this chapter would have easily fit into the prior chapter; online networking and professional connectivity is a theme that runs through their work as well. The first three teachers in this chapter—Larry Ferlazzo, Jennifer Roberts, and Catlin Tucker—are all teachers I first learned about through Twitter or blogging, and they were also part of Accomplished California Teachers, the teacher leadership group I helped direct for several years.

Larry Ferlazzo, English and Social Studies
Luther Burbank High School, Sacramento

Those of us who know Larry Ferlazzo's work have trouble believing that he sleeps. In addition to teaching, Larry writes books—eight at last count (some with coauthors). Larry blogs for *Education Week Teacher* and produces podcasts, both under the title "Classroom Q&A" and distinguished by their substantive inclusion of expert voices from the field. Larry also blogs on multiple personal websites, each with its own focus, including his "Websites of the Day" blog with thousands of curated lists of useful articles and resources.

What's his secret? Perhaps copious caffeination? Actually, for someone whose productivity seems almost frenetic, Larry is surprisingly mellow and soft-spoken. His patient demeanor is well-suited to working with English language learners (ELLs), who make up the bulk of Larry's students and whose needs are at the forefront of much of his writing and advocacy. In addition to teaching and writing about teaching for ELLs, Larry has devoted considerable effort to parent engagement, motivation, and classroom management, and has books on all three topics. His parent engagement efforts resulted in a school program that sends teachers to visit the home of every new student each year. Everything he focuses on as a writer comes from success in the classroom, school, and community, as I see from spending a day with him at Luther Burbank High School in Sacramento.

Larry's morning history classes consist of two classes meeting at the same time in the same place. Half the students are studying world history, and half are learning US history, and all are receiving support for English language development. The concentration of ELL students in one classroom helps Larry deliver instruction in ways that support language growth along with content mastery. He splits his time between the two classes, and while he's with one group, the other works collaboratively on material he provides, supported by a bilingual teaching aid, Alma Avalos. She and Larry both speak Spanish, which can be helpful for many of their students; other students' first languages include Arabic and several Asian languages.

This instructional approach, having two classes in the room at once, reflects considerable administrative respect for Larry's skills and knowledge. For many teachers, this arrangement would be too challenging, maybe impossible. Larry feels well-supported and valued at the school, and in fact, has often written about the strong leadership provided by principal Ted Appel. Larry's unique teaching situation works in large part because of the trusting relationship with his administrator. Larry knows he isn't being set up to fail when he is given a variety of challenges within his teaching assignment.

After the history classes, Larry has his English Language Development (ELD) classes. Again, there are multiple levels in one period. Students spend part of their time working on computer-based language exercises and part of their time working on writing, helping each other and working individually or in small groups directly with Larry. Regarding the computer exercises, students probably have little idea how exhaustively Larry reviews various options to support their learning. Primarily for the benefit of his students, and secondarily for his professional peers who read his blog, Larry has reviewed hundreds—maybe thousands—of websites, applications, computer programs, and other resources to support ELLs. When they're not meeting with him, Larry has students working on different exercises, depending on their particular needs: Some students are engaged in a story-based program, while others are concentrating on vocabulary related to housing and household items. When students have a chance to work directly with Larry, he offers consistently warm and enthusiastic appraisals of their writing. There are suggestions and instructions for improvement as well, though Larry is wise to recognize that learning to write is a years-long process. In the short term, Larry is making it clear to his students that they *are* communicating in writing; their meaning comes across however imperfectly, and his response supports their motivation to continue writing.

One of Larry's students has only been in school for a couple of weeks. I don't mean he transferred from another school—he is actually new to schooling. After a decade of living on the streets in El Salvador, this young man is trying to adjust to much more than a new culture and a language; he's adjusting to being a student. I watch briefly as a peer helps him navigate one of the computer-based exercises, which is challenging for a high school student unaccustomed to using computers. He's learning to spell (and type) very basic sentences after hearing them on the computer. It's painstakingly slow, though in the time that I'm observing, he perseveres and shows no frustration. I hope the novelty of the experience is positive and life here is going to be better than what he left behind.

I also hope he won't be discouraged when he's expected to sit through standardized tests, including portions requiring academic writing in English, which will be outrageously inappropriate for him. Larry and his colleagues could help him make astounding gains in the next year or two, but the demands of standardized tests will still greatly exceed his skills. The idea that Larry or his colleagues might be held accountable for the results of such mismatched testing should offend any sensible person, yet that's that type of shoddy educational policy favored in many parts of the country. (Accountability is not the problem, but there are better ways to approach it, which are detailed in the next chapter.)

Though Larry has written books about classroom management and student motivation, there's nothing overtly different about his classroom. I'm observing his students at work, observing him with them, and the word that comes to mind is "authentic." It's not like the teacher-author is some kind of salesman demonstrating the contents of his books, nor is everything in his classroom managed to perfection. What's abundantly clear is he has worked on the relationships in the classroom. Students are responsive and welcoming as Larry moves among them, often smiling when he approaches to observe their work or provide some help. With some students, he'll offer feedback and guidance in a combination of Spanish and English. He responds warmly to their efforts as well, acknowledging strong cooperative work and noting individual progress with essays they're writing.

In the afternoon, Larry switches from teaching English language instruction and history classes for ELLs to a course called Theory of Knowledge, part of the International Baccalaureate (IB) curriculum. IB is an international educational program of advanced study and certification, with certain requirements for schools and comprehensive end-of-course exams, similar to the Advanced Placement program offered by the College Board. About half of Larry's students are in the IB program, while the other half are taking the course out of interest, but without doing the full IB curriculum. The philosophical nature of the course provides quite a contrast to Larry's earlier classes; as he puts it, "I go from reviewing vowel sounds in the morning to teaching about Plato in the afternoon."

Today, students are examining ethical dilemmas, the kind of hypothetical situations that generate rich and sometimes heated discussions, and rarely offer any "right" answers. If you were in a life-threatening emergency with limited time and resources to effect rescues, how would you decide who to save first? Are there situations in which you could sacrifice one life to save others? Is torture justifiable if it could produce information that would prevent an act of mass murder? Larry's students wrestle with these questions and also have to identify what kind of thinking, knowledge, or moral framework would guide their decisions. To keep conversations flowing and everyone engaged, Larry has students working in small groups, giving every student more opportunity to speak and contribute to the whole. Like the group work I observed in Larry's morning history classes, this approach supports both engagement and language development.

One of Larry's main areas of professional focus is student motivation. Beginning with his book *Helping Students Motivate Themselves: Practical Answers to Classroom*

Challenges, Larry has always emphasized the importance of intrinsic motivation, insisting that we can't "give" students motivation. To help students develop their own motivation, Larry looks for opportunities to put students in charge of aspects of their own learning. The group work mentioned above helps in that regard. The issue of grades can be tricky with regard to motivation, as we direct students to focus on extrinsic motivators, even though intrinsic motivation leads to better learning. Since grades are unavoidable, Larry helps students internalize the process, making self-assessment and "defense" of grades part of his classes. While the teacher provides standards, exemplars, and instruction, students can learn to assess their own work effectively. When students have to analyze their work, assign a grade, justify it, and defend it if questioned, Larry says, "About ninety percent come out 'right.' They get the same grade I would give. About five percent underestimate. The final five percent overestimate, and they have to meet with me to persuade me if they want the higher grade."

Prior to teaching, Larry worked as a community organizer for many years, and took away some key lessons that apply to teaching students and working in a school community. Obviously, relationships are central to the work in both of these areas. The goal of relationship-building is to help everyone achieve shared goals, though the organizer or teacher should not see their role as doing anything for others that they can do themselves. While Larry's effect on his broader school community is hard to observe from his classroom, I get glimpses of it in conversation with his principal, Ted Appel, and a colleague and coauthor, Katie Hull Sypnieski. (Katie and Larry co-wrote *The ESL/ELL Teacher's Survival Guide: Ready-to-Use Strategies, Tools, and Activities for Teaching English Language Learners of All Levels*). In my conversations with them, what they know and share admiringly about each other's work speaks to the value of trust, communication, and collaboration in helping teachers and students thrive.

Jennifer Roberts, English
Point Loma High School, San Diego

Of all the teachers in this book, Jennifer Roberts would have to be the one whose teaching is most visible to the outside world. She doesn't think of her class blog in terms of broadcasting to the world, however; it primarily serves her students as a resource and a time machine.

At the start of a ninth-grade English class, Jennifer asks students to recall some prior work. Activating memories of prior work is a common and valuable technique to help students make the most of a lesson. "Let's go back in time," she begins. "Who can remember what we were doing one week ago today?"

One student confesses, "Ms. Roberts, I can't remember what I had for breakfast," and another offers, "We took a quiz about that stuff that you and some other English teachers were talking about."

Jennifer replies, "That's accurate, but let's get more specific."

I hear the sound of a keyboard clicking, and a student leaning over a Chromebook says, "Wait! I'm going back in time *right now.*"

Jennifer smiles: "And how are you doing that?"

"9thEnglish.blogspot.com," the student answers. And if you want to see what Jennifer's ninth-grade English classes have been doing at Point Loma High School in San Diego, you, too, can go to that blog. There, you'll find summaries of each lesson, links to resources, instructions for submitting work, and a course calendar. Jennifer excels not only at organization, but also at technology integration that makes it easier for her and her students to stay organized. Jennifer's facility in the use of technology comes from lengthy and consistent practice, and training to become a Google Certified Instructor. She has a reduced teaching assignment in order to spend more time supporting the use of technology in her school. Much of Jennifer's expertise has been shared for years through her blog (www.litandtech.com) and more recently through her book *Power Up: Making the Shift to 1:1 Teaching and Learning* (co-authored with Diana Neebe). The reference to "1:1" means that every student has a personal device (tablet, Chromebook, laptop computer), making technology and the internet available to every student at any time during their school day.

In the dialogue above, one of the students mentions a quiz. That quiz was a "pre-test" designed to see what students might already know about rhetoric, and the terms *ethos, logos,* and *pathos.* Once students recall the activity, Jennifer shares her findings with the class: "When you were asked in descriptive terms, you understood the text you were reading and how the author tried to persuade you. What we need to work on is labeling it accurately." And with that, Jennifer shows a short animated video in which the narrator explains the use of each rhetorical strategy in a boy's attempts to persuade his mom to order a pizza for dinner. A link to the video appears on today's agenda so if any student is absent or just wants to review the video independently, it's easy to find on Jennifer's "time machine" blog.

After students view and briefly discuss the video, Jennifer assigns them to small groups to reread an article about extreme sports, this time analyzing and discussing the rhetoric using the technical terms. The use of Chromebooks makes it possible for students to read and highlight the article without using paper or highlighters. Students are collaborating as they make the case for *ethos, logos,* or *pathos* in different parts of the article, and if students persuade their partners to change a response, it's possible to change the color of highlighting on the digital text. When they're done, Jennifer will be able to view everyone's work online—no papers to collect. Jennifer has designed these groups with a certain balance in mind. All year long, she observes and tracks her students' strengths, needs, interests, tendencies in group work, and depending on the type of task, she designs and organizes groups differently.

If all this digital management leads you to picture Jen constantly leaning over her laptop computer, that's not the case. Most of this work occurs outside the classroom, leaving Jennifer unencumbered and free to move around the classroom. Jen checks in with groups, monitoring their progress, and when she intervenes, it's primarily to coach students regarding discussion and interaction; she wants them regularly checking their thinking collaboratively, pushing each other to make the case for their analysis and interpretation. When the group process concludes, Jennifer leads the full class through a discussion of the article. When there are different opinions, she doesn't rush students to settle on one correct idea; rather, she suggests alternatives and poses hypothetical questions showing how students can test their own thinking: "Now, if that quote [in the article] came from a professor instead of a child, what would we say? Would that still be *pathos?*" Her students are all engaged and following along. I smile to myself seeing how Jennifer enjoys the interactions, challenging students with difficult material and guiding them through new thought processes.

The direct connections among Jennifer's teaching, school responsibilities, and professional writing are abundantly evident. Her book features vignettes of best practices taken from a variety of middle school and high school classrooms, making the book more useful for teachers of other grades and subjects. It's clear from watching Jennifer for a day and from reviewing her class blog that what she writes is simply what she does, and it works to improve teaching and student learning.

Catlin Tucker, English
Windsor High School, Windsor

As noted earlier, Catlin Tucker was among the educators who joined Accomplished California Teachers, and "accomplished" is a perfect word to describe her. She has authored or coauthored four books about teaching; the most recent, *Blended Learning in Action: A Practical Guide Toward Sustainable Change,* (coauthored with Tiffany Wycoff and Jason T. Green) was released in October 2016. (The term "blended learning" means that to a significant extent, students are engaged in coursework through digital means and with more flexibility or autonomy, yet still spending significant time in the classroom with the teacher as well.) In addition to the books, Catlin has her own blog (catlintucker.com) and is a regular contributor on the topic of education technology for the professional journal *Educational Leadership.* When she's not teaching, Catlin is a sought-after instructor in technology integration and has speaking engagements around the country. Her primary job, however, is teaching ninth- and tenth-grade English classes at Windsor High School, in the Sonoma County town of Windsor.

To clarify, Catlin teaches both ninth and tenth-graders in each of her classes; the curriculum is structured such that, over a period of two years, students receive the same instruction and materials, though the sequence varies. This approach works because there's no difference between ninth- and tenth-grade English the way there is between biology and chemistry, or algebra and geometry. Gunn High School in Palo Alto (where Roni Habib teaches; see Chapter 12) has long used the same approach. Placing ninth and tenth graders in one class has the advantage of fostering some intergrade relationships among students and exposing ninth graders to the ways that tenth graders have learned to work in high school. When Catlin organizes groups of students for various activities, she's intentional about mixing the grade levels, which helps groups start work more quickly and proceed more efficiently.

The only day I could schedule my visit to Windsor was October 31, so my observations are not coming on a typical school day. Halloween is much more of an event in elementary schools, though at Windsor there are some students wearing costumes today. Catlin joins in the fun, dressed as a flower child from the 1960s, with a floral garland in her hair and feather earrings, a corduroy vest, and bell-bottom jeans. Other than the costumes, there are a couple of other Halloween elements in the day. For a quick and fun exercise in the importance of providing and paying attention to specific details, Catlin has students take three minutes to write a description of a scary monster, then three minutes to draw a picture based on the description. Then, students randomly receive one of their classmate's monster descriptions and have three minutes to attempt a drawing based on that description. The activity ends with a challenge to students to match up each pair of drawings based on the same description, which is sometimes easy and sometimes surprisingly difficult.

One other nod to Halloween is that Catlin reads her classes a story titled *I Need My Monster*, by Amanda Noll. While the story is selected for its Halloween connection, reading aloud to students is something Catlin does somewhat regularly. Though they're sophisticated high schoolers much of the time, students can still enjoy some of the simpler pleasures of their younger years. These readings are just for fun, though she hopes in these few minutes per week to build a sense of community in the class and to demonstrate the inherent appeal of good storytelling.

With regard to technology integration in Catlin's classes, I observe her students more often engaged in activities and discussions that are not making direct use of technology. Class begins with students taking some time to read their current book, Maya Angelou's memoir *I Know Why the Caged Bird Sings*. While they're reading, Catlin is circulating through the room to check up on students' reading annotations, a quick way to gain some insights into students' work habits and their thoughts about the text. Later in the period, students will engage in small-group discussions about the reading as well. Another nontech activity has students reviewing vocabulary by trying a "Word Sneak." Based on an improvised comedy routine on *The Tonight Show*, the goal is for students to integrate vocabulary words into a conversation as naturally as possible.

A class vocabulary activity provides some insight into Catlin's approach to technology integration, though the technology is not central to the exercise. In addition to the "Word Sneak," students are also reading aloud some ministories they've written at some point earlier in the week, with each story integrating all the words from the current vocabulary list. The class has selected the stories to be shared, having read each other's work on Schoology prior to today's class. (Schoology is a learning management system, or LMS, also described in Chapter 9.) In this way, the technology use has supported a class activity that's fun and interpersonal, without putting students in front of screens for a longer portion of their school day. Another example of technology in the course but not in the classroom comes up when Catlin reminds students about recent and upcoming work shared in a Google Drive folder. (Google Drive allows users to create, store, and share work online through Google accounts, and allows multiple users to modify a file at the same time.)

Technology use that's most directly observable during the class involves a grammar review, with students collaboratively identifying complete and incomplete sentences on an interactive online platform called Socrative. There are many ways Socrative can help a teacher share content or questions, then gather student responses. The advantage of this technology is that the teacher can collect real-time feedback to see what students understand, then decide to review material further, move on, or perhaps note the need to provide extra support for some students. During today's class, Catlin's students are using a gaming mode in Socrative; each group is entering its responses to the interactive grammar quiz using one group member's personal smartphone. Correct answers advance the group's rocket-ship icon displayed on a screen at the front of the classroom. Catlin is mindful that competition among students can be fraught with problems; winning and losing can both give students a false sense of self-esteem and potential, and it's preferable to cultivate intrinsic rather than extrinsic motivation. However, occasional, brief, low-stakes group competition among students can add some fun and energy to a potentially dry activity, like reviewing a grammar lesson.

Over the course of a single class period, I don't see technology taking over Catlin's instructional time or dominating her classroom. Yet I've observed directly and indirectly how she and her students enhance their collaboration using at least three different interfaces—Google, Socrative, and Schoology—and the only devices used in the class are students' own smartphones. In a sense, seeing only occasional use of technology is a sign of smart technology integration, the goal of which is to enhance good teaching rather than intrude on it. While tech skills are essential for students' future learning and work, Catlin's philosophy regarding technology is not focused on the device and interface: "It's all about engagement and student voice, letting students generate their own questions and ideas." In correspondence with Catlin several months later, she describes how she helps students take ownership of their learning experience: "We're ending the year with what I call 'free range' literature circles. Students select books and are working in groups to design an entirely student-led unit. It's amazing to watch them take all the skills they've learned this year and use them to create units that reflect their strengths and interests. I gave them a set of nine skills they needed to demonstrate mastery of over the course of the unit, but that's the only guidance I provided. The rest is up to them!"

Jim Burke, English
Burlingame High School, Burlingame

The teacher-author who works nearest to my home and whom I've known the longest is also the best-known to my fellow English teachers around the nation. Jim Burke's books about English teaching are practically required reading in our field. In fact, some of his books, *The English Teacher's Companion* in particular, have been required reading for some teachers-in-training. It was a fellow English teacher, Jennifer Abrams, who introduced me to Jim at the annual convention of the National Council of Teachers of English (NCTE), in the mid-1990s. Since then, Jim has authored over twenty books and has coauthored, edited, or contributed to many more. He also created an online community called the English Companion (englishcompanion.ning.com), an active and engaged group of English teachers numbering over 45,000.

For me to spend a day in Jim's classroom seemed comparable to being a line cook invited to visit the kitchen of a world-renowned chef. It's not only that I wanted to see Jim's teaching firsthand, but I was also curious to see how he'd make use of the volumes of instructional materials he's created. The visit turned out to be as educational as I hoped, but not in the ways I anticipated. Not even close.

Burlingame High School, in the town of the same name, is about a half-hour from my home, but I've never been there before. Jim's classroom is on the corner of an older building near the front of the campus, with a view of athletic fields and a tall stand of eucalyptus trees. There are no Jim Burke posters or plaques to be seen, however.

In fact, during my day observing Jim, I don't see any of his books, or any lessons or handouts from his books. The day's lessons are well-designed, providing each class with opportunities to read, write, converse, and even listen to a *Marketplace* podcast; this particular episode of the popular public radio program focuses on companies engaging in marketing based on generational assumptions. I find out later that the podcast idea came to Jim just last night. He thought the students would enjoy the format and react to the attempt of the older generation to label and commodify their generation. Instead, students question the premise of the report, and it turns out many don't feel a strong sense of generational identification. In one class, that conversation leads Jim to mention the song "My Generation" by The Who. He promises a complete vocal rendition with air-drum solo if his students finish their work with enough time left, though it's clearly one of those jokes teachers tell more for their own amusement.

Watching Jim in the classroom has been worthwhile, but it's the conversations outside the classroom that are more revealing. His classroom demeanor is warm but not effusive, serious but not humorless. Jim's passion for teaching English is more evident in the wide range of his work and in his tirelessness—his almost unreal capacity to teach, write books and articles, consult for professional organizations, and train teachers. Somehow he fits in time for family, and judging by the number of book and article references he dropped in our conversations, he finds ample time for reading as well. "It can be energizing to spend extra time delving into something deeply. I talk about passion with my students. You know, it's your job in life to find something fascinating, challenging, worthy of your time. I'm fascinated by teaching English and figuring out what makes things work for kids and groups."

And it's clear Jim still strives to figure it out, even after teaching for more than twenty years and producing about twenty books. The students are always new, of course, and I see how Jim makes an effort throughout his day to check in with students individually, either asking questions or following up on prior conversations. Then, there's the podcast lesson that didn't quite take hold. There's the puzzlement over why class structures that worked well in previous years aren't helping students manage their work flow this year. On a broader level, there's the constant evolution of culture, kids, and technology.

Jim talks about his work overall using an organic, holistic phrase: "living in the classroom." It means knowing your students, interacting with them in a way that is relaxed and supportive, yet still academically challenging. It means that the materials and the learning are managed, rather than the young adults we work with. "We're dealing with the realities of different kids, in different classes, with different needs and dynamics, and they vary from day to day," Jim says. "Sometimes random things come along, random inspiration, in the moment, and things click. It's unpredictable. Windows of opportunity open up that aren't on lesson plans; you have to have flexibility to veer off and maximize student engagement." Jim values the freedom to be flexible and creative. Developing new lessons and approaches requires acceptance of imperfection and occasional failure. He contrasts this view of teaching with others that "aim to anticipate everything, manage and control everything."

An English teacher who wants to anticipate and manage everything *could* read Jim's books and gain insights into every level of instructional design, from the broadest inquiry into essential questions, to unit and lesson design, to specific handouts and procedures. Ironically, that's not how Jim would do it. Still, I'm sure I'll be pulling his books off my shelf now and then for years to come, when I need some ideas or inspiration.

Jeremy Adams, Social Studies
Bakersfield High School, Bakersfield

My visit with Jeremy Adams at Bakersfield High School offers a number of contrasts to the time I spent with Jim Burke. I've never met Jeremy before my arrival, haven't read his books prior to the visit, and know relatively little about him. Tim Allen of the Carlston Family Foundation (see Chapter 6) suggested I spend a day here, telling me multiple times what a wonderful teacher Jeremy is. Tim's judgment in these matters is excellent, though he wasn't the first to notice: Jeremy has been honored by several organizations and was named Kern County Teacher of the Year in 2012. He's also an adjunct professor at California State University, Bakersfield.

Jeremy's first book, *Full Classrooms, Empty Selves,* is a teaching memoir, a reflection on Jeremy's own education and journey into teaching, and his search for meaning and virtue in education. He digs deeply into history and philosophy, asking pointed questions about the cultural shifts and trends that challenge his way of thinking about education and civics. There are no easy answers, no comforting bromides. In the end, it feels like a fight with cynicism that ends in a draw. The book's conclusion notes, however, that it captures a moment in time for Jeremy; it is not the sum of his professional experience or identity. He has since written a second book, *The Secrets of Timeless Teachers: Instruction that Works in Every Generation.* To the extent that his first book wrestled with trends and turbulence in culture and education, the second book establishes anchors—asserting that there is such a thing as "timeless teaching" for starters, then identifying the core habits that distinguish great teachers in any generation. The time I was able to spend with Jeremy showed me the intellect and passion behind the book and how deeply he cares about his students, school, and work.

Bakersfield High School is among the oldest high schools in the state and has a distinctive campus with city streets running through it. (The streets are closed to through traffic during school hours.) Jeremy's classroom is in the same building as the school theater and across G Street from the main administration building, where I check in at the start of the school day. I notice a mural that celebrates "Driller Tradition"—a reference to the region's oil drilling history. Tradition is something they take seriously here. Jeremy is a perfect example: He's an alumnus of the school, now teaching where his father also taught for twenty-five years. The school likes competition and spectacle, Jeremy tells me, noting that they've won more state football championships than any other high school. He has put his unique stamp on the school with the creation of a new tradition, The Constitution Cup, a government and history trivia competition held annually in their 1,600-seat theater. Organizers build up the event's theatricality with smoke machines, music, and lighting, and have successfully solicited videorecorded questions for the competition from governors, members of Congress, and Supreme Court justices.

When Jeremy allows me a moment to introduce myself to his classes, I briefly share my purpose in visiting, and add, "I'm a Driller for a day." To an extent that surprises me, that line works, eliciting nods and smiles from high school students more than I think I'd encounter at another school. I've had some positive interactions with students at many schools, but I can't recall a place where so many students talked to me on their way out and made me feel welcome. They say things like *thanks for coming* and *hope you enjoyed your day,* and the most endearing valediction: "Once a Driller, always a Driller!"

I should have asked if it's a coincidence that Jeremy's classroom is in the same building as the theater. It's not just The Constitution Cup that might make it appropriate, but also the way that Jeremy treats the classroom as his stage, even though teachers are often advised that it's "better to be a guide-on-the-side than a sage-on-the-stage." Jeremy's teaching methods are surely more varied, but today is an appropriate day for such teacher-centric choices, because he has just returned from Washington, DC, where he was in the House of Representatives gallery for the 2015 State of the Union address.

His students are attentive to his stories and asks questions about every facet. The mere opportunity to be there is something Jeremy describes as "'beyond bucket list.'

I never thought I'd go." He narrates the whole process of arriving at the Capitol, passing through security, and the eventual arrival of the President. "Someone told me I looked like a child in a candy store," he says of the moment he stood up, clapping, tears coming to his eyes. Though it's palpable in his narration, he tells students explicitly that he felt a great sense of optimism and patriotism, and an appreciation for the traditions and institutions, while clarifying that this is a nonpartisan enthusiasm and not an endorsement of the President or his party.

Behind the scenes, Jeremy had the chance to meet some members of Congress and describes how honored he was to meet civil rights movement icon John Lewis in particular. He also recalls a moment more amusing than profound, giving someone instructions about taking a good picture with an iPhone, only to find out later she was Laurene Powell Jobs (the widow of Steve Jobs).

Tales from DC take up only part of the class period. It's the start of the second semester of school. For sophomores, it's time to study World War I, and Jeremy has them thinking about the difference between a cause and a trigger: The assassination of Archduke Ferdinand was the trigger for the war, but the underlying causes—long-standing conflicts—were broader. Seniors are starting the transition from a semester of AP government to AP macroeconomics; today, they're exploring the difference between micro and macroeconomics.

My interactions with Jeremy outside the school prove instructive as well. We grab a midmorning cup of coffee at Dagby's; Jeremy calls it "the hipster hangout" in the old downtown section of Bakersfield. He runs into a former student who's eager to say hello and catch up for a few minutes. After school, Jeremy wants to enhance my Bakersfield experience and insists we visit Dewar's Candy Shop just down the street from the school, for one of their ice cream sundaes. We drive separately as we'll be parting ways shortly, and as his car enters the parking lot, one wheel catches the curb at an odd angle, leaving Jeremy with a rapidly deflating tire. Nonetheless, we go inside and spend a half hour or so talking about educational philosophies over ice cream sundaes. Jeremy is extremely well-read, his opinions about education informed not only by educational research, but also by history, philosophy, and classics. At the same time, he's quite curious and solicits my opinions and impressions as much as he offers his own.

Our time for casual conversation is running out, as Jeremy has to solve his tire problem. He remains constantly upbeat, though; not that he's happy to have a flat tire, but complaining about it wouldn't fix anything. Jeremy focuses on the positive. As he told me earlier, "I teach a lively and fascinating subject to the best students at the best high school in the county, with an extraordinarily supportive administration behind me. I have said many times that I am the luckiest teacher in Kern County." His students are similarly lucky to have a teacher who is so committed to them and so knowledgeable and interested in constant learning for them and for himself.

For great teachers, the distinction between teaching and learning is minimal. Doing our best work always involves learning about the individuals we're working with and more about our subject, as well as trying new ways to help students. Similarly, we can only be truly effective in our professional and local community when we learn ways that build relationships and mutual understanding. We learn continually through teaching, and we learn intentionally, based on analysis and reflection. You can see that thread particularly in high-quality teacher training (see Chapter 5), in National Board Certification (see Chapter 7), and in the instructional practices and habits of educators profiled in this chapter. As these teacher-authors demonstrate, writing has much in common with teaching: Both processes demand a combination of broad vision and attention to detail, an openness to examination, and a commitment to improvement.

Building on Strengths:

How California Can Improve Public Education

Adam Ebrahim surveys students working in his human geography class at Fresno High School.

You've now read about more than sixty California public schools and even more teachers and education leaders, all of whom are helping students learn and thrive. In the news, in politics, and too often even among ourselves, the single story told about public education is negative. Let the examples in this book mitigate the danger of the single story. Every time you walk or drive past a public school, assume the best: There are well-trained, highly skilled, dedicated, caring, and effective teachers working in that school. Bet on it. On any given school day, keep in mind that the teachers and schools profiled in this book are all at work, all making a positive difference for students. There are dozens of additional schools I hoped to visit but couldn't fit into my travel plans. There are hundreds more I could find through social media and networking, thousands more that would be worthy of profiling here.

That's all the good news. We can't stop there, however, lest we fall into the same "single story" trap. So what now?

Do we need a higher concentration of outstanding teachers in many of our schools? Yes. Do our teachers need better training and continual professional learning? Yes. Do California public schools need to improve and evolve? Emphatically, yes.

Improving public education is too often approached as a *personnel* problem, too many "bad teachers" and not enough good ones. The first flaw in that thinking is that good teaching is often contextual. Put me in another school or district, and I may not be as effective. Pluck certain teachers out of a dysfunctional situation, and they may thrive. The vast majority of teachers start out neither great nor awful; if our society ends up with "bad teachers" it's because we have a system that neglects both average teachers and schools overall. We will not create a better teaching force operating from negative assumptions about the people doing the work now. The sparks of creativity and innovation, the desire to excel at teaching—they're already there. Improving public education is a *systems* problem; systemic improvement will produce and sustain better work by everyone, while motivating a broader pool of applicants to join in the work.

In conversations with friends and colleagues, during and after these school visits, I was often asked about my conclusions from this project; most people asked about *the best* school or teacher, or the one best thing to do for school improvement. Clearly, there was no singular best teacher, nor do any simple solutions work for an incredibly complex system, involving such a diversity of people and places.

And yet, I have reached some conclusions. The broadest of these, and perhaps the key to other improvements, is that we need everyone who cares about public education to offer a vote of confidence—literally, when the ballot presents opportunities to support public education, and figuratively, when confronted with negative stereotypes or flawed assumptions. Anthony Bryk and Barbara Schneider spent years leading a team of researchers studying a group of Chicago elementary schools. They demonstrated that trusting relationships among the adults in a school community had a positive causal effect on student learning.[5] (That effect was indirect. Trust among adults doesn't cause children to learn; it causes teachers and principals to engage in more robust improvement efforts.) Trust must be earned, of course, though all of us can approach a situation or relationship inclined or disinclined to extend trust. That you've read this book suggests you may already be inclined toward trust. We can share in the effort of expanding that trust, and hopefully, in the work of education advocacy.

On more specific policy matters, I offer these parting thoughts, observations, and recommendations for how we might best direct our efforts to advocate for public education.

Equity in School Funding

Most teachers and schools are stretched too thin to reach their full potential. When a system is overstressed and under-resourced, there are two options for relief: Reduce the stress or add resources. Reducing the stress on schools would essentially mean increasing services to California's children, 23 percent of whom live in poverty, with another 24 percent in low-income families (slightly above poverty level).[6] Until we make incredible progress in solving poverty and income inequality, adding resources for schools to better support children is both the practical and moral choice. In the past few years, California has pulled itself out of a period of worst-in-the-nation funding levels for public education, but we still have much to do.

The inequity across districts is stark. Keep in mind that educating English language learners and children in poverty requires more resources for both students and teachers; *equitable* support would provide greater funding for districts with higher concentrations of needy students. Districts with very low numbers of students or very broad geographic areas also incur higher costs per student. State efforts to supplement funding for needy students are described in the next section, though the overall gaps remain wide. Complicating potential equity solutions is the fact that roughly 130 California school districts are "basic aid" districts, receiving significantly less state funding because local tax revenues for schools in those districts exceed what the state allocates. These districts tend to be smaller, suburban, or rural districts with a stronger tax base. You can see the differences below: I've compared four basic aid school districts to four "revenue limit" (regular) school districts. Each comparison focuses on unified (K–12) districts, with similar enrollment figures, in the same region, using 2014–15 figures provided by the California Department of Education.[7]

Paso Robles Unified School District:	$8,786 per pupil
San Luis Coastal Unified School District:	$11,653 per pupil, or 33% more
Tustin Unified School District:	$7,952 per pupil
Newport Mesa Unified School District:	$11,492 per pupil, or 45% more
New Haven Unified School District:	$9,519 per pupil
Palo Alto Unified School District:	$16,067 per pupil, or 69% more
Gonzales Unified School District:	$9,390 per pupil
Carmel Unified School District:	$17,843 per pupil, or 90% more

Skeptics question if more spending produces better results. Of course, that question is typically about controlling taxes and spending for *other people's children* (to borrow the title of Lisa Delpit's book on cultural differences in education). Through their actions, however, wealthier families and communities convey their belief in the connection between spending and results, consistently finding ways to invest more in their children's schools than the state would otherwise spend. Still, the skeptics deserve an answer. An examination of forty years' worth of data from American school systems showed that "a 20 percent increase in per-pupil spending each year for all 12 years of public school for children from poor families leads to about 0.9 more completed years of education, 25 percent higher earnings, and a 20 percentage-point reduction in the annual incidence of adult poverty."[8] If that's the effect of a 20 percent increase, consider the implications for the funding gaps shown above.

Here in California, we've had our own experiment with increased funding for needy schools: The Quality Education Investment Act (QEIA) became law in 2006, as part of a legal settlement from a school-funding lawsuit brought against

Governor Schwarzenegger by the California Teachers Association. The resulting eight-year, $3 billion supplemental funding for low-performing schools provided valuable support to reduce class sizes, improve teacher learning and collaboration, and bring in additional support for students.[9] I saw the direct benefits of QEIA funds at Brookfield Elementary in Oakland, Riley Elementary in San Bernardino, and Luther Burbank High School in Sacramento. In 2012, Californians passed Proposition 30, temporarily raising the state sales tax from 7.25 to 7.5 percent and temporarily raising income taxes on those earning over $250,000 per year. It was neither the first nor the last attempt to address school funding via the ballot. Ultimately, short-term, patchwork solutions need to give way to sustained equitable funding for California's children and public schools.

At the high school level, equitable funding and staffing would make it possible for all schools to offer seven classes instead of the typical six. Students who are taking all the necessary prerequisites for college at a rate of six classes per semester have little room for anything else in their schedule, which limits electives such as journalism, yearbook, the arts, and technology courses. Districts with more funding often support high schools that offer a seven-period schedule. Students benefit not only because they have one-seventh more opportunity every day to learn something new, but the "extra" courses they can take are often the electives that make such a difference in so many students' lives, in terms of both passions and practicalities. It's a shame that Californians can't fund all high schools at a level that would provide equitable access to such enriching learning experiences.

Local Control Funding and Accountability Plans: The California Way

As of 2013, California has begun providing supplemental funding for schools that serve concentrations of students with greater needs, specifically children in low-income households, English language learners, and children in foster care. It's a step in the right direction, though, as we've seen, neighboring basic-aid districts might still spend much more per pupil, not even counting the significant fundraising conducted on behalf of these schools through associated nonprofit foundations. The increase in state funding has coincided with new flexibility for districts to decide locally how to allocate funding, which is why the new approach is called the Local Control Funding Formula (LCFF). With fewer state rules regarding specific uses of money, districts are now required to seek teacher, parent, and community input to determine budget priorities. Just as significantly, these stakeholders also help determine how the district will be held accountable, through a mechanism called the Local Control Accountability Plan (LCAP).

The LCAP represents a shift toward more sensible policies regarding school and district accountability. When Congress passed the federal No Child Left Behind act, (technically, a renewal of the Elementary and Secondary Education Act), schools became accountable for raising test scores continuously until every student in America supposedly achieved proficiency in English language arts and mathematics. The law went into effect in 2002, and the target year for meeting this impossible goal was 2014. As that year approached, schools were overhauled or closed with increasing frequency, based almost entirely on test scores. People complaining about the flaws in this reform strategy were often characterized as having low expectations or wanting to evade accountability entirely. The validity of NCLB criticisms became increasingly apparent as the damage spread: narrowed curriculum, testing fatigue, cheating scandals, and most important, no evidence that a focus on standards and testing had achieved the desired effects on student learning.[10] Tensions between state and federal policy will continue to be worked out as we transition to new federal law and guidelines: In 2015, Congress replaced NCLB with the Every Student Succeeds Act (ESSA), and each state now has responsibility for devising its own implementation plan for the 2017–18 school year.

The creation of LCAPs is one of the signature policies of "The California Way," a progressive agenda supported by Governor Jerry Brown, the State Board of Education, and Tom Torlakson, the State Superintendent for Public Instruction. Instead of repeating the failed cycle of expecting improvement through state-mandated standards, testing, and rankings, these leaders have revised the accountability paradigm by bringing stakeholders together locally to discuss specific details about what matters most in education and how to ensure schools address the right priorities. For now, the de-emphasis on standardized test scores and school rankings is welcome by many of us in education and is consistent with the practices in highly regarded educational systems in other countries. As ESSA takes hold at the federal level and we pass through the transitional phase following the adoption of Common Core standards and assessments, the overemphasis on test scores may return.

While I support "The California Way," it's still important to acknowledge that these policies present challenges of their own. In conversations with people living and working in large districts, I haven't heard great enthusiasm for local control accountability plans so far. For example, consider that the Los Angeles Unified School District serves hundreds of thousands of students and more than 600 square miles, spanning regions and municipalities that feel little connection to each other, and sometimes minimal attachment to the district. It's not surprising that district-level meetings and processes fail to create a sense of new possibilities there.

However, in smaller districts, the shift can be significant. Through my work with the CalTURN, I've had the chance to sit at the table observing as union leaders and district administrators collaborate to develop and improve their LCAP process in specific, practical ways. It's exciting to hear about the inclusion of parents and high school students in these processes and meetings. I've heard district teams describe how the conversation is shifting as more people gain access to a process that articulates a vision and a set of goals in schools. I encourage anyone interested in public education to inquire about their district's Local Control Accountability Plan. Go a step further and get involved. If the LCAP is allowed to become another obscure bureaucratic exercise in compliance, Californians will have squandered a chance to improve public education.

Libraries with Full-Time Professional Librarians

If we are committed to deeds and not just words regarding a quality education for all students, libraries and librarians should be virtually sacrosanct. A thriving library, like the arts, should require no additional justification in schools. Arts and libraries have played a central role in civic and cultural life longer than schools have existed. But if you ever encounter a skeptic who wants additional justification, you can rest assured that research studies consistently demonstrate the value of librarians and libraries in improving student learning.[11]

The outdated image of libraries involves bookshelves and card catalogs and librarians who alternate between keeping children quiet and stamping due dates into books. The best contemporary libraries, in cities and schools, are hubs of information, activity, and learning, in ways that are flexible, personal, collaborative, and technological. Within schools, libraries may be the single clearest representation we have of what education is, what it does, what it means. A library's quality is often a barometer of a district's commitment to quality education for all students; after all, the library is the one classroom that serves all students (and teachers), and the librarian is the one teacher with that breadth of responsibility. The three librarians profiled in this book embraced that responsibility with creativity and zeal: Kay Hones (San Francisco Unified, Chapter 7), Sarah Morgan (Merced High School, Chapter 9), and Kelly Spector (NEW Academy, Chapter 13, in the section focused on Genein Letford).

Not all California schools have libraries, and even fewer have professional librarians. Our collective approach to library staffing is frighteningly shortsighted. It's difficult to summon language strong enough to lambast California's failure in this regard. In 2011, the national ratio of students to teacher librarians is roughly a thousand to one.[12] California continues to lag far behind; in 2014–15, we had over seven thousand students per librarian.[13]

Of course, having a high-quality library is expensive: It requires full-time staffing, with a certificated teaching librarian, and classified support staff to assist with both teaching and managing the library. Quality libraries are open throughout—if not beyond—the school day and offer a diverse and contemporary collection of books and periodicals (in print and digital formats, visual and audio), along with access to myriad digital archives, academic journals, and databases. Libraries require an investment not only in personnel and materials, but also in the physical space, which should be clean, comfortable, and furnished to support both instructional and recreational activities. What better way is there to support reading than to make the place with all the free books into a recreational destination on campus?

School Nurses and Professional Counselors

Due to confidentiality issues and the sensitive nature of their interactions with students, I didn't directly observe school counselors and nurses, but decades of personal experience and some indirect observations from my travels all lead me to offer a hearty endorsement for their work. When students are dealing with long-term health issues, social-emotional problems, or challenges in their home or neighborhood, those concerns are not left at home. Dr. Victor Carrion, professor of psychiatry and behavioral sciences at Stanford University Medical Center, has published research suggesting that in high-poverty, high-violence, urban areas, as many as 30 percent of children may have undiagnosed post-traumatic stress disorder. Another study by Dr. Carrion found that experiencing even one significant "adverse event" in childhood (such as neglect, exposure to drug addiction, an incarcerated parent) caused a jump in the rate of health and behavioral problems. Exposure to four or more types of adversity put children at *thirty times* as much risk for behavioral and learning problems.[14]

To some extent, all teachers practice a bit of nursing and counseling, but there are always problems beyond our limited abilities in these areas. We receive a modest amount of training to help students with diabetes or to administer epi-pen injections to arrest a severe allergic reaction, yet most of us have little actual experience dealing with medical emergencies. The number of medical crises and deaths at schools may be quite low in absolute terms, but such statistics offer little consolation when inadequate medical staffing contributes to a student injury, illness, or death at school.

For a general education population, professional organizations recommend one nurse for every 750 students, and a much lower ratio for students with special health needs. California's statewide ratio is one nurse for every 2,640 students (using 2013–14 data).[15]

With regard to counseling, students have needs spanning a broad emotional and psychological spectrum. Teachers may have the skills and knowledge to support students coping with limited and somewhat ordinary challenges, but more acute concerns arise frequently, and students with such needs deserve and require assistance from trained professionals.

There has also been increased scrutiny of student suspensions in recent years, putting schools under intense pressure to address student behavior problems without removing students from school. It's uncomplicated for principals to lower their suspension rates to comply with district and state directives; they simply stop suspending students. Yet without an accompanying significant increase in the amount and quality of counseling in schools, simply keeping troubled students in the building serves no one well. Many of my friends who teach in Los Angeles Unified say classroom and campus climates have deteriorated noticeably because their principals lost the option of suspension but received little if any compensatory assistance to effectively address behavioral problems at school.

On a day-to-day basis, we can take some comfort in the ways that an experienced teacher like Martha Infante holds a class together at Los Angeles Academy Middle School (see Chapter 11), keeping troubled students engaged in academics while also trying to improve their self-monitoring and impulse control. In the long run, we're asking far too much of such great teachers. We're placing these teachers at risk and jeopardizing their career longevity. We're also woefully underserving students who need more than great teaching to overcome the challenges in their lives.

Additionally, at the secondary level, we expect school counselors to provide academic advising and course selection guidance. In high schools, college and financial aid application processes and other career advising also land in the counseling department. The professionally recommended ratio is one counselor for every 250 students.[16] The national average is one counselor per 477 students, and in California, we have only one counselor for every 945 students.[17] In a state with so many students whose parents may not be fluent in English and may be unfamiliar with our higher education system, the lack of counseling represents a significant inequity that harms both students and our state's interest in developing a highly skilled and well-educated citizenry.

The next several recommendations are grouped according to specific areas where policy decisions are concentrated. However, as we consider these separate areas, we must maintain an overarching concern with teacher retention as we head into a period of anticipated teacher shortages nationwide. To that end, people involved in designing and implementing policies in these areas have a special responsibility to ensure increased diversity in the teacher workforce. We must examine and remove existing barriers that disproportionately keep people of color from becoming or remaining teachers. New policies must not only avoid creating barriers, but also proactively address and improve systemic conditions that drive teachers of color out of the profession or limit their opportunities when they stay.

Teacher Salaries

Attracting and retaining skilled employees is essential to any workplace. Our school system is not just another workplace, however. I don't need to belabor the unique importance of schools in our society. What requires our attention is the shortage of teachers in California.

In 2016, the Learning Policy Institute (LPI) published a report on California's teacher shortage, detailing a variety of causes and solutions. Regarding compensation, the report notes that "since the early 1990s, teacher salaries have been declining in relation to other professional salaries. Even after adjusting for the shorter work year, teachers earn 15 to 30 percent less than individuals with college degrees who enter other fields, depending on the field and the region."[18] Salaries are not the sole driver in any labor market. However, if salaries are too low, in either relative or absolute terms, then workers will go elsewhere. Relatively low salaries drive teachers to work in districts with higher pay (typically wealthier communities), and drive some teachers to leave the profession for higher pay in other sectors (especially scientific and technological work). In areas with a high cost of living, teacher pay is often too low to cover rent and other basic expenses. The LPI report also notes that carrying student debt is a deterrent to prospective teachers; they recommend state and federal programs that either prevent teaching candidates from taking on debt or forgive student debt over a period of years for graduates who enter and stay in the teaching profession.

Efforts to stabilize the teaching workforce may incur costs, but those expenses are partially offset by savings. Teacher turnover generates nationwide annual costs estimated to be as high as $7 billion.[19] Depending on whether we count schools or students, California's share of that cost would be 10 percent or more. Reducing turnover also improves students' achievement.[20]

Dealing with the numbers in teacher compensation can be a tricky proposition, considering the unusual working hours and calendar, and the variables in pension contributions and other benefits. (There's also the fact that teachers on average spend several hundred dollars on their classrooms and student supplies—a nifty, billion-dollar-plus annual subsidy to American public education that you won't read about too often.) Summer break is another complicating factor in discussion of teacher salaries. However, if we use the forty-hour workweek as the standard unit of measure, the average teacher is putting in much more than a summer's worth of work over the course of the school year. Most teachers continue to do some school work over the summer, though the amount has not been quantified, as far as I know, and any average would distort the huge variability in summer work. Here's another way to look at it: If the average American teacher works fifty-three hours per week for forty weeks, that's equivalent to working slightly more than forty hours per week, *every* week.[21]

The Teacher Salary Project also has some good resources on teacher pay, including some important information about comparing current teacher salaries to past salaries, adjusting for inflation, and comparing teacher salaries to those of similarly qualified and experienced professionals in other fields.[22] Looking at the facts and figures overall, I think it's clear that teachers as a whole need higher salaries, especially in the first half of their careers.

Teacher Preparation and Induction

My own teaching experience began prior to my entrance to the Stanford Teacher Education Program (STEP), so I was even more prepared to take advantage of its benefits. The most important part of STEP for me was the opportunity to work at one school for an entire school year. Most teacher preparation programs move student teachers around during the year, with the intended and valid goal of providing a more varied experience. My fellow STEP alumni typically agree that the benefits outweigh the costs when we stay in one place. Seeing one or two more schools has a slight benefit, but not as great as that derived from the experience of one school year with one set of students. By the end of that year, STEP graduates are better prepared for the sharply increased workload that comes with the first year of teaching.

Although I didn't always know the background of the teachers I visited, knowing when and where a teacher had been trained helped me understand the teachers' approaches to their practices and their longevity. I won't belabor the skills and leadership traits of the STEP alumni I've already highlighted in prior chapters: Haydee Rodriguez, April Oliver, Marciano Gutierrez, and Karl Lindgren-Streicher. I can add, however, that the STEP graduates I've taught with are consistently effective teachers who make substantial contributions within their departments and across campus.

Attention is increasingly being paid to the quality, or lack of it, in teacher preparation programs overall. Linda Darling-Hammond, among the world's foremost experts on teacher training, was the faculty sponsor of STEP for many years until she relinquished that position shortly before this book was written. She summarizes the characteristics of quality teacher training that we should advocate for in the state and country:

> *[Effective teacher education] programs include tight coherence and integration among courses and between coursework and clinical work in schools, extensive and intensely supervised clinical work integrated with coursework using pedagogies linking theory and practice, and closer, proactive relationships with schools that serve diverse learners effectively and develop and model good teaching.*[23]

While teacher training in general may need improvement, the problem is one of commitment and execution rather than a lack of ideas about what to do. It's logical and demonstrable that improvement follows from better preparation for teaching, better supervision and support for novices, and better coordination among systems. Some programs—most famously but not limited to Teach for America (TFA)—claim they can produce a "highly qualified teacher" in much less time. It strikes me as a step backward for the profession to make that argument and to promote short-term commitments rather than envisioning a career in teaching. There are also serious equity issues in placing less-prepared teachers with short-term commitments in schools where students need more stability and even better trained teachers.

To further capitalize on good teacher training, schools and districts should ensure that induction programs offer enough support for new teachers without saddling them with excessive burdens in the area of documentation, analysis, and reflection. Part of this goal can be accomplished by making sure that new teachers don't receive the most challenging teaching placements. For example, schools sometimes hire based on what needs to be covered in the schedule. If the English department at a high school has five open class periods, but they're in three or four different courses and grade levels, it would be wiser to adjust the schedules of current teachers before hiring a new teacher, so that the new teacher has a more manageable teaching assignment. Established, experienced teachers must take *more* than their share of the challenges if we hope to retain new teachers. Reducing the teaching load for a new teacher is even more useful, though costly in the short term; however, considering the high costs of teacher turnover, workload reduction could provide some return on investment, offsetting some of that cost.

Teacher Leadership and Career Pathways

This issue is near to my heart and the subject of much of my work outside the classroom. As an associate director of Accomplished California Teachers from 2009 to 2013, I worked closely with Anthony Cody, my co-associate director Sandy Dean, and Dr. Linda Darling-Hammond to produce a report sharing teacher leaders' views on leadership and career pathways in education. A team of about a dozen teachers from all over the state spent months discussing the issues, reading relevant literature and studying existing models. Our conclusions were largely consistent with other groups that have studied the issue: Teachers generally feel disempowered in education policy, locally and beyond, and seek opportunities to exercise leadership and influence without having to leave the classroom entirely. The report, "Promoting Teaching Quality: New Approaches to Career Pathways and Compensation," can be downloaded from my personal website; the same page includes a link to another important report, "Greatness by Design," produced by the California Department of Education to examine the future of teaching in our state.[24] Interested readers outside California might want to investigate state-level approaches to promoting teacher leadership in New Mexico and Iowa, and also examine the work of the Center for Teaching Quality (CTQ) and the National Network of State Teachers of the Year (NNSTOY).

I previously focused considerable attention on multiple schools and educators who help illustrate the benefits of teacher leadership, so I won't revisit the point here. However, I am encouraged that state- and national-level attention has been directed to this cause. The goal of differentiating teacher career pathways based on expertise and demonstrated leadership must be linked to teacher compensation as well. While typical performance pay models fail when they're based on simplistic outcomes, we should pay teachers more if they have demonstrated advanced qualifications and taken on additional professional responsibilities.

When districts overly rely on top-down leadership, they tend to invest too much authority in fewer people or in specific programs, and these are among the least stable pieces of the education puzzle. Assistant superintendents and program directors come and go. Various curricular decisions are changed without teacher control or input, and teachers' frustrations mount as every year or two seems to bring a professional learning "reset"—new people, new materials, new technology, new priorities. Teacher leadership in areas of curriculum and instruction has the potential to expand the professional skills and improve the stability of districts and schools. Nonteachers tend to think in terms of fidelity of implementation in these situations, ensuring that every teacher sticks to the adopted program. Teachers tend to think in terms of fidelity to students, exercising their own judgment regarding classroom materials and practices. That approach may slow down the implementation of worthy programs, but it can also mitigate the damage from those that are inadequate. In conversations with the teachers I visited, the greatest complaints about standards and instruction were from those who felt they were always on the receiving end of district mandates. Teachers who had more autonomy, input regarding their work, and opportunity to lead—at schools like Cleveland Elementary (Pasadena) and Live Oak Elementary (Fallbrook), Union Middle School (San Jose), Lincoln High School (San Francisco), and Design39Campus (Poway)— were highly energized in their work and spoke of administrative support rather than hindrances. Teacher-led schools (see Chapter 8) provide the strongest possible response to this problem.

There are politicians and school board trustees who would prefer to keep teachers in their place, largely as the passive recipients of instructions and mandates from their superiors. That's an attitude that needs to be challenged for multiple reasons, including the latent sexism it reflects in a profession characterized by mostly female practitioners and mostly male leadership. In addition, the expansion of teacher leadership is ultimately about allowing input from better informed and more engaged professionals whose voices and expertise will lead to improved education policy at every level.

Teacher Evaluation (and Misuse of Test Scores)

As I noted at the outset of this chapter, we err by viewing school improvement as a personnel problem rather than a system problem. Nowhere is this error more apparent than in the misdirected focus on teacher evaluation. To borrow an oft-used metaphor, it's like we're trying to raise heavier livestock by improving how well and how often we weigh the animals.

I spent almost two years studying and writing about teacher evaluation, helping to produce a policy report on the topic for Accomplished California Teachers.[25] The potential value of our recommendations depends first on shifting the view of evaluation from a compliance and accountability focus to a teacher-growth focus. We advocated a more robust form of teacher evaluation, tied to clear standards and leading to relevant professional learning opportunities. Evaluations should be carried out by trained evaluators, including professional peers (and not only administrators). We supported the idea that evidence of student learning should be part of evaluation, though used to promote analysis and reflection rather than to reach summative judgments regarding teaching quality. We categorically rejected the increasingly common but unjustified use of standardized test scores as evidence of student learning.

To an outsider, I see how that may seem illogical: Last year's test measured student learning, so this year's test should measure the contribution the teacher made to student learning. In fact, an abundance of research demonstrates that student test scores are only marginally affected by schools but are predominantly an artifact of factors outside of school, mostly relating to in one way or another to indicators and effects of poverty. That idea is not in dispute. The debate arises from the fact that teachers are the top influencers on test scores among all influences *within* schools. However, although those effects can be demonstrated using huge data sets involving thousands or millions of students, the effects are too unstable at the individual level to be true measures of teacher effectiveness. If we use student test-score growth to rate teachers using what are called "value-added measures" (VAM), the year-to-year volatility is too high to make the measures reliable or useful. Advocates of VAM say that multiple years' worth of data will smooth out that volatility, but they cannot account for the dozens of other variables that change in any given year of a teacher's work. Placing high stakes on a measure that's volatile and outside the teacher's control is simply bad policy, and it hasn't worked. The approach has divided the education community—and not along teacher-administrator lines. Many administrators have sided with teachers against test-based evaluation, most notably in New York, where hundreds of principals joined a coalition to oppose state policy on teacher evaluation. Test-based evaluation has also produced a variety of lawsuits and cheating scandals—predictable outcomes when people feel threatened and relatively powerless.

No professional organizations in educational research and measurement endorse the use of standardized test scores for teacher evaluation. The fact that standardized tests are not validated measures of teacher effectiveness is a monumental obstacle, but technical and complex enough that few policy makers seem interested in understanding it, as they hasten to appease the general public's appetite for teacher accountability. For more extensive reading and citations regarding the numerous problems with test-based teacher evaluation, I recommend consulting the National Education Policy Center (nepc.colorado.edu), VAMboozled.com (created by Dr. Audrey Amrein-Beardsley of Arizona State University), and FairTest.org.

Progressive Unionism and Labor-Management Collaboration

Teachers unions are the largest organizations of teachers, the ones that completely encompass grade levels and subject areas, representing teachers from all types of schools and districts, communities and regions. Our collective ability to make a positive difference in public education is certainly evident when it comes to budgets, politics, and the law. That doesn't mean that I've agreed with every position CTA has taken over the years (I'm less familiar with the California Federation of Teachers, or CFT, which also represents teachers around the state). However, our unions are still fundamentally democratic in nature, with elected teachers representing us in processes that establish organizational priorities and policies. Just as I think our society will be better off with broader participation in elections and civic life, so do I believe our unions will be stronger and more effective with maximum participation among members.

The idea of union effectiveness should be understood as more than advocacy for salaries, benefits, and working conditions. These items are certainly essential parts of unionism, but we need to be about more than that. The two other facets of progressive unionism are professional practices and social justice.

Being the most effective professional educators possible is the best way to persuade the public and policy makers to listen to and work with us to address labor-related issues. To that end, unions must take a more active interest in the quality of teaching and better publicize existing work in that area. CTA organizes teaching conferences around the state and includes discussion of teaching practices in its publications. Local units must follow suit by taking a more active role in guiding and supporting professional learning for their members. In their book *United Mind Workers: Unions and Teaching in the Knowledge Society,* researchers Charles Taylor Kerchner, Julia E. Koppich, and Joseph G. Weeres suggested that—similar to guilds in various trades and crafts—the union should be responsible for hiring teachers and ensuring the quality of their work. That idea also surfaces in *Teaching 2030: What We Must Do for Our Students and Our Public Schools . . . Now and in the Future* by Barnett Berry. It would be a seismic shift for teaching, completely dissonant with most current assumptions about roles, responsibilities, and accountability in public education. I don't know if it would work or not. I do know that there's a misconception in the general public that unions are unconcerned with teaching quality and focused on protecting mediocre or weak teachers. The best way to combat that misconception is by not limiting ourselves to talking points, but rather taking actions that are unambiguously focused on improving teaching and learning in every classroom. Working with administrators and school boards to pursue our common interest in student learning, we will establish a higher degree of trust that serves our other interests as well.

However, it's not enough for teachers to focus on schools if we really want what's best for our students and communities. When accused of not doing enough for kids, we are quick to note that the out-of-school factors shaping their lives are stronger than the effects of schools, a point which garners wide consensus in education research. If we're all in agreement that the effects of community, family, and society at large are more powerful than schools overall, then teachers, unions, and anyone claiming to advocate for children's well being, must also have a broader vision of what constitutes support for students. Unions must actively seek substantive engagement with parents and community leaders to learn more about their strengths, values, and aspirations, and how we can work together to meet challenges. We can't rely on community support for teachers simply by virtue of being teachers. We must be willing to give as much support as we hope to receive.

Three of my school visits were driven at least in part by a desire to observe places where labor-management collaboration has yielded greater teacher voice and impact on professional practices. Those three were Encina Prep (San Juan Unified), Design39Campus (Poway Unified), and Gahr High School (ABC Unified). I previously noted that ABC Unified has received state and national recognition as a leader in labor-management collaboration, which improves student learning by strengthening the entire organization. And while the district-level collaboration is still a work in progress, the union in Fresno Unified has made strides in community engagement, taking the initiative to organize multiple community meetings for discussion of the LCAP. Both teachers I observed in Fresno, Adam Ebrahim and Hilary Levine, were leaders in that union. If we're smart, unions will continue such efforts, organizing civic engagement activities in places and times that work for community members, with food, child care, and translation services included as needed.

Californians are not well served by legal actions, bills, or propositions intended to undermine unions. The most prominent recent example was *Vergara v. California*, in which plaintiffs (represented by an organization called Students Matter) claimed that certain teacher job protections expose mostly minority students to a disproportionate number of ineffective teachers, thereby violating students' rights under the state constitution. They rationalized their strategy by arguing that unions obstruct legislative solutions, making judicial actions the only viable recourse.[26] In the 2014 trial, despite mixed evidence on the issues, Judge Rolf Treu ruled in favor of the plaintiffs. One section of his surprisingly concise ruling relied on his own hypothetical reasoning about school personnel operations, without any reference to evidence presented in trial. The ruling was appealed, and I was proud to be included in a "friend of the court" (*amicus*) legal brief delineating flaws in the lower court's findings. Other teachers profiled in this book who also signed on as "friends of the court" include Rebecca Mieliwocki, Jessica Pack, Alicia Hinde, Marciano Gutierrez, Adam Ebrahim, and Sarah Kirby-Gonzalez (in her capacity as a school board trustee). In April of 2016, a three-judge panel of the appellate court unanimously overturned the lower court ruling, citing many inadequacies in the trial evidence and errors in Judge Treu's legal reasoning. Students Matter appealed that ruling to the California Supreme Court. In August 2016, just before this book went into publication, that appeal was denied, marking the end of the Vergara case.

If teacher job protections negotiated and supported by unions were inhibiting quality teaching, you might expect states and nations without such protections, or without unions, to produce better educational outcomes. No such trend exists, nor, to my knowledge, has even been suggested. In fact, strong quantitative research using ten years of data comparing states and districts leads to the opposite conclusion: Strong unions have a positive effect on teaching quality and student achievement.[27]

Battling with unions through the courts, legislature, or ballot will only stiffen political resistance and exacerbate disagreements. A political "win" over unions will not motivate better teacher performance. You cannot compel people to excel. The better approach to reform is to highlight positive examples and aim to replicate the conditions that make such work possible and sustainable. From what I've heard and seen, negotiation and collaboration among stakeholders produces mutual buy-in and *shared responsibility for success*. Schools and districts that adopt such approaches are not immune to tensions and disagreements, but they navigate challenges together because they understand there is no one-sided success; labor and management both depend on *the other's* effectiveness to be most effective themselves.

Capturing the Spark

We all care about the quality of public education. Most of us have an insecurity about it as well, whether we're teachers, administrators, parents, policy makers, concerned community members, or any combination of the above. That insecurity has some value as it means we're not complacent; we know we can do better than we're doing now.

Insecurity becomes a problem if we are constantly looking around to see what everyone else is doing, focusing on deficiencies, convincing ourselves that we don't measure up to the best schools or the best teachers. Education has a long list of "best practices," some of which warrant the name more than others.

Instead of focusing on best *practices*, I prefer to ask that we focus on best *conditions*. It's like we're taking a tour of a hothouse, marveling at the exotic orchids and birds-of-paradise. We're so focused on the plants that we're not thinking about the soil, the water, the temperature and the humidity. We don't all need orchids. We do need to understand how plants grow. We don't need to help schools import the best practices of other schools. We need policies and working conditions that allow teachers, school leaders, and communities to create their own best practices that are informed by others, yet based on their own strengths, which arise from their unique contexts.

Capturing the spark means not being distracted by the flames. You can't replicate the schools in this book, copy and paste their programs, or clone the teachers. Nor do you need to. The sparks are already close at hand, if you recognize and cultivate the potential in your community, schools, teachers, and students.

Guide to Teachers Online

Blogs, websites, and Twitter feeds of teachers featured in the book (alphabetical by last name). Twitter feeds can be searched through a Twitter mobile application or desktop platform, or viewed in your web browser by adding the unique user name to the URL: http://twitter.com/

Jeremy Adams
Blog: theeducatorsroom.com/author/jeremyadams1976
Twitter: JeremyAdams6

Laura Bradley
Website: laurabradley.me
Twitter: LAMBradley

Jim Burke
Website: englishcompanion.com
Twitter: EnglishComp

Larry Ferlazzo
Blog: larryferlazzo.edublogs.org
Blog: engagingparentsinschool.edublogs.org
Twitter: LarryFerlazzo

Martha Infante
Blog: dontforgetsouthcentral.blogspot.com
Twitter: AvalonSensei

Genein Letford
Blog: geneinletford.blogspot.com
Twitter: GeneinLetford

Karl Lindgren-Streicher
Blog: historywithls.blogspot.com
Twitter: LS_Karl

Jessica Pack
Website: packwomantech.com
Twitter: Packwoman208

Jennifer Roberts
Website: litandtech.com
Twitter: JenRoberts1

Catlin Tucker
Website: catlintucker.com
Twitter: Catlin_Tucker

Heather Wolpert-Gawron
Website: tweenteacher.com
Twitter: TweenTeacher

Recommended Viewing and Reading

Films

American Teacher (2011)
Vanessa Roth, Brian McGinn, co-directors
Ninive Calegari, Dave Eggers, Vanessa Roth, producers
www.theteachersalaryproject.org/american-teacher-the-movie
Examines the daily lives of four teachers struggling to balance demands at work and home, with insufficient salaries.

Beyond Measure (2014)
Reel Link Films, Vicki Abeles, producer/director
http://beyondmeasurefilm.com/
Documentary examines how education must change to meet students' needs in ways not typically valued or measured by schools.

Crenshaw (2014)
Lena Jackson, producer/director
https://vimeo.com/101591828
Short documentary taking a critical view of how Los Angeles Unified School District undermined promising reform efforts at Crenshaw High School and pushed through an unpopular, destabilizing school reconstitution program instead.

Defies Measurement (2015)
Shine On Productions, Shannon Puckett, producer/director
https://vimeo.com/122720631
Documentary film about a unique elementary school in Emeryville, California, celebrated for its focus on holistic education and environmental awareness, that was closed due to low test scores and replaced by a charter school.

The Inconvenient Truth Behind Waiting for Superman (2011)
Grassroots Education Movement
https://vimeo.com/41994760
Teachers and parents in New York responding to the more famous *Waiting for Superman* detail ways in which New York City favored charter school operators while forcing community schools into unviable situations and eventual closure.

Mitchell 20 (2011)
Randy Murray Productions, Andrew James Benson and Randy Murray, directors
www.mitchell20.com
Narrated by Edward James Olmos, this feature-length documentary tracks the career-changing experiences of twenty teachers pursuing National Board Certification together at Mitchell School in Phoenix.

Most Likely to Succeed (2015)
Greg Whiteley, producer/director
www.mltsfilm.org/
Documentary film shows a year of project-based teaching and learning at a San Diego high school, with numerous education experts sharing perspectives on innovative approaches to education.

Books *(by authors other than the teachers profiled in this book; for information about their books, please see the teacher's website or blog, listed in Appendix 1)*
21st Century Skills: Learning for Life in Our Times
Bernie Trilling and Charles Fadel
Jossey-Bass, 2009
Describes how education must evolve to meet student and societal needs for greater flexibility, collaboration, communication skills, problem solving, and critical thinking in the information age.

Drive: The Surprising Truth about What Motivates Us
Daniel H. Pink
Riverhead Books, 2009
Though not directly about education, this book continually informs my thinking about teaching, working within a school, and what motivates people in any complex and challenging endeavor.

#EdJourney: A Roadmap to the Future of Education
Grant Lichtman
Jossey-Bass, 2014
The author drove around the United States and visited sixty schools that had promising and innovative instructional practices and academic programs.

The Educator and The Oligarch: A Teacher Challenges the Gates Foundation
By Anthony Cody
Garn Press, 2014
Building from efforts in his blog "Living in Dialogue," Anthony Cody describes the Gates Foundation's outsized influence and negative impact on American education policies and practices.

The Flat World and Education: How America's Commitment to Equity Will Determine Our Future
Linda Darling-Hammond
Teachers College Press, 2010
The foremost expert in American education examines research and international models that suggest how American education must evolve and improve to meet the needs of all students in the modern economy and world.

Identity-Safe Classrooms: Places to Belong and Learn
Dorothy M. Steele and Becki Cohn-Vargas
Corwin, 2013
The authors examine ways in which student identity affects classroom and school dynamics, and offer exemplary practices and strategies educators can use teachers to make school "identity safe" by valuing all aspects of student identity and seeing differences as individual and community assets.

Improbable Scholars: The Rebirth of a Great American School System and a Strategy for America's Schools
David L. Kirp
Oxford University Press USA, 2013
Immersing himself in the schools and community of Union City, New Jersey, Kirp reveals how a coordinated effort and hard work by all stakeholders in a community can turn schools around.

Inside the Black Box of Classroom Practice: Change Without Reform in American Education
Larry Cuban
Harvard Education Press, 2013
Cuban examines why it is so hard to create and sustain change in classrooms and schools.

Mission High: One School, How Experts Tried to Fail It, and the Students and Teachers Who Made It Triumph
Kristina Rizga
Nation Books, 2015
Building on reporting she did for *Mother Jones* magazine, Rizga uses four years' worth of school-based observations and interviews to take readers deep into San Francisco's Mission High School, showing how education policy can be at odds with the people and practices that make a school successful and respected in the community.

Professional Capital: Transforming Teaching in Every School
Andy Hargreaves and Michael Fullan
Teachers College Press, 2012
The authors cite copious research and examples from educational systems around the world to build an argument for broad changes in policy and practice that put teacher expertise at the center of educational leadership.

The Public School Advantage: Why Public Schools Outperform Private Schools
Christopher A. Lubienski and Sarah Theule Lubienski
University of Chicago Press, 2014
Examining ample research, data, and statistical analyses of various educational outcomes for all students across all types of schools, the authors argue that our public education systems do a better job than their nonpublic counterparts.

Reign of Error: The Hoax of the Privatization Movement and the Danger to America's Public Schools
Diane Ravitch
Knopf, 2013

One of the most influential books in education reform debates, *Reign of Error* challenges the underlying assumptions that have led policy makers to try to fix schools through strategies that have failed to solve our problems. While child poverty soars and educational infrastructure languishes, corporate-influenced education reform focuses on new standards, more testing, school choice, and tougher evaluations, despite shaky evidence that these approaches will help.

The Teacher Wars: A History of America's Most Embattled Profession
Dana Goldstein
Anchor, 2014
A fascinating history of the status of teachers and public schools in American life, revealing how we tend to make the same mistakes repeatedly, focusing on the wrong metrics and the wrong levers to bring about better teaching and learning.

Teacherpreneurs: Innovative Teachers Who Lead But Don't Leave
Barnett Berry, Ann Byrd, Alan Wieder
Jossey-Bass, 2013
Profiles individuals and highlights opportunities for teachers to take on significant leadership roles without giving up teaching.

Teaching 2030: What We Must Do for Our Students and Our Public Schools: Now and in the Future
Barnett Berry, et. al.
Teachers College Press, 2011
The Teacher Solutions team examines all the ways that schools and teaching will change in the near future and what we should do to improve teaching and schools to be ready for success in a new era.

This Is Not a Test: A New Narrative on Race, Class, and Education
José Luis Vilson
Haymarket Books, 2014
Blending elements of a memoir, teaching narrative, and social commentary essay, New York City teacher, blogger, and activist José Luis Vilson challenges readers to confront systemic racism and issues of social class that perpetuate inequality.

Trusting Teachers With School Success
Kim Farris-Berg and Edward Dirkswager, with Amy Junge
R&L Education, 2012
Arguing that teacher-created and teacher-led schools hold promise for improving education, the authors offer a wide-ranging and finely detailed comparison of schools with various approaches to leadership and governance.

ACKNOWLEDGMENTS

Capturing the Spark has been a long time coming, and I owe so much to so many people who made a difference along the journey.

Sandy Dean directed the National Board Resource Center at Stanford University during my years as a support provider for National Board Certification candidates. Her dedication to better teaching and teacher leadership has undoubtedly benefited hundreds of educators and thousands of students. My fellow candidate support providers helped me develop a broader understanding and a professional voice; among those peers, Tammie Adams, Laura Bradley, Kay Hones, and Silver White went a step further and supported me directly in this project.

Sandy Dean warrants another acknowledgement, along with Anthony Cody, for bringing me in to help establish and run the leadership network Accomplished California Teachers (ACT). For about six years, we had the privilege of working to amplify the voices of skilled teachers around the state, dedicated to the idea that effective education reform must be not only informed, but also driven by skilled teachers. I learned from them constantly, and their combined insights and passion made it a pleasure to work together.

Dr. Linda Darling-Hammond, at the Stanford University Graduate School of Education, was our champion in establishing and sustaining ACT for as long as possible and has continued to offer support, guidance, and opportunities to me and many other teachers working for the improvement of public education. Her contributions to the profession are immense, as teachers and education leaders around the country will attest.

Dr. Barnett Berry, founder and CEO of the Center for Teaching Quality (CTQ), gave me my first opportunity to learn from and interact with teacher leaders from around the country, by inviting me to join the Teacher Leaders Network (TLN). He also generously provided the Foreword for this book. CTQ has been a continual source of support and inspiration, from my early participation in an email list-serve group, to the current virtual networking in the Collaboratory. There are too many CTQ friends to thank everyone individually; however, I have been particularly supported and inspired by Bill Ferriter, Nancy Flanagan, Jane Fung, John Holland, Susan Graham, Bill Ivey, Kathie Marshall, Renee Moore, Lori Nazareno, Cindi

Rigsbee, Ariel Sacks, Claudia Swisher, Mary Tedrow, José Vilson, and once again, Anthony Cody.

John Norton was the virtual heartbeat of TLN for a number of years and now runs MiddleWeb. He's played a unique role in supporting and encouraging so many of us as writers and advocates. John certainly deserves more thanks than I have space to offer, but if you look at the acknowledgements section of other books by teachers connected to CTQ, you'll see John thanked, over and over—quite a legacy!

For over a decade, I've been fortunate enough to work with wonderful teachers and staff at Palo Alto High School. I've seen dedicated and talented teachers, year-in and year-out, across disciplines, always inspiring me to improve my teaching and continue my own learning. My thanks to Letitia Burton for invaluable lessons about understanding and caring for all our students, and for opening her classroom to me as I began this work. Rachel Kellerman's sense of mission and drive has shaped my thinking about libraries and also influenced this project.

My principals at Palo Alto High School, five of them going back to 2002, have always been supportive in ways that made my teaching better and my career sustainable. Now, more than ever, I appreciate how valuable it is to have leaders whose first inclination is to say "yes." In particular, Kim Diorio's enthusiastic support has been a great help to me. Over the years, Palo Alto Unified School District staff have also helped me understand teaching and education more broadly; thank you Jennifer Abrams, Kelly Bikle, Burton Cohen, Becki Cohn-Vargas, Scott Laurence, Max McGee, and Kevin Skelly.

My union sisters and brothers at the Palo Alto Educators Association, the California Teachers Association (CTA), the CTA Institute for Teaching (IFT), and the California Teachers Union Reform Network (CalTURN), you've been *my* teachers, role models, and sources of inspiration: Tom Alves, Teri Baldwin, Sheila Bell, Pat Dolan, Dick Gale, Triona Gogarty, Eric Heins, Kelly Horner, Mary McDonald, Kate McKenna, Candy Smiley, Dean Vogel, Christal Watts, Yale Wishnick—and especially, Shannan Brown. Much appreciation also to my fellow participants in the IFT Think Tanks.

At a time when I hadn't discussed this book with anyone beyond friends and family, Samer Rabadi of Edutopia agreed to listen to an idea I wanted to run by him. It was a mere postscript to a longer and unrelated conversation, but I took great encouragement from his response. Others who have asked useful questions and offered insights about writing and publishing include Dave Burgess, Larry Cuban, Dave Eggers, John Fensterwald, Brad Herzog, Alex Kajitani, Reed Malcolm, and Dave Martinez. For additional advice and feedback that shaped my approach and influenced my thinking, I want to thank Delaine Eastin, Kim Farris-Berg, Kristoffer Kohl, Grant Lichtman, Sandra Pearson, Susie Richardson, Barry Schuler, Jamie Schwartzman, and Mark Simon.

Life on the road, up to two weeks at a time, was made more pleasant when I occasionally avoided hotels and enjoyed the generous hospitality of friends and family. Many thanks to Karen and Michael Alexander, Inger and Rob Avery, Lisa Alva and Troy Wood, Sue and Ken Dickson, Irma and Al Hogan, Alysia and Paul Krafel, Angela and Tony Reed, Jennifer and Kris Roberts, Keila Snider and Jesus Jimenez. And though our coffees and lunches didn't make it into the book, meeting you made the journey that much sweeter: Scott Bedley, Tim Bedley, Jo-Ann Fox, David Theriault and Sean Ziebarth.

In recent years, I've written enough blog posts to fill *two* books, but writing one book turned out to be harder than I anticipated. My developmental editor, Julie Feinstein Adams, stuck with me as a months-long project extended beyond a year. Her honesty, critical insights, and concise feedback made a great difference in how this book evolved. Ruth-Anne Siegel's cover design helped translate *Capturing the Spark* into visual form, to great effect. Marla Markman provided the copy editing and expert project management to see me through the final steps of this multiyear project, for which I'm immensely grateful.

ENDNOTES

1. S. Childress, A. Samouha, D. Tavenner, & J. Wetzler, "Dissatisfied Yet Optimistic: Moving Faster Toward New School Models," NewSchools Venture Fund website, August 31, 2015, www.newschools.org/wp/wp-content/uploads/Dissatisfied-Yet-Optimistic-final.pdf.

2. Esther Quintero, "The Social Side of Education Reform," Albert Shanker Institute website, April 2016, www.shankerinstitute.org/sites/shanker/files/SSoER%20Research%20Primer%20Final_1.pdf.

3. Coincidentally, my trip to Los Angeles included time spent at the headquarters of 826LA, where I had a chance to visit my former student, Annie Vought, and learn more about the program from Executive Director Joel Arquillos. I highly recommend that teachers and schools in Los Angeles and the San Francisco Bay Area look into the programs and support offered by 826LA and 826 Valencia. They also have programs in a few other large cities outside California. And if you're in the Echo Park neighborhood of Los Angeles, check out the 826LA retail storefront on Sunset Boulevard, the highly amusing Time Travel Mart.

4. The Annie E. Casey Foundation is a good source of information on these problems. See aecf.org.

5. Anthony Bryk and Barbara Schneider, *Trust in Schools: A Core Resource for Improvement* (New York: Russell Sage Foundation, 2002).

6. "California Demographics of Low-Income Children," National Center for Children in Poverty website, April 6, 2016, http://www.nccp.org/profiles/CA_profile_6.html.

7. "Current Expense of Education," California Department of Education website, Feb. 25, 2016, www.cde.ca.gov/ds/fd/ec/currentexpense.asp.

8. C. Kirabo Jackson, Rucker Johnson, Claudia Persico, "The Effect of School Finance Reforms on the Distribution of Spending, Academic Achievement, and Adult Outcomes" (Working Paper No. 20118, National Bureau of Economic Research, May 2014), doi: 10.3386/w20118.

9. Multiple studies of QEIA have been conducted by Vital Research of Los Angeles and can be accessed via the California Teachers Association website: www.cta.org/qeia.

10. Michael Hout and Stuart W. Elliott, ed., Board on Testing and Assessment, Division of Behavioral and Social Sciences and Education, and National Research Council, *Incentives and Test-Based Accountability in Education* (Washington, DC: National Academies Press, 2011). Available from National Academies Press website, http://www.nap.edu/catalog/12521/incentives-and-test-based-accountability-in-education.

11. See resources from the website for the American Association of School Librarians (part of the American Library Association): www.ala.org/aasl/research; and the *School Library Journal* research collection: www.slj.com/category/research/.

12. The precise ratio is 1,023:1. The most recent available national data is from 2011. See "Digest of Education Statistics," from the National Center for Education Statistics website, nces.ed.gov/programs/digest/d13/tables/dt13_213.20.asp.

13. The precise ratio is 7,218:1. See "Statistics about California School Libraries," California Department of Education website, www.cde.ca.gov/ci/cr/lb/schoollibrstats08.asp.

14. Erin Digitale, "Childhood Trauma Linked to Higher Rates of Mental Health Problems and Obesity, Says Stanford/Packard Psychiatrist," Stanford Medicine News Center website, June 8, 2011, http://goo.gl/T87Lmw.

15. "2013-2014 Ratio of School Nurses to K–12 Students by County," California School Nurses Organization website, Feb. 9, 2015, www.csno.org/uploads/1/7/2/4/17248852/california_map_of_nurses_ratio_and_rank_2014.pdf.

16. American School Counselor Association, "The Role of the School Counselor," n.d., www.schoolcounselor.org/asca/media/asca/home/rolestatement.pdf.

17. "Research on School Counseling Effectiveness," California Department of Education website, www.cde.ca.gov/ls/cg/rh/counseffective.asp.

18. Linda Darling-Hammond, Roberta Furger, Patrick Shields, and Leib Sutcher, *Addressing California's Emerging Teacher Shortage: An Analysis of Sources and Solutions* (Palo Alto: Learning Policy Institute, 2016), 18.

19. National Commission on Teaching and America's Future, "The High Cost of Teacher Turnover," 2007, http://nctaf.org/wp-content/uploads/2012/01/NCTAF-Cost-of-Teacher-Turnover-2007-policy-brief.pdf.

20. Matthew Ronfeldt, Susanna Loeb, and James Wyckoff, "How Teacher Turnover Harms Student Achievement," *American Educational Research Journal* 50, no. 1 (2013): 4–36.

21. *Primary Sources: America's Teachers on Teaching in an Era of Change* (Scholastic Inc. and the Bill and Melinda Gates Foundation, 2013).

22. http://teachersalaryproject.org/facts-about-teachers-2/

23. Linda Darling-Hammond, "Constructing 21st-Century Teacher Education," *Journal of Teacher Education* 57, no. 3 (May/June 2006):300–14. doi: 10.1177/0022487105285.

24. "Resources," DBC Education website, see "Leadership," http://dbceducation.com/resources-page/.

25. Again, see my website resource page: http://dbceducation.com/resources-page/.

26. What Students Matter and other reform groups consider to be union obstructionism is generally an effort to avoid the negative educational consequences of flawed bills. Unions do not oppose all change; the rejection of the specific arguments and legal strategy in the *Vergara* case should not be construed as blanket opposition to negotiated improvements in education labor policies.

27. Eunice S. Han, "The Myth of Unions' Overprotection of Bad Teachers: Evidence from the District-Teacher Matched Panel Data on Teacher Turnover," (Working paper series, Labor and Worklife Program at Harvard Law School, 2015).

INDEX

CPSIA information can be obtained
at www.ICGtesting.com
Printed in the USA
BVOW06s0024140517
484087BV00013B/397/P

9 780997 686807